PEOPLE
BUSINESSES

To Johanna

PEOPLE BUSINESSES

Making Professional Firms Profitable

ROGER PARRY

BUSINESS BOOKS LIMITED

First published in 1991 in Great Britain by
Business Books Limited
An imprint of Random Century Limited
20 Vauxhall Bridge Road, London SW1V 2SA

Random Century Australia (Pty) Limited
20 Alfred Street, Milsons Point, Sydney
New South Wales 2061, Australia

Random Century New Zealand Limited
9–11 Rothwell Avenue, Albany, Glenfield
Auckland 10, New Zealand

Random Century South Africa (Pty) Limited
PO Box 337, Bergvlei, South Africa

Set in Bembo by 𝔸 Tek Art Ltd,
Addiscombe, Croydon, Surrey

Printed and bound in Great Britain by
Butler & Tanner, Frome, Somerset

British Library Cataloguing in Publication Data
A catalogue record for this book is available from the British Library

ISBN 0-09-174661-2

CONTENTS

ACKNOWLEDGEMENTS

The idea for this book came from my colleagues in the various consulting, advertising and PR firms I have been lucky enough to work in and from discussions with professionals in law, accounting, design, market research and architectural businesses.

Many of the people I spoke with felt there was a gap in the literature about managing professional service firms – *People Businesses* is an attempt to fill that gap.

To write this book I have interviewed more than a hundred professionals ranging from trainees to the chairmen of public companies across the whole range of professional services. I am grateful to each of them for their time and their insights. It would be impossible to name them all and invidious to name only a few. Where they are directly quoted in the text I have identified their professional area but only in a very few cases have I used their names.

I acknowledge the help of many journalists and academics whose work I have read and I am grateful for their permission to quote from it. I must particularly thank Dr David Maister of Boston who is one of the leading consultants in this area. He has written extensively on the subject and generously given me advice on this manuscript and allowed me to reproduce some of his work.

My thanks to Lucy Shankleman of Business Books Limited for consistent good advice and encouragement and to her colleague Martin Liu whose editing skills have made the text far more readable and the ideas much clearer. I am indebted to Karen Bruce for producing the figures which I hope help to clarify the concepts described. Any factual errors and other mistakes which remain are, of course, my own.

Roger Parry
London 1991

PREFACE

In 1986 the international advertising agency J. Walter Thompson (JWT) made profits of some US$26 million on its revenues of US$649 million. A profit margin of 4 per cent. In 1987 JWT was taken over by new management and by 1989 it was making profits of US$75 million on revenues of US$751 million. A margin of 10 per cent. The extra US$49 million of profit was a product of tight financial controls.

By 1990 WPP Group plc – the publicly listed company which worked the magic on the JWT margins – was having major problems of its own losing more than 70 per cent of its stockmarket value when shareholders became concerned that its aggresive expansion programme had caused it to take on too much debt. A victim of over-ambitious growth.

Also in 1990, one of the world's best known design companies, Michael Peters Group (MPG), went into liquidation having seen its share price tumble from 278p to just 5p. According to the *Sunday Times*, one insider concluded: 'What has happened at MPG is the culmination of years of bad management'.

A few months later one of the world's largest accounting firms, Laventhol & Horwath, filed for bankruptcy after a disastrous period of badly managed growth resulting in bad debts and malpractice litigation.

Most large professional practices – accounting, consulting, legal and architecture firms and so on – are private partnerships, so their profits are not disclosed. Their performance is less visible than that of JWT, their failings less spectacular than those of WPP and MPG. For them partner compensation rather than profit is a more realistic measure of performance, but this compensation varies hugely between the well run and the less well run businesses offering similar services.

The *Financial Times* (7 February 1991) quoted leaked documents which revealed that just before the merger of the two accounting firms in 1989 to create Ernst & Young the partners in Ernst &

Whinney were set to earn US$263,000 while those in Arthur Young were to get US$191,000 – a difference of 38 per cent.

The figures for the gross fee income per partner of leading firms (see Appendix) shows that there are very wide variations. Even though take-home pay remains a closely guarded secret some partners are, clearly, much better off than others – again as a result of good management.

Professional service firms are organizations through which skilled individuals carry out complex work for other people. In many cases the management of the firm itself comes a poor second to serving the client. However the great professional boom in the 1980s is now over and the firms which prosper will have to look to their own management abilities as well as their professional skills. Many professionals are too busy being good professionals and too focused on their clients to manage their own firms well. The lack of attention to management of the firm itself leads to lower profits and can threaten the long-term viability of the organization. In the past this has not mattered too much as the relatively closed nature of many professions meant that financial rewards were great. In the future, as competition increases, firms will have to look to their bottom line to generate the profit necessary to ensure survival.

This book suggests ideas for running professional firms more effectively with a view both to improving client service and to allowing the professional employees and the firm's owners to reap the financial rewards of good management.

INTRODUCTION

More than 70 per cent of the working population in the Western countries are now employed in service organizations. It is by far the most important sector of the economy: but ask those who are involved in it and it would appear, particularly in the professional services sector, to be one of the worst managed. Managing processes and goods seems to be easier than managing people.

The 'service industries' include a very broad range of activities – from airlines to advertising agencies, hotels to hairdressers. Within the services sector, the *professional* service firms (such as accountants, lawyers, architects, advertising agencies and public relations consultancies) are an important sub-group and the main focus of this book.

Depending on the exact definition used, about one person in ten works in a professional service firm. These are the businesses where highly trained people are the main assets and where salaries are the main cost items. Known as people businesses they are the organizations about which it is often said, critically, their assets go up and down in the lift.

Professional practitioners devote great care and attention to doing their clients' work – if they did not they would soon be out of business. In many cases, however, those same professionals give little thought to running their own firms. By devoting so much time to solving their clients' problems they often ignore the task of managing and building their own businesses. They often waste money and squander profits and can miss the opportunity of building a really substantial firm.

The professional management skills of manufacturing and production are well established and well documented. Phrases like 'economies of scale' and 'learning curve', derived from manufacturing production, are now common vernacular. Professional service firms have not enjoyed the same degree of management attention and considerably less thought has gone into describing them and suggesting ways they can be made to work better.

This book is principally about professional service firms, but many of the observations hold true for other types of organization. To decide if this book is directly relevant to a particular business ask the following questions:

- Does the business provide solutions to clients' problems?

- Do these solutions require work to be done by trained and specialized people?

- Do clients reward the business for solving their problems with either fees and/or commission?

- Are the main tasks of managers in the business to recruit people with, or who can be trained to have, specific professional skills and then to assign those people to do client work?

- Does the business employ more than two people who pool their efforts to share the costs of overheads, marketing, administration and so on?

If the answer to each of these questions is yes then the book will be useful for that business and you are probably describing a professional service firm.

People Businesses contains ideas about what makes these types of business profitable and successful. Although the book uses examples drawn from certain types of professional firm the basic ideas and suggestions are applicable in almost all professional businesses. The objective is to provide a framework which gives a better understanding of how professional firms work and to describe management tools which can allow them to run more effectively.

Running a professional firm, just like any other business, involves a series of trade-offs and compromises. Each chapter in this book is intended to give a perspective on one or more of those trade-offs. Certain major themes, such as understanding the profitability of each client and the ratio of the number of senior to junior professional staff, are discussed in several chapters, but on each occasion they are viewed from a different perspective. The reader may start at the beginning and work through to the end, but the book can be dipped into at particular sections.

OUTLINE OF THE BOOK

This book is structured into six main parts, each of which is subdivided into individual subject chapters. Each part groups together a set of ideas about a particular aspect of professional firm management. Each chapter is organized to suggest ways of answering the sort of questions managers seek to answer. These questions are listed at the start of each chapter.

At the end of the book there is a summary section containing 20 propositions for effective management of professional service firms.

PART I: SERVICE FIRM CONCEPTS

What ideas are useful in describing and understanding professional service firms?

- Definitions – developing a common language

- Business system – five basic tasks

- Economics – how the business works

- Service challenges – managers' main concerns

- Management ideas – unique aspects of professional firms

- Service offering – how the firm compares with others

- Management tools – useful techniques

Service firms are a special type of organization – a grouping together of professionals who can sell their services to clients more effectively by working as a group than they could by working alone.

Most managers of professional firms regard running the business as a secondary part of their work ('clients come first') and do not have access to ideas and models which help to manage the firm. Without management concepts like those used in manufacturing (economies of scales, diminishing returns, etc.) it is difficult to run a professional firm to its greatest potential.

The first part of the book describes the nature of professional service firms. It covers what sort of activities fall under this definition, how these firms work, where the money comes from and where it goes.

It describes the key economic and organizational characteristics of professional service firms and explains what makes them profitable. It provides the ideas and models which managers should find useful. The chapters in the first part describe, in theory, the ideas and frameworks that are used throughout the book and which managers will find valuable in thinking about their business and can use as a starting point for making their firms more effective.

Part I provides professionals with the vocabulary and the concepts to help them understand their own firms better and to think of them as businesses which are run to make a profit.

PART II: LEVERS OF PROFITABILITY

What can the managers of professional firms do to make their businesses more profitable?

- Profitability – the measure of success

- Client profitability – a firm is not a charity

- Product profitability – sell what you do best

- Balance of staff numbers – chiefs and indians

- Billing rates – the price of service

- Staff utilization – getting people to do the right things

- Working capital – do not become a banker by accident

- Housekeeping – watching the pennies

- Profitability – the right attitude

The second part looks at those aspects of the firm which are within the control of managers and identifies specific actions which are taken to maximize profit. This part focuses purely on the actions required to increase the amount of money available for the firm's owners – it focuses of the profit perspectives of the general management issues covered in the rest of the book.

By breaking down the crude aggregate profitability figures for the firm as a whole, it is possible to uncover the underlying profit contribution made by each client and, where relevant, each product.

The best profit performance comes from avoiding hidden subsidies to clients, either as a result of doing more work than they paid for or by running up costs which do not get paid. The best use of resources comes from planning ahead to ensure that the maximum amount of available professional time is spent on client work.

PART III: PUTTING PEOPLE FIRST

How do you get the best from the firm's key asset – its people?

- Recruitment – getting the best people

- Evaluation – identifying the best people

- Retention – keeping the best

- Motivation – getting the best out of people

- Assignment – making the best use of people assets

- Training – making people more valuable

- Support staff – not professionals but critical to success

- The people shortage – professionals are an endangered species

The third part is about how to manage people: but it is not about how to be a personnel manager. Given that more than 60 per cent of a firm's operating costs will probably be professional staff salaries, this aspect of management deserves special treatment.

People, their motivation and welfare must be a primary concern for *all* managers in professional firms. Like the cliché about war being too important for the generals, people in service firms are too important for the personnel experts alone. A professional firm which leaves people management to a specialist department is almost certainly giving this key area too low a priority.

PART IV: RUNNING THE BUSINESS

How should you control the day-to-day operations of the firm?

- Who should own the business?
- Management structure – everyone is a manager
- Leadership – more than just managing
- Management information – taking the pulse
- Quality control – keeping up standards
- Client relations – keeping the customer satisfied
- Getting paid – giving real value for money
- Premises – don't cut corners
- Technology – always buy the best

This part looks at the major decisions that need to be taken about how to structure, resource and operate the business. It considers the tactics of managing professional service firms as opposed to the strategy. It covers the things managers should be thinking about on a day-to-day basis.

Every professional must have some element of managerial responsibility. It is not possible simply to get on with client work and leave the running of the firm to the management. Senior managers must aim to create a culture in which the responsibility for good management of the firm's resources (mainly people's time) is shared by all.

PART V: BUILDING THE BUSINESS

How do you grow the firm AND stay profitable?

- Organic growth – the natural way
- Joint ventures/strategic alliances – finding partners
- Acquisition/merger – a marriage of convenience?
- Managing growth – getting bigger *and* staying profitable
- Marketing – meeting customers' needs
- New business – winning the 'beauty contest'

Part V is about how to get bigger and, crucially, how to plan growth so that it is achieved profitably. Growth is desired by most professional firms and is necessary if junior people are going to realize their ambitions of promotion.

Unfortunately, growth can be the hurdle at which professional firms fall as they are often unable to get bigger *and* make money. Those firms that expand by acquisition can actually go into liquidation when acquired businesses, purchased with debt, perform below expectations. The safest way to grow is through winning new business and finding the staff to service it.

PART VI: STRATEGY

Where should you take the firm in the future and how should you get it there?

- Customers – the market-place
- Competitors – the profession/industry
- The company – the firm itself
- Service offering/positioning
- Business plan
- Getting rich

This final part deals with the key decisions a professional service firm must take in respect of how and where it intends to compete. Once this has been decided, there are still crucial questions to be answered about the firm itself.

A framework for the development of strategy is suggested based on an analysis of customers, competitors and the company itself, leading to decisions about the service offering and business plan.

The formulation of strategy is, essentially, done by answering questions. This part poses the main questions. And how partners and managers can maximize their personal wealth is covered at the end of this part.

PART I

SERVICE FIRM CONCEPTS

What words and ideas are useful in describing and understanding professional service firms?

When I first started I had hundreds of hours of tuition about how the law works, how the courts work and how the profession works. I was given a whole new vocabulary. Unfortunately we were never given any words about how a law firm worked.

Associate, legal firm

To start this book it is necessary to define what is meant by professional service firms and to describe the key characteristics of this type of business. It is also necessary to develop a vocabulary and a framework of ideas which describe what these organizations are and how they work.

PEOPLE

Professional firms are the classic people businesses – that is, those where the applied skills of people are the main service. The people are not just employees doing tasks which require relatively low skills in a labour-intensive process. They have professional knowledge and techniques, acquired through training and practice, which are not found in many other people, and which they seek to sell. The firm is the mechanism through which they sell those skills to clients – skills which the clients usually do not have themselves. It is not simply a matter of providing substitute labour for a task which the client does not have time to do itself, but of providing specific professional services which are hard to do well by the clients themselves.

1

PROFIT

Professional service firms have a simple set of economics yet are unlike any other sort of business. The two main things driving the level of profit are concerned with:

- Maximizing the income derived from billings
- Minimizing the salary costs

Management is mostly focused on improving the utilization of professional staff and ensuring that growth is both controlled and profitable.

Professional firms have a unique business system and face specific management challenges. The main features of such firms are that: their output or product is intangible and perishable; for the most part the services they provide have to be carried out in locations near to the clients; it is very difficult to ensure a consistent quality of service over time.

STRATEGY

Fundamental to taking management decisions about how to determine the strategy, structure and operations of a professional firm are a number of key concepts:

- The *staff pyramid* of senior, middle and junior professionals – the shape of the pyramid has a fundamental effect on the sort of work the firm can do and on its profitability. Keeping the pyramid balanced as the firm grows is always a problem

- The *client service techniques* of client relations, project management and application of professional skills at all of which the firm has to excel

- The *client service package* of expertise, experience and execution – which must be balanced to the needs of each client

MANAGEMENT TOOLS

There are certain management tools which are useful in running professional firms. These include:

- Techniques of *cost allocation* based on how professionals spend their time

- An assessment of *profitability* of each client

- The use of *client audits* to monitor the nature of the relationship between the firm and its clients

- Specialized *quality control* measures aimed at improving the consistency of the firm's services

Part I is the most theoretical part of the book in that it covers the frameworks and concepts which can be useful in describing and understanding professional service firms. Some readers may want to skip this part and go to subsequent parts of the book which contain more practical examples of the applications of these ideas. Readers who are interested in the theory of professional firms should look at the books in the reference list, and, in particular, the work of Dr David Maister who pioneered many of these theoretical frameworks.

1

DEFINITIONS

What is meant by professional service firm?

---

*I've no idea if we're a professional service firm. We like to think
we're professional, we do give service of sorts and we are running a
business. I don't really care about an exact definition but I am
always open to ideas which can make us more profitable.*

Director, PR consultancy

Identifying a group of organizations which have the same sort of
characteristics and the same sort of problems and opportunities
gives managers the chance to learn from the way things are done
in similar but different businesses to their own. Furthermore, it is
useful because trying to define what is meant by professional
service firms can provide insights into what makes some work
better than others. To clarify what is meant by a professional
service firm it is useful to consider what it is *not*.

WHAT PROFESSIONAL FIRMS ARE NOT

Clearly all businesses need people, so the simple existence of
employees does not define a people business. A possible, but
rather rigorous test would be to calculate the ratio of the value of
assets in the business to staff costs and describe professional
service firms as only those above a certain ratio. For example, a
fully automated chemical plant, that has fixed assets (machines,
robots, buildings, etc.) with a value of £100 million and employs
500 people at a total annual salary cost of £10 million will give a
ratio of staff costs to assets of 10:100 or 0.1. A legal firm in rented
premises with leased equipment that owns assets worth only
£10,000 and employs 20 people at a total annual salary cost of £1
million will give a ratio of 1,000,000:10,000 or 100.

Figure 1.1 shows various industries ranged along an axis of
intensity of labour costs, from mainly asset-based to mainly

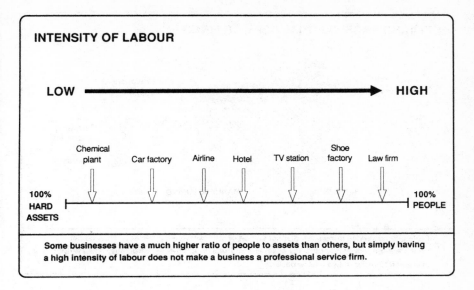

INTENSITY OF LABOUR

LOW ➡️ HIGH

Chemical plant · Car factory · Airline · Hotel · TV station · Shoe factory · Law firm

100% HARD ASSETS   100% PEOPLE

Some businesses have a much higher ratio of people to assets than others, but simply having a high intensity of labour does not make a business a professional service firm.

Figure 1.1

people-based. Taken alone, however, this dimension of people to assets is too simplistic. In some cases, such as the shoe factory shown in the figure, the ratio of people to machines is simply the result of a decision by the company to use people and not machines. The value added per head is low and the end product is tangible and can be placed in a warehouse unlike the product of true people businesses. A professional firm delivers a product which cannot be stored away. It adds value by helping its client to solve a problem or by doing some service on behalf of the client.

Figure 1.2 contrasts a service business with a retailer and manufacturer and the comparison offers another way of defining a professional firm. The differentiation of the service business from a classic manufacturing company is relatively simple as there is no physical end product as with the manufacturer. The distinction is, however, more complex with some types of manufacturer, particularly those manufacturing processes where there is a high element of service involved in creating the product. A newspaper publisher, for example, has many similar character-istics to a professional service firm in that it organizes people to work as journalists; but it differs in that it produces its output *irrespective* of specific client orders or requests. The publisher, in effect, simply hopes someone will buy its newspapers. Similarly a TV station produces and broadcasts programmes in the hope

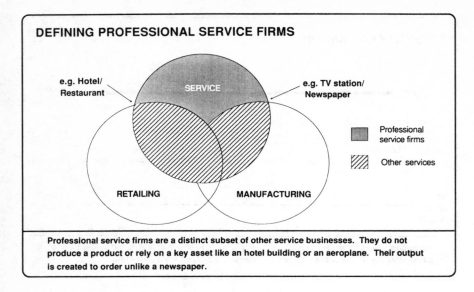

DEFINING PROFESSIONAL SERVICE FIRMS

e.g. Hotel/
Restaurant

e.g. TV station/
Newspaper

SERVICE

Professional
service firms

Other services

RETAILING

MANUFACTURING

Professional service firms are a distinct subset of other service businesses. They do not produce a product or rely on a key asset like an hotel building or an aeroplane. Their output is created to order unlike a newspaper.

Figure 1.2

that someone will tune in. For the purpose of this definition they are more like a manufacturing company. They create a tangible product even though the bulk of their costs are salaries.

Much of retailing involves providing a service to customers by way of expert advice as well as making the products available. The main difference is that the retailer's staff only work in the store or warehouse in order to sell the product or service. They do not create a solution or provide a service through their own efforts. In retailing the people are part of an overall business system which delivers value to the consumer rather than providing that value as individuals selling their professional skills. The role of most people in retailing is to act as a delivery mechanism which requires a relatively low degree of skill.

The distinction from professional service firms becomes even more blurred in those areas of business where the service level is greater than in retailing (such as in hotels, restaurants or amusement parks) – but again the main purpose of the people in their jobs is to act as a delivery mechanism for a hard asset (the hotel building, the aircraft fleet, the rides and features of the park). Without these hard assets the jobs would not exist. In professional service firms the people provide a service as their main goal. It is the service which clients are paying for not the use of an asset with service thrown in.

WHAT PROFESSIONAL FIRMS ARE

Having looked at various types of business to eliminate those which are not considered to be professional service firms, we must now try to establish what professional firms are. To begin with we can create a list of characteristics common to a professional firm:

- The majority of the firm's costs are salaries

- People in the firm tend to have shared professional skills

- Clients reward the firm by paying time-based fees or commissions related to the size or value of the job

- Employees of the firm tend to serve several clients over time

- Senior members of the firm try to spread their time across many clients to leverage their expertise in the most profitable way

- Professional progress in the firm happens with increasing tenure, age and skills

- Each client will require a unique service-package tailored to meet its individual needs

The outputs of professional service firms on behalf of clients can vary considerably but include documents, court appearances, advertisements, press releases, drawings and so on. Although these are tangible manifestations of the firm's work they are not, with rare exceptions, *products* in that they do not have an intrinsic value and cannot be sold to others. They are specific manifestations of the client service package. Another distinguishing feature of professional firms is that the performance of the individuals in their professional capacity is very obvious to the client and important to the success of the firm.

Figure 1.3 shows a variety of businesses which have high levels of staff costs. However in the professional firm it is the individual as opposed to staff in general who make the difference. It is the individual effort for which the client is paying. That is not to say that a particular worker in a shoe factory or an hotel does not have a high impact on the final product – but in professional firms it is the skill and application of the professional that the client is specifically seeking rather than just a good pair of shoes or a comfortable night's stay. Indeed, most professional services could be provided by individuals without the support of a firm. But the economics of being part of a firm with the ability to share costs and to use their experience to manage and guide others makes firm membership attractive for most individuals.

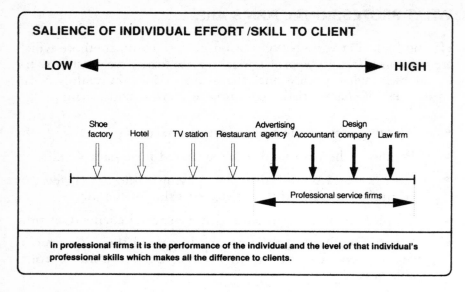

Figure 1.3

In his book, *Service Management*, Richard Normann talks of service firms being personality intensive (rather than simply labour intensive) meaning that clients are very aware of the individuals who service them. He describes the interaction between the firm's staff and the clients as 'the moment of truth,' that instant in which the service is delivered, face-to-face. Staff in professional service firms are constantly having such 'moments of truth' in their daily work with clients in a way that a back-room employee of a hotel or the pilot of an aeroplane does not.

WHO ARE THE SERVICE FIRMS?

There are three broad sub-groups of service firms:

- Skilled service providers such as accountants
- Transaction managers such as stockbrokers
- Service system providers such as fast food restaurants

The ideas in this book are most relevant to the skilled service providers – who are the true professional firms – but many of the book's observations can be applied to transaction managers. Service system businesses have some similarities with professional firms but managing them is much more to do with achieving capacity utilization and improving the delivery system to the customer than it is to do with managing professional people.

Skilled service providers

These firms tend to be rewarded by clients on the basis of time spent providing the service. Some will work at agreed hourly rates. Some work on the basis of a percentage commission related to the size of the job. Some will quote a fixed price for an agreed service and base their estimate on how long they think it will take to complete the work and how many of their people will be involved. The group of service businesses, which are the main focus of this book, includes:

Accountants
Actuaries
Advertising agencies
Architects
Colleges
Consulting engineers
Decorators
Dentists
Designers
Doctors
Economic consultants
Electricians
Employment agencies
Executive recruiters
Golf professionals
Hairdressers
Interior designers
Investment banks (advice services)
Investment managers
Lawyers
Management consultants
Market research firms
Marketing consultants
Morticians
Plumbers
Prostitutes
PR agencies
Psychiatrists
Ski instructors
Stockbrokers
Tutors in language schools, etc.

All these types of firm have very similar economics and problems of capacity management and growth. One can argue about exactly which of the above list are *professionals* but is often simply a matter of how long a type of business has been in existence before it generally enjoys the professional label. When they first started, management consultants did not have the same status as lawyers or accountants but now are certainly thought of as professionals.

Whole industries such as advertising, public relations, management consulting and even psychiatry have been invented to solve client problems. In some cases the clients' problems have been discovered or at least identified, isolated and described as a prelude to the creation of the industry. For example, it is desirable, and in most cases a legal necessity, for companies to have an independent audit of their financial statements – hence the creation of the profession of auditors. Similarly if it were deemed necessary that all companies must provide an analysis of the tennis prowess of all their employees then a new profession would be born – and with it a new set of tennis excellence criteria, annual conferences, specialist magazines, professional bodies, standards and ethics committees, and the rest of the intellectual luggage that comes with a new profession.

Some people reading the above list might strongly argue that tennis and golf professionals or ski instructors are simply not professionals in that they do not go through a lengthy educational process. From the perspective of this book, however, they are directly analogous to other professional firms in the way that they could organize themselves and the way they interact with clients.

There tends to be considerable overlap between the products or output of professional service firms and their names are not always exact guides to what they actually do. Accountants, management consultants, marketing consultants, lawyers, even advertising agencies and public relations consultants might all include drawing up a business plan or writing a corporate brochure among their list of services. Tax advice can come from lawyers, accountants, investment bankers or management consultants. This convergence of professional services has important implications for recruitment and retention of staff and for the development of strategy.

Transaction managers

Transaction-based businesses are those which conduct a sale or purchase on behalf of their clients. These firms tend to be rewarded with percentage commissions on the transaction. They provide a service for their clients but that service is nearly always in the execution of a sale or purchase. In some cases there is a sliding scale which reduces the percentage as the size of the transaction increases. However, there is no reason why they should not operate on time-based fees. The group includes:

Banks (certain functions)
Bookmakers
Building societies (certain functions)
Casinos
Estate agents
Foreign exchange bureaux
Insurance brokers
Investment banks (certain functions)1
Media buyers
Stockbrokers (certain functions)
Travel agents

These businesses have economic and management issues that are similar to the core professional firms. The main difference is that they have a different basis of remuneration. Looked at in some ways, an advertising agency could be regarded as a transaction manager in that in many cases it is remunerated on the basis of the amount of media space and time it has purchased on behalf of its client. An estate agent which charges on the basis of its marketing and communications costs and the time spent by its staff, as opposed to a percentage of the value of the property sold, could be defined as a skilled service provider.

In general there is a trend for commission systems to break down and for transaction managers to be rewarded by fees which reflect the work done rather than the size of the transaction. A classic example of this change is the legal work of domestic property conveyancing in Britain where solicitors traditionally charged fees based on the value of the house being sold rather than the complexity of the task. So outrageous did this become that people started doing the work for themselves and in response many solicitors radically changed their basis of charging to reflect time spent on the client's behalf rather than the value of the transaction. In Canada it is quite common to see signs in lawyers' windows advertising a fixed price list for basic services like house purchase and drawing up wills. In time such price competition will inevitably spread to other countries.

Service system providers

There are other types of service businesses where the output is a service rather than a product, and which, while clearly not in manufacturing, have characteristics different from *professional* service firms. Although some of the concepts in this book are relevant to them they fall into a category of their own. They are businesses which operate a service system requiring, for the most part, a relatively low level of skill as most of the people employed carry out well defined tasks which form part of an overall service delivery system. These include:

Airlines
Banking (certain functions)
Bars/pubs
Distribution
Education
Fast food
Hospitals
Hotels
Insurance
Newspapers
Magazines
Publishers
Radio stations
Repairs
Restaurants
Retailing
Television stations
Transport

Clearly within these business are some very highly skilled jobs such as airline pilots, teachers, hotel managers, journalists and engineers. These individuals could very well be described as professionals and said to work in a profession but they do *not* work in professional firms. These skilled professionals within service system businesses, *as individuals*, are subject to many of the issues covered in this book such as recruitment, training and retention of skilled people. However, the economics of their companies will be driven by different forces from those affecting the more closely defined professional service firm.

PROFESSIONAL SERVICE FIRM FOCUS

Professional service firms are, as described above, a broad group of businesses with many common characteristics. One characteristic, above all, tends to unite them which is that, as organizations, they tend to worry far more about serving clients than about running their own business. The rest of this book is devoted to trying to redress the balance and to help managers focus on the issues of their own business.

2

BUSINESS SYSTEM

What model can be used to describe the basic tasks of a professional service firm?

I'm a designer. I design things. I help clients by designing things for them and they pay me. I am not part of a production process. I design and that's the beginning and the end of it.

Junior Executive, design consultancy

The business system of most professional service firms comprises a five-step sequence as shown in figure 1.4. All work, in practice, can be characterized as a client assignment whether it is a 20-minute haircut or a five year-long advertising campaign. Each of the steps in figure 1.4 represents an element of the client assignment.

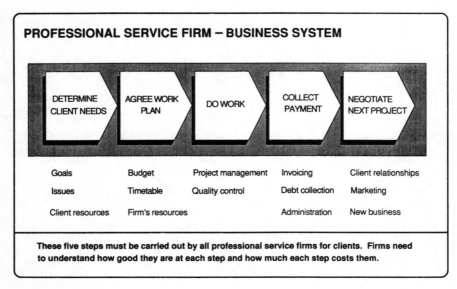

PROFESSIONAL SERVICE FIRM – BUSINESS SYSTEM

DETERMINE CLIENT NEEDS	AGREE WORK PLAN	DO WORK	COLLECT PAYMENT	NEGOTIATE NEXT PROJECT
Goals	Budget	Project management	Invoicing	Client relationships
Issues	Timetable	Quality control	Debt collection	Marketing
Client resources	Firm's resources		Administration	New business

These five steps must be carried out by all professional service firms for clients. Firms need to understand how good they are at each step and how much each step costs them.

Figure 1.4

The importance of defining and recognizing a business system is that it enables the firm to think about its business in manageable chunks. It allows the firm to think about how its costs build up in an assignment; how its resources must be deployed; how its profits may be maximized; and how it can beat the competition. To be successful a firm must not only be good at each of the steps but must be able to do them cost effectively. If, for example, the managing director or senior partner is the only person in the firm capable of successfully negotiating the next project then the firm's ability to grow will be constrained by his or her availability.

1 DETERMINE CLIENT NEEDS

At the heart of a successful professional relationship is an investment of time and effort at the very start of the process to ensure the firm is directing its resources correctly.

The vital preliminaries

This first step can come as a result of an approach by the client following advertising or promotion by the firm, or it may come from the firm directly approaching the prospective client. It very frequently comes from an existing client who seeks solutions to new problems. It will involve senior people in the firm in identifying exactly what the client wants. It is the stage of defining the problems and opportunities facing the client and defining the client's needs in such a way that the firm's professional skill can be applied to them. Defining the issues and getting the client to agree them, is one of the most valuable parts of any professional service.

Identify client goals

With the inevitable involvement of senior people this first step can be costly – but it cannot be ignored. If the client is left to define its own problem it may well start the relationship off on the wrong basis and will often seek the cheapest and quickest solution. It is vital to involve senior people from both sides at this stage to ensure that both the client and the firm agree on the same objectives.

During this step clients frequently get very frustrated when a service firm redefines their problem. If, for example, an advertising agency, appointed to boost sales of the product to young people in the west of the country, says it wants first to consider the overall positioning and distribution of the product nationally, the client may not feel comfortable with the shift of emphasis. When management consultants tell clients that the problem that they have defined for themselves, such as productivity in division X, can only be addressed in the context of the overall strategy of the entire business clients may feel they are being rail-roaded. In reality the professional firm may be providing very good advice.

So as a first step, a clear set of *goals* for the professional relationship itself must be established. It is important that both the firm and the client clearly understand and agree on the reason for their relationship, what both will get out of it and what will *not* be attempted or promised. At the broadest these goals may be, for example, to appoint a legal firm to handle all and any legal work that may result from the prospective client's business activities. At its narrowest it may be for a public relations firm to get the client's chairman profiled in a particular Sunday newspaper.

A clear definition of who does what and what is expected will avoid conflict and disappointment later on.

Other issues to resolve

Other key issues concerning the relationship may include, for example:

- Who, within the client organization, will be regarded as *the client* for the purpose of giving instructions and approval?

- Will the appointment of the firm be made public?

- Will the firm have office space on the client's premises?

- If the client has other professional advisers, how will the firm work with them ? How will the various advisers communicate – will each report direct to the client or will one of the firms be given the task of controlling the others and passing their reports on?

One issue almost certain to arise will be the exact basis of charging. Will it be hourly or daily fees, an estimated fixed fee for the job, or will the firm charge a percentage of the value of a transaction undertaken, etc? The agreed basis will often determine the way the work plan of step two is constructed. The same service can be provided by the same firm under a variety of different charging mechanisms. These are considered in detail in part IV in chapter 31, 'Getting paid'.

Client resources

The firm must also establish at the very beginning, even before a work programme is devised, what resources the client will be able to make available to the project and the firm. For example the existence of in-house printing facilities might affect the costs of using an advertising agency or PR consultancy. Similarly availability of in-house legal staff or financial analysts will change the size of the team needed to be provided by a legal firm or management consultancy. Having looked at goals, issues and resources the service firm should have a clear understanding of the client's needs and of the client's organization and expectations. The firm should normally send the client a memorandum describing its understanding of the situation to ensure that the client agrees.

The step is a fundamental part of building a good client relationship which is considered in greater detail in chapter 30 in part IV.

2 AGREE WORK PLAN

This can be a difficult stage of the process during which the basis of charging and probable budget is established. This again will frequently require the attention of senior members of the firm and will usually determine the overall profitability of the relationship.

Competitive pitches or 'beauty parades' occur during this step. Usually the firm will have to outline a work plan before the new business pitch to provide some idea of budget and levels of proposed service. Once the pitch has succeeded and the firm has been selected a detailed work plan will be agreed.

Budget

During the detailed planning of the work it may become clear that the original budget discussed during the pre-assignment phase will be inadequate. It is very common for the client to call for additional resources to be made available as the opportunity or problem becomes better defined. A frequent mistake is for firms to allow themselves to be bullied into sticking to the original budget but expanding the objectives and thus taking on the project as a potential loss maker. It is critical to agree, up front, with the client that the firm must be correctly rewarded for its efforts.

Timetable

Attempting to agree a timetable often throws up cultural differences between the client and the professional advisors on what is meant by urgent. Although some people might imagine that professionals want to spin out projects, most professional firms work to much tighter deadlines than their clients. Timetables must be realistic. While a professional firm might expect its own highly motivated, highly paid associates to complete a piece of research in five days it is quite unrealistic to expect the same of a client's salaried middle management.

If projects are designed with a critical path that requires abnormal performance by the client's own people in terms of collecting data or doing research, the timetable will almost certainly slip and this will be the fault of the firm not the client: the development of a sensible and realistic work plan should be one of the skills the professional firm brings to the table.

Firm resources

A major problem for most professional firms is the future availability of their own staff. This is compounded by the need to undertake a constant balancing act to ensure that each client has available to it enough time from the right professional experts at the right stage of the project.

This availability problem can develop into a physical bottleneck in certain types of firm with special facilities when, for example, three advertising campaigns simultaneously require the attention of an in-house video editing machine. But more often it is to do with the availability of individuals with the right skills.

Yet another complication which should be discussed with the client is the issue of balancing the work assignments of an individual with the sort of training and experience that individual needs to get on in the firm. These issues are covered in more detail in part III, chapter 21, 'Assignment'.

3 DO THE WORK

This is normally the most lengthy stage during which the firm applies its resources, techniques of project management and professional skills to the task as agreed with the client.

During this phase, the senior firm members can usually step back to allow the juniors to do the actual work and simply ensure that there is adequate supervision and regular contact at a senior level with the client.

Project management

Clients will require regular updates of progress. Professional firms should ensure that these progress reports are delivered by themselves to senior clients rather than having information about alleged progress, or the lack of it, filter up through an internal system. One individual from the firm's team should have clear responsibility for the progress of the work and for the management of the firm's resources. It is this individual who will be responsible for keeping to timetable and to budget.

This project management role is concerned with the effective use of resources and is seperate from the client relationship role which is more concerned with achieving clear communication.

Quality control

During the project, rather than after it, the firm must have in place a system for quality control to ensure that the team is delivering at the standard the client was promised. Creative directors of advertising agencies who do not see the finished advertisements until the client presentation or corporate identity specialists who do not subject their teams' ideas to critical appraisal *before* the client meeting will run into trouble.

QUALITY CONTROL

The junior members of a public relations team were working for a holiday company. They had prepared a series of briefing documents for the media which described their client's product and compared it very favourably with the competition, and which drew out the weaknesses of competing brands and included very unfavourable customer testimonials about competitors. Unfortunately the junior team members were unaware that their client was about to purchase one of the much criticized competitors and that the acquisition would be announced at the press conference along with new product news. The consultancy chairman was aware of the acquisition but had been too busy to review the material before the client saw it.

The issues related to project management, quality control and the use of a relationship manager to ensure the client is happy are covered in detail in part IV, 'Running the Business'.

4 COLLECT PAYMENT

This a straightforward process but it raises the issue of cash management as the firm must ensure it does not subsidize its clients by allowing them late payment. In most cases payment will be made regularly during a project with a performance-related bonus, if applicable, being paid at the end.

Invoicing

The firm must ensure it has a good system for issuing and chasing up invoices and must make certain that the client *really* understands the basis of the charges. Badly laid out and confusing invoices are a very common problem in service firms, where projects are negotiated by senior people with a close regard to the client's way of working but invoices are sent out by a very junior executive in the accounts department having been directly generated from a computer system. Often these invoices are sent to the named senior client who, apart from being reminded of the cost of the professional services, will find them incomprehensible and often littered with unexplained extra charges.

Debt collection

Collecting payment is very much part of the overall professional relationship and firms should take lessons from the best restaurants to ensure that the bill is presented with a high degree of clarity and charm. Smile when you ask for money!

Administration

Firms must ensure they have good, basic accounting systems in place to monitor unpaid debts and give early warning of possible bad debts. The finance or accounts department should constantly remind account directors of any payment problems being experienced with their clients. All too often the client service teams are unaware that all their efforts are not being rewarded.

The management of working capital is one of the key elements of profitability and is covered in part II.

5 NEGOTIATE NEXT PROJECT

It is at this stage that it will become clear whether the client feels the value of the service justifies the cost. It may well be that the client does not require an immediate new work–package but if the client feels it is getting good value for money repeat assignments will follow at some time. However, some professional firms develop a bad name for the pressure of their salesmanship and their desire to stay involved: 'once they are in you'll never get them out,' is a charge often levelled at management consultants. 'The lawyers simply make more work for themselves,' is another common sentiment. In general, though, it is quite legitimate for a firm to look for more work as the basic proposition to the client must be that the value added by the firm greatly exceeds the fees paid.

Client relationships

The process of seeking new work from existing clients will again involve senior people but follow-up projects will always be less costly than seeking completely new clients. The importance of building and maintaining a long-term relationship with a client that goes on far beyond individual projects is described in detail in chapter 30 in part IV.

Marketing

Finding work from both existing and new clients involves all the activities of marketing the firm to bring it to the clients' attention which are described in detail in chapter 38 of part V. This involve decisions about positioning the firm and pricing its services as well as promoting the firm through advertising and so on.

New business

The process of seeking to win a client assignment is expensive and must be approached in a disciplined fashion. This is described in chapter 39 in part V.

TYPICAL BUSINESS SYSTEMS

Two examples of typical business systems of professional firms are given below; the first is for a hairdresser and the second for a management consultant.

HAIRDRESSER'S BUSINESS SYSTEM

Identify client needs
After discussion with client, it is agreed that the hair has grown too long and a haircut is required. Special services such as perms and tinting are not wanted.

Agree work plan
To make the job easier the hair will be washed and, given the hot weather, conditioner will be used. It is agreed that the whole process will take 40 minutes so the client will be on time for lunch and the standard charge is £13.

Do the work
The hair is washed, cut and dried.

The client agrees that some mousse to give it body is a good idea and agrees to buy some of the salon's own conditioner to use at home as it seems to have worked so well.

Collect payment
The conditioner cost an extra £2. Change is given from a £20 note in the form of five £1 coins in the hope of a tip.

Negotiate next project
A card is presented with the stylist's name and telephone number. It is agreed that the customer should not leave it so long next time. It is explained that haircuts are half price on Wednesday afternoons.

STRATEGY CONSULTANT'S BUSINESS SYSTEM

Identify client needs
The client wishes to open a new supermarket but the board is split on the location.

The client's chairman needs an outside opinion to resolve the deadlock. He needs to be able to show the decision is based on objective criteria related to local market conditions.

Agree work plan
The consultant will analyse the market in the two alternative locations. The work will take three months and cost £200,000. The client wants to delay the project by two months to accommodate staff holidays. The firm resists. A team of four consultants is assigned to work with the client's own management.

Do the work
Data is collected and analysed. The client's management and suppliers are interviewed. The project is completed four weeks late. A recommendation is made.

Collect payment
The invoice is delivered after a lunch with the chairman during which the value of the study was discussed.

Negotiate next project
The firm explains that the work done has helped it to devise a store location model which the client could use to test all new store locations.

3

ECONOMICS

In professional firms where does the money come from and where does it go? What can be done to make the firm more profitable?

I have a completely intuitive sense of whether a business is making money. If I walk around an agency I can tell you from watching people and chatting to them if its profitable. There's just a certain right number of people to do the job and a certain feel of how busy they should be.

Chief Executive, agency network

Understanding *how* a professional firm works and knowing *why* some firms are more profitable than others is the basis for successful management. The whole of part II is devoted to practical actions which increase profits. This chapter describes the basic ideas that are useful in thinking about how professional firms run.

Although it is very simplified, the five-step business system process described in the previous chapter characterizes all professional service firms. Similarly their fundamental economics are equally universal in terms of where their money comes from and where it goes.

HOW MUCH TO CHARGE?

In theory the value added to the client's business will be more than or equal to the price the client is prepared to pay for the professional service. This fee or commission collected by the firm will be large enough to cover its costs and will leave the firm with an acceptable gross profit. What is acceptable will always vary and, ultimately, will depend on what value individuals place upon their time. While it is acceptable for professional service firms to be seen as successful and profitable they should not be seen to take this to extremes. The accountant who arrives in a Ferrari must raise questions about the size of the fee he or she charges you.

For those firms which are in public ownership the level of declared profit will be quite visible to clients, and firms which are felt to be overly profitable can experience difficult client relations when negotiating fees. Conversely those firms which are known to be unprofitable can have their professional reputations dented. Who wants to get advice from people who can't even run their own shop well?

Neither response is quite rational. Clients should judge a firm on the quality of its service to *them* rather than its overall performance as a business. It is, however, often the case that the best run and most profitable firms *do* provide the best professional service and badly run firms can go out of business, which is inconvenient for clients.

INCOME/COSTS

The typical picture of costs and income for the professional service firm is shown in figure 1.5. Although the relative sizes of the individual blocks of income and cost will vary greatly from business to business, the basic components will remain the same.

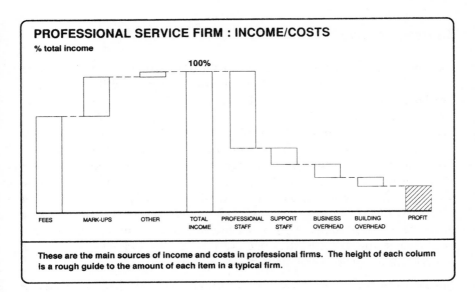

These are the main sources of income and costs in professional firms. The height of each column is a rough guide to the amount of each item in a typical firm.

Figure 1.5

Sources of income

Each professional firm will have its own unique mix of sources of income, but most will have some money coming in from each of the three categories described below.

Fees are those sums charged to clients for the services done on their behalf – they are the direct reward for the professional time worked by members of the firm. They may be calculated on an hourly, daily, weekly, or even yearly basis. For firms paid on a commission basis, the fees or commissions are calculated as a percentage of the size of the job or the value of the transaction.

Mark-up is that additional percentage charged to clients for goods or services purchased on their behalf by the firm. In the case of a law practice the amount of income from mark-up is likely to be small or non-existent. In the case of the old-fashioned model of an advertising agency the so-called media commission (in effect a mark-up on the actual cost of media paid by the agency) represented the vast majority of the income of the business.

Other includes such things as interest earned on the money received from clients before it is paid out on the clients' behalf to the ultimate suppliers of goods or services. This once formed a significant part of the income of advertising agencies who paid the media for time and space some time after the clients had paid them.

Sources of costs

As with sources of income each individual firm will have a unique profile but, by and large, all professional firms will look fairly similar in respect of their cost base.

Staff costs are by far the biggest of the firm's outgoings. This is the primary characteristic of the professional service business. These costs include salaries, national insurance, bonuses, car costs, health insurance, and so on. It is always useful to separate the costs of professional staff from the salary packages of administrators and support staff. However remember that many of the fee-earners devote some of their time to general administration and some of the support staff (e.g. secretaries) contribute directly to specific client projects.

Business overheads are those costs which are not directly charged to the client such as stationery, postage and telephones but which are incurred as a necessary part of running the firm. The overheads which are paid directly by the client do not form part of the firm's operating cost base.

If overheads are incurred on behalf of clients but are *not* passed onto the client for payment (either because of a policy decision or oversight) then these costs must be recorded as associated with that client and used in the calculation of client profitability.

Building overheads include items such as heat, light, rent and rates. These are costs which are necessary to allow the firm's staff to work but are not directly related to client projects – as such it is most unlikely that these can be charged directly to clients. They tend to be fixed and related to the number of people employed rather than the volume of work being done.

Both building overheads and business overheads need to be controlled as excessive spending will clearly eat into profits. However given the nature of the people who work in professional firms and the relatively high salaries paid an obsessive attention to saving pennies on overheads is usually counterproductive.

The bottom line

Profit is the excess income after all costs have been deducted and before taxes are paid. For public companies very high profits can be a source of embarrassment as both clients and staff may feel the firm is doing too well at their expense. This is not such an issue for partnerships as the profits are simply distributed to the partners or directors. The only true measure of profit in these firms is total partner compensation – which is usually secret.

In response to critical clients, highly profitable, publicly owned, service firms must stress that the value of their service is not directly related to the size of their profits. After all would any rational traveller avoid flying Singapore Airlines just because it is more profitable than other carriers? Far from charging excessive fares or cutting corners Singapore's high profits are a function of its own cost structure and management skills.

THE INCOME EQUATION

The fees or commissions charged to clients are nearly always the largest single element of income for a service firm. An understanding of the building blocks of this income source is fundamental to running the business.

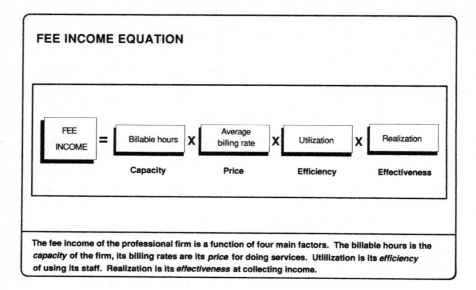

Figure 1.6

A firm's income will depend on how many professional hours it has available for sale (capacity); on how much it can charge for each hour (price); on how many of the available hours are actually worked (efficiency) and how many of those worked hours are actually paid for by the client (effectiveness of collecting income). Even those businesses like advertising agencies which operate on percentage commissions have, in effect, a similar equation. Instead of charging an hourly rate they receive commission income but in order to service their clients they must work a certain number of professional hours. The effective price of each hour worked can, therefore, be calculated. There are four elements to the fee equation:

- Billable hours
- Average billing rate
- Utilization
- Realization

Figure 1.6 illustrates the fee income equation.

Billable hours

The total number of billable hours available is a function of the number of professionals the firm employs. It will also depend on the number of hours the firm believes its professional should be available for work. Every firm must make its own policy decision on this. A corporate law firm, for example, might expect its professionals to work a 50 hour week for 48 weeks a year, implying a capacity of 2,400 hours. It must be understood that this is simply a target figure around which the firm can do its planning as opposed to some legally enforced employment condition.

Average billing rate

The average amount per hour charged by the firm to its clients for the services of professionals is, in effect, its average price per hour.

In setting its price per hour the firm must take into account how much value the client feels it is receiving and also how much competing firms are charging. The ultimate control on the firm's price is the decision by the client to forego the professional service or to employ someone on the client's own staff to do the work if the price becomes too high.

The same concept of average billing rate holds true for commission based businesses even if they do not quote a price per hour for their work. If, for example, an advertising agency handles a £1 million account its income might be £150,000 (15 per cent). If the agency devotes 1,000 man hours to servicing that account then its *effective* average billing rate is £150 per hour. If the agency only devoted 500 hours to the same account its effective rate would double to become £300 per hour.

Commission-based businesses that 'cheat' their clients by under-servicing large projects by having few people do relatively few hours are, in effect, charging very high hourly rates. They will tend to lose out in the long run as the clients will fire the firm, feeling they do no get value or good service. Also the firm's competitors will be able to offer the same service for a much lower price. Equally by over-servicing – having many people working many hours for a client and bringing the effective hourly rate down low – the firm will make a financial loss on serving the client. In effect the firm will be giving away the services of its staff at well below what they could be earning doing other work.

Utilization

This is the number of billable hours which are *actually* spent on client work as opposed to training, administration and unassigned ('on the beach') time.

Utilization will usually decrease with seniority. A typical firm might aim for 50 per cent utilization of directors and 85 per cent utilization of executives. Achieving utilization rates is a matter of capacity planning and marketing. It is quite possible to have utilization rates in excess of 100 per cent if people actually work more client hours than set in the billable hours target.

Realization

This is the percentage of billed work *actually* paid for by the client. Sometimes there are bad debts, sometimes clients haggle over fees. High realization is a function of good financial systems, good client relations, realistic pricing and high quality work.

FEE EQUATION EXAMPLE

A public relations consultant who is a sole practitioner goes to work for 40 hours a week for 48 hours a year. Her total billable hours are 1,920 (40 × 48).

She tells her clients she will work for them at a cost of £50 a hour – her *billing rate*. As she works alone this is also her average billing rate. If she worked with a partner who charged £30 an hour and who worked the same number of hours the *average billing rate* of their two person firm would be £40 per hour.

She actually manages to work on behalf of clients for 1,200 hours during the year. The rest of the time she is doing adminstration, training, etc. Her utilization is 62.5 per cent (1,200/1,920).

Of the 1,200 hours she billed to clients at £50 an hour she might have hoped to receive £60,000. In fact because of bad debts and disputes over fees she actually got £50,000 – a realization rate of 83 per cent.

Her *effective billing rate* for the year was thus £26 per hour, this being the total income of £50,000 divided by the total hours worked of 1,920.

ECONOMICS OF A PROFESSIONAL FIRM									
	NO. IN GRADE	TOTAL BILLABLE HOURS	USE*	AVERAGE HOURLY RATE**	TOTAL FEE INCOME £000	TOTAL SALARY COSTS £000	% OF INCOME	% OF COSTS	RATIO INCOME/ COSTS
Directors	5	10,000	50%	£130	£650	£750	12%	33%	0.87
Managers	10	20,000	80%	£90	£1,440	£600	27%	33%	2.40
Executives	30	60,000	90%	£60	£3,240	£900	61%	40%	3.60
TOTAL	45	90,000	83%	£71	£5,330	£2,250	100%	100%	2.37

* Use = Utilization = % of billable hours charged to clients
** Rates charged to clients, i.e. price

Utilization and the billing rate are the main drivers of direct profitability for each of the firm's three layers of professional staff. The excess of fee income over salary costs goes to cover the firm's overheads.

Figure 1.7

Figure 1.7 shows a typical professional firm of 45 people with its income and costs. For simplicity the fee income model shows only three layers of professional staff – directors, managers and executives – and ignores trainees and support staff. It assumes 2,000 billable hours for each professional. Again, for simplicity, the income side shows only fees from serving clients and ignores income from mark-ups.

In law firms and management consultancies where work is charged by the hour the model is an accurate reflection of the economics. For commission and transaction based businesses, like advertising agencies, the income is not actually produced as a result of hours billed but professional staff are, in effect, operating at a billing rate which can be calculated by assessing the number of hours worked and the income generated.

The point to note from figure 1.7 is that the executive group generates 3.6 times its cost in fee income compared to the directors at 0.87 and the managers at 2.4 times. This is a function of the billing rate (the firm's price which is dictated by the competition in the market) and the salary packages (the main costs which are dictated at the junior levels by the job market and at a senior level by the directors' own decisions on how much money they can take out of the firm). The directors (or shareholders) will enjoy the greatest profits when the billing ratios are greatest. In the short term this can be achieved by charging the clients at greater than the market rate or paying the professionals at below the market rate. However, assuming that no firm can get away with this overcharging or underpayment for long, the source of sustainable high profits is, ultimately, the efficient use of professional staff and good management which comes back to utilization and realization.

A common and major error made by people acquiring professional firms is to assume that the high profitability which they observe at the time of purchase is a result of efficient operations and can be sustained. It is, in fact, often a result of an aberration in high billing rates or low salaries and is unsustainable. Cautious purchasers of professional firms should look for a consistent picture of high utilization and realization as well as fees and salaries which reflect prevailing market conditions. Astute purchasers might look for firms which have a good client base but are poorly managed in terms of low utilization and so on.

4

SERVICE FIRM CHALLENGES

What are the main problems which have to be overcome by the managers of professional service firms?

How do clients know good PR when they see it?
PR Consultant

If I don't work I don't eat. It's not like owning a factory.
Designer

You just can't do it on the telephone. I must have enough frequent flyer miles to get a free 747.
Consultant

You know that thing about only being as good as your last job — well that's our business.
Copywriter, advertising agency

There are certain challenges, specific to professional service firms, which managers must recognize and overcome for the firm to be successful. These are:

- Intangibility of service
- Perishability of service
- Localness of service
- Consistency of service

Figure 1.8 shows the main responses to each of these challenges.

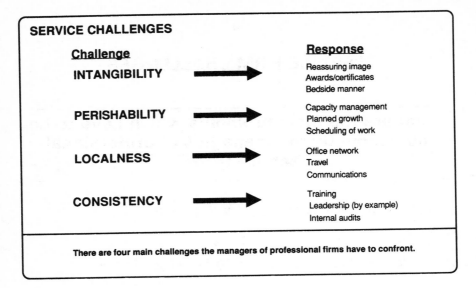

Figure 1.8

INTANGIBILITY

The sumptuous reception areas and well displayed creative awards of advertising agencies; the wood panelling and certificates of qualifications of lawyers – are no accident. In circumstances where the actual product of the business is hard to see and touch these physical props provide a level of reassurance. Far from being a vainglorious squandering of clients' money the investment in image-enhancing elements is of great assistance to firms in winning new business and in retaining existing clients.

Perceptions of quality

Since clients cannot easily judge the quality of the professional service itself they need to be impressed with the overall service package. Service professionals need a good bedside manner to reassure the client that things are going well.

PERCEPTIONS OF QUALITY

In 1989 two friends went into hospital within a few weeks of each other for minor operations. One went to a smart private hospital in London's West End, the other to a large

National Health teaching hospital. After the event the two recounted very different experiences. The private patient could not speak highly enough of the food, the surroundings and the attentiveness of the staff. The public sector patient remembered rudeness, bad food and a general sense of being out of control. In the event the actual operations were both probably perfect but the patients, being unable to comment on the actual core professional service, simply reacted to the package.

The same is true for lawyers, accountants, public relations people and all other professionals. The very intangibility of their service and the difficulty for clients to assess it means that the overall delivery system, not just the execution of the specific professional skill itself, must be made to work.

PERISHABILITY

The fact that services tend to be consumed at the same time as they are produced throws up the problem that service, unlike products, cannot be stockpiled. Successful service firms must have good systems for capacity management and planned growth to ensure they do not, through over-optimistic forecasting, have surplus, expensive staff where not required.

Firms need to develop good client relationships if they are to schedule work to fit in with the firm's ability to deliver rather than the client's needs. This is discussed further in chapter 21.

To ensure that staff are available to meet demand when it is there and to avoid having too many unused people (which will bring down utilization rates) firms must investigate the use of freelance, part-time and temporary staff to cope with seasonal peaks and troughs. This is discussed in chapters 24 and 37.

The marketing effort must be geared to keeping professionals as fully occupied as possible. The flow of new business must be managed to reflect the firms projected future capacity. This is covered in chapters 38 and 39.

LOCALNESS

As well as being delivered in real time professional services are also usually delivered in a certain place − consultancy work, advertising advice, legal assistance and so on are often delivered at the client's office. Although professionals can and do travel extensively and sometimes operate out of hotels, a firm which wishes to grow beyond any one city will need a network of offices. To prevent clients feeling neglected the firm must give a high priority to good communications with frequent telephone calls, faxes and letters to provide full information about progress. In some cases professional firms install dedicated fax lines or electronic mail links in a client's office to help maintain a close client relationship.

The management of the issue of localness is covered in chapters 33 and 37.

CONSISTENCY

Once a firm grows beyond more than a handful of professionals, providing a consistent quality of service becomes a critical problem. This is partly a challenge of supervision but also of recruitment and leadership. If a firm is going to sustain a reputation for a certain level of excellence it must ensure that *all* professional staff have a clear, and consistent, belief about what is and is not acceptable.

Regular quality checks – sometimes called internal audits – of client work must be carried out. Professionals should present their recent past and current work to their peers in the firm who are best able to assess its quality in the context of the firm's own standards.

Achieving consistency is covered in chapter 29.

5

MANAGEMENT IDEAS

What ideas or models are useful in describing and operating professional firms?

I guess the main management task is deciding, with our clients, who does what and then we go and do it.

Management consultant

There are three management concepts which are very useful in understanding service firms and how they function, how to structure the firm, what to charge clients, how fast to grow the firm and so on. They provide a language and a set of terms with which to describe the professional firm. These concepts are:

- Staff pyramid
- Client service techniques
- Client service package

STAFF PYRAMID

There is no single correct way to structure a professional firm but broadly all firms exhibit three levels of hierarchy as shown in figure 1.9. Although the name given to each layer will vary from business to business, the existence and function of the three levels will be very familiar to all. Each level is characterized by its role within the firm, its reward structure and the skills it brings to client work.

Sructure of the pyramid – leverage ratio

An important characteristic of a professional firm is its *leverage ratio* – the balance between the three levels of the pyramid. The most appropriate ratio will depend on the nature of the firm's

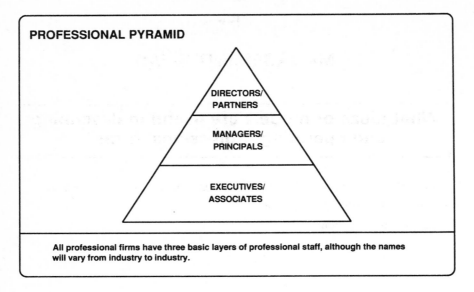

Figure 1.9

service and the demands of its clients. There is no universally correct ratio, but certain types of firms in certain markets will benefit from being either flat or steep – the two main types of pyramid structure:

- Flat or broad base where there is a high ratio of junior staff to seniors

- Steep or narrow base where there is a low ratio of junior staff to seniors – i.e. a relatively larger number of senior staff

The flatter the pyramid and the broader the base the greater the leverage enjoyed by senior people. Figure 1.10 contrasts the economics of a flat pyramid with that of a steep structure and shows that the combination of a small number of directors with a large number of highly utilized executives creates the significantly greater profits in the flat model. To operate a business like this directors will have to be very good at bringing in new work and will have to be able to spread themselves thinly across a large number of clients.

In the flat model the role of the director is more that of rainmaker (new business winner) and elder statesman. In the steep, narrow base, model directors tend to be more involved in

STAFF PYRAMID - FLAT VS STEEP

GRADE	NUMBER IN GRADE	BILLING RATE	UTILIZATION	INCOME* £000's	SALARY COSTS £000's	SURPLUS** INCOME £000's
FLAT PYRAMID : BROAD BASE				**Profit per director = £216,000**		
Directors	5	£130	50%	£650	£750	(£100)
Managers	10	£90	80%	£1,440	£600	£840
Executives	30	£60	90%	£3,240	£900	£2,340
TOTAL	45			£5,330	£2,250	£3,080
STEEP PYRAMID : NARROW BASE				**Profit per director = £62,000**		
Directors	10	£130	50%	£1,300	£1,500	(£200)
Managers	15	£90	80%	£2,160	£900	£1,260
Executives	20	£60	90%	£2,160	£600	£1,560
TOTAL	45			£5,620	£3,000	£2,620

* Assumes total of 2000 billable hours
** Surplus prior to meeting firm's overheads which are assumed to be £2m

The flat structure produces a much higher leverage and a greater profit for distribution among the directors.

Figure 1.10

the actual work. A firm which builds its reputation on the counselling of clients by experienced, senior staff would find it hard to become a flat pyramid business because the very qualities the clients value, such as regular access to senior firm professionals would be almost impossible to deliver and require the larger numbers of senior people typical of a steep structure.

Clearly the flat alternative offers a better profit to the directors but this can only work if the structure fits the needs of clients and the operation of the market. The shape of the pyramid is discussed in more detail in chapters 11 and 26. The problems of growing a firm with a flat pyramid are covered in chapter 37.

CLIENT SERVICE TECHNIQUES

Professional service firms need to excel at the following skills:

- Client relations
- Project management
- Application of professional knowledge/expertise

Broadly speaking the three techniques correspond to the three layers of the pyramid hierarchy. Each level of seniority tends to

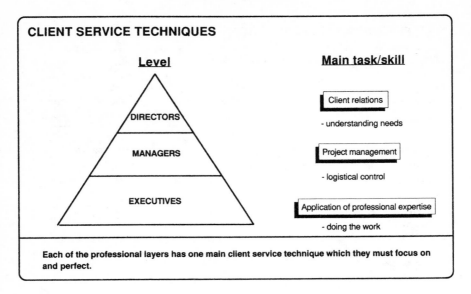

CLIENT SERVICE TECHNIQUES

Level — Main task/skill

DIRECTORS — Client relations / - understanding needs

MANAGERS — Project management / - logistical control

EXECUTIVES — Application of professional expertise / - doing the work

Each of the professional layers has one main client service technique which they must focus on and perfect.

Figure 1.11

focus on one of the techniques. Figure 1.11 illustrates this in terms of identifying the prime task of the people at each level; although this is an oversimplification as clearly all members of the firm will need to exhibit all of the techniques to some degree.

The balance of these three techniques will depend on the type of firm and the type of client work undertaken; for example, some firms may adopt a uniform approach and be consistent in their approach towards all clients. Others might have different work groups within the firm, each with a different focus and different balance of the skills. But each of these techniques must be taught within the firm to ensure all its professionals achieve an acceptable level of competence.

The development and application of these key techniques is discussed in part IV.

CLIENT SERVICE PACKAGE

Each client will require a different mixture of professional value from its service firms. In all cases the service package will be based on:

- Experience
- Execution
- Expertise

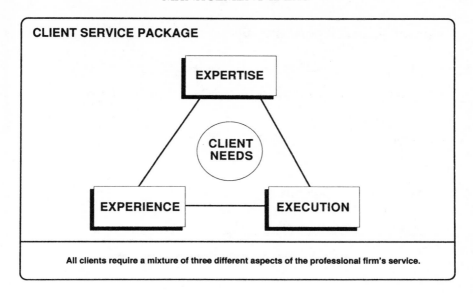

Figure 1.12

As shown in figure 1.12, it is unlikely that one firm will exhibit a consistent mix of the three elements and in fact the three broadly different types of client package can show up as different types of project within one firm. Within an industry various firms tend to develop the reputation of being stronger at one of the elements. Thus some advertising agencies are thought of as highly creative (expertise-based) while others are known to be very efficient (execution-based). Some management consultants will be seen as good at helping clients go through the traumas of a merger (experience-based) others will be known for installing financial systems quickly and cost-effectively (experience and execution).

These professional value terms (expertise, experience and execution) have been variously describes as the three Es – expertise, experience and efficiency ('brains', 'grey hair' and 'procedure', respectively) by Dr David Maister in his book *Professional Service Firm Management*; and, firms designated 'strong ideas', 'strong service' and 'strong delivery' firms in a joint paper on the management of architectural firms (Weld Coxe *et al*). Figure 1.13 shows these alternative approaches.

Clearly a firm would like to be regarded as excellent in all three areas but many firms tend to emphasize one more than the others simply because it helps them to differentiate themselves from competitors.

Large firms will often develop internal divisions or practice

SERVICE PACKAGE DESCRIPTIONS

ELEMENT	FEATURES	Maister* Description	Coxe** Description
EXPERTISE	One-off projects Creative	BRAINS	STRONG IDEAS
EXPERIENCE	Practical solution Knowledge based	GREY-HAIR	STRONG SERVICE
EXECUTION	Good systems Attention to detail	PROCEEDURE	STRONG DELIVERY

* *Professional Service Firm Management* by David Maister
** *Charting Your Course* by Coxe, Hartung et al, in *Architectural Technology*

Management writers characterize the three service elements in different ways.

Figure 1.13

areas each of which has its own characteristic balance. For example, a large law firm may have different practice areas corresponding to each client service type; the expertise element will be seen most strongly in things like a libel action requiring very high levels of litigation skills; the experience element will predominate in the negotiation of an international merger where a large number of legal complexities can be dealt with from experience; execution projects are those such as commercial property conveyancing where a strict, flawless routine is called for. Alternatively with public relations, a small group of contested-bid specialists might form a firm based on this expertise; a broad-based corporate public relations firm assisting clients with regular communications will be mainly experienced-based; a consumer PR firm concerned only with media relations will need flawless execution.

Although in reality it is never as simple as the examples given, all firms will have a mix of clients and projects, the principal in general holds good. If managers feel the whole firm (or a particular project) requires an emphasis on a certain balance of the three elements they must ensure that all other aspects of the firm such as recruiting, training and assignment are consistent with this approach. This is discussed further in part IV.

ACHIEVE BALANCE

Professional firms cannot be organized into a rigid, clear unchanging structure as clients' needs and the market change over time. A key management task is to find, and maintain, the balance between the potentially conflicting demands of:

- Flat versus steep pyramid
- Three client service techniques
- Three types of service package

The firm's structure, recruitment, training and operations must be changed to reflect the changing balance. Unsuccessful firms are usually those which do not recognize this reality and try to operate with one type of structure while offering clients a different type of service.

LACK OF BALANCE

A successful London consumer PR firm decided it wanted to break into the lucrative contested bid area. The firm's chief executive had the necessary skills. The consumer firm had enjoyed a flat, wide base pyramid and had excelled at project management, with the bulk of its clients requiring experience and execution skills. Senior staff set the targets – junior staff did the work

The new clients, involved in contested bids, required expertise skills and close client relations. Attempting to use the firm's junior staff to serve the clients was unsuccessful as they lacked the necessary professional abilities and credibility.

The firm tried to recruit more senior staff to meet the needs of bid clients but this unsettled its structure making it uneconomic to service consumer clients. Having what amounted to two inconsistent business systems running in parallel destabilized the firm.

The questions the managers of professional service firms should ask themselves are:

- Who are my target clients?
- What service packages do my target clients require (in terms of expertise, experience and execution)?

- What balance of techniques will the firm need to service the clients (in terms of client relations, project management and professional expertise)?

- What structure is appropriate? (in terms of flat or steep)?

- Will the business operate profitably with that structure?

- Will the firm be able to grow and maintain this structure?

The balance must reflect the clients' needs at any one time and must be preserved as the firm grows if a successful and profitable formula is not to be lost.

6

SERVICE OFFERING

How should a firm position itself to clients?
How can it describe the nature of its services?

You can't be all things to all men. Clients seek us out because they know our real skill is attention to detail. We're not that creative but we are really a safe pair of hands.

Director, advertising agency

They come to us for good ideas. I think it is true we are difficult people but we are the most creative.

Director, advertising agency

In terms of positioning firms have to be clear what they believe their clients want and then be equally clear that they have assembled the right resources, directed in the right way, to deliver it.

WHAT BUSINESS ARE WE IN?

Professional firms should be clear about how they position their services in the market place. This will help them in a number of ways:

- Marketing – clients can understand what service the firm is offering, if it meets their needs and if they are prepared to pay for it

- Recruitment – people will understand what sort of firm they are joining

- Management – the resources and operation of the firm will be consistent with the positioning

A firm can position itself at different places along a number of dimensions:

- High cost/low cost

- Knowledge(experience)-based/technique(execution)-based

- Consulting only/hands-on, turn-key, implementation

The decision on where to position the firm is a matter of strategy and is dealt more fully with in part VI. The remainder of this chapter describes the framework and ways of thinking about positioning.

RELATIONSHIP AND CONTRIBUTION

One way of approaching the question of positioning is to use a hypothetical model based on:

- The *relationship* with the client which is based on the type of service techniques employed (the degree to which the client values the firm purely for its professional skill or, at the other end of the scale, for its counselling ability)

- The *contribution* the firm makes to the client from the client service package (the degree to which the client wants the firm for its experience or for its execution skills)

Taking these two ideas and developing them further within a framework gives the basis for figure 1.14. One axis describes the *relationship*, ranging from a strong counselling and communications-based approach at one end (where the firm is very involved in the relationship with the client); to a very clinical, surgical, knowledge-based relationship at the other end (where the firm is mainly valued for its knowledge). The other axis describes *contribution*, moving from expertise based work where the firm is mainly called upon for its skills which have been built up over time (skills which the client does not have) to execution-based work where the firm is valued for its ability to get things done (things which the client prefers not to do for themselves).

Adjectives have been added to the axes in figure 1.14. that might be associated with the different types of positioning. To give a flavour of each positioning the names of fictional detectives, each with their own style, is placed in each box.

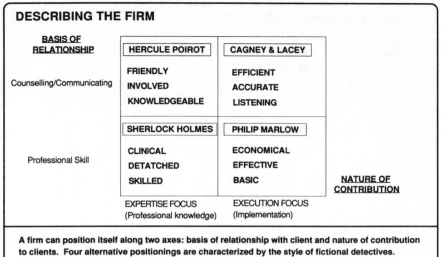

Figure 1.14

The positioning of a firm's service along each axis will mainly be a function of what clients want and are prepared to pay for. A client of a strategy consultant with very action-oriented internal management might only require the strategy described (high professional skills, high expertise) –they want the Sherlock Holmes approach (without the implementation skills of Dr Watson!). In effect Holmes solves the case and the police (the client's own people) do the dirty work. Another client may require the consultant to become far more involved in the implementation of the strategy (high relationship as well as detective expertise) requiring the Hercule Poirot way of doing things.

Figure 1.15 shows the possible positioning of some of the services offered by accounting and legal firms. Very small firms might position themselves in just one box but most firms will offer a range of services. Managers must be aware that the different positioning implies a different set of economics and a different business system.

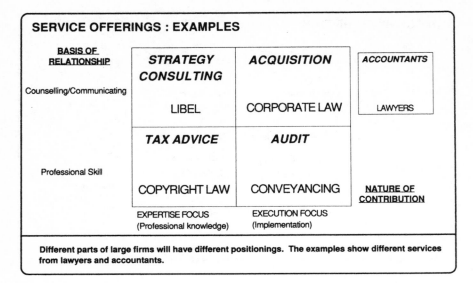

SERVICE OFFERINGS : EXAMPLES

BASIS OF RELATIONSHIP	*STRATEGY CONSULTING*	*ACQUISITION*	ACCOUNTANTS
Counselling/Communicating	LIBEL	CORPORATE LAW	LAWYERS
	TAX ADVICE	*AUDIT*	
Professional Skill	COPYRIGHT LAW	CONVEYANCING	NATURE OF CONTRIBUTION
	EXPERTISE FOCUS (Professional knowledge)	EXECUTION FOCUS (Implementation)	

Different parts of large firms will have different positionings. The examples show different services from lawyers and accountants.

Figure 1.15

MAISTER MODEL

The leading professional services consultant Dr David Maister has developed the framework shown in figure 1.16 to describe various positionings in terms of medical services.

The *pharmacy* services are those where clients have a good idea of what is needed and simply want something provided quickly and at low cost. Audit work or house conveyancing are analogies from accountancy and law. To be effective in this positioning the professional firm must ensure high utilization rates and have relatively junior staff doing the bulk of the work.

The *nursing* services are for clients wanting a higher level of interaction and counselling. The problems to be solved may be relatively routine but unlike the 'pharmacy' the client needs more hand-holding to see the value in the service. The professional skills required are relatively low but the client service skills are much higher. To reflect these additional skills the firm probably uses more senior people and charges more accordingly.

The *surgery* services are those where the client needs the high level professional expertise of the professional but does not feel the need to become involved in the process. Much of the work of commercial architects will fall into this area. It will also be the positioning of information technology consultants within an

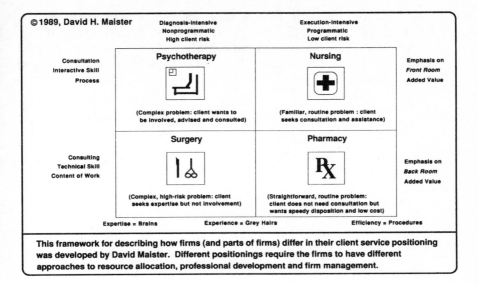

Figure 1.16

accounting firm. Firms working in this way will have to recruit and keep the best technical experts in their field.

Psychotherapy requires a high level of client involvement as well as strong professional expertise. The solution to the problem is unlikely to be the application of a routine procedure. Firms will have to have a large number of senior people available to provide this sort of approach.

Dr Maister's work is a rich source of ideas and theoretical frameworks and readers who want to go further into the theory are strongly recommended to read his book *Professional Service Firm Management*.

FIT WITH CLIENT NEEDS

In terms of high- or low-cost positioning a firm has to consider its ability to deliver to client expectations and its own circumstances. A legal firm with prestige offices in the centre of a capital city is unlikely to be able to do routine conveyancing work as cheaply as one in the suburbs. Equally the small local firm will be unlikely to attract the staff to handle complex commercial issues. However both firms can be equally profitable and successful.

The positioning of a firm's services is not the same as the positioning of the whole firm itself. While it is unlikely that one firm can have both low-cost and high-cost elements it is quite possible to have both knowledge-based and technique-based services on offer.

7

MANAGEMENT TOOLS

What techniques are useful in running a professional firm?

In terms of knowing what's going on I've always found the analysis of time-sheets to be the single most revealing insight.
Manager, accounting firm

Professional service firms will benefit from management tools which have been specifically designed with regard to the economics and issues of such firms. Manufacturing industry has developed specific techniques such as cost/benefit analysis, capital budgeting using internal rates of return and so on. The main tools of use in professional firms are:

- Cost allocation
- Client profitability
- Client relationship audits
- Internal quality control

This chapter, briefly, outlines each technique. They are discussed in much greater detail in later chapters of the book.

COST ALLOCATION

In well-run firms there will be a clear link between income from each client and the costs incurred in servicing that client. It is theoretically possible to allocate all the costs of running the firm such as heat, light and rates to individual clients but in practice this is unwieldy and unnecessary and provides no insights.

The principal cost is peoples' time and everything else tends to flow from this. Given this fact the basis of most cost allocation is to analyse how people spend their time by requiring professional

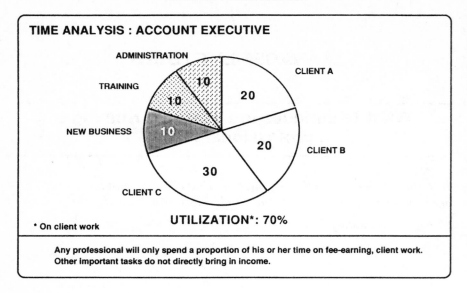

Figure 1.17

staff to fill in time-sheets. Figure 1.17 shows a typical time-breakdown for an account executive or other middle-ranking professional derived from an analysis of time-sheets. In most firms time will be split between various clients, general administration tasks and projects aimed at building the firm such as training. In the example shown the executive is achieving a 70 per cent utilization rate. That is to say 70 per cent of his or her hours are being spent on fee-earning client work.

Even in those businesses where clients are not billed on the basis of hours worked the firm should calculate how professionals spend their time so managers can calculate the cost of doing various activities. Time-sheets are more important as a cost calculation mechanism than they are as are as a basis for charging clients.

In addition to professional time other costs such as directly identifiable overheads (printing, messengers, telephones, etc.) should be allocated to all clients and to the main activities of the firm. The firm also needs to understand how much recruiting or training really costs when professional time and identifiable overheads are included.

The collection and use of cost information is described in much greater depth in parts II and IV.

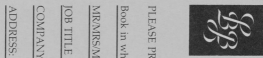

If you would like to join our mailing list and receive our twice yearly catalogue, with details of our wide range of books on every aspect of business and management, please fill in this card and send it to us.

PLEASE PRINT

Book in which this card was found:
_____

MR/MRS/MS: _____ INITIALS: _____ SURNAME: _____

JOB TITLE (if applicable): _____

COMPANY (if applicable): _____

ADDRESS: _____

_____

_____ POSTCODE: _____

BUSINESS BOOKS LTD.

Customer Mailing List

Random Century House

20 Vauxhall Bridge Road

London SW1V 2SA

CLIENT PROFITABILITY

The income and costs breakdown for a typical client are shown in figure 1.18. The fees shown in the figure may have been negotiated in advance and paid to the firm on a project–cost basis or they may have been calculated retrospectively based on the number of hours worked for each client.

The mark–up income will depend on the value of goods and services purchased for clients and how big the percentage mark–up is. This will vary according to the nature of the client project.

On the cost side the professional time comes directly from the time–sheets. The cost is calculated by knowing the total cost of employing someone and the total number of hours worked and hence the cost per hour to the firm.

Direct overheads are those which can be identified as clearly incurred as a result of servicing the client.

Any costs which were charged directly to the client would generate a small mark–up or handling charge which would appear as income under the 'handling' or mark–up line.

Allocated overheads are things like rent and rates. These are judged to be incurred in about the same proportion as the fraction of the firm's total professional staff time devoted to the client. In truth whether these overheads are allocated by client or just treated as a central cost makes little difference to controlling the firm. As a basic principle the only overheads worth allocating are

---

TYPICAL CLIENT PROFITABILITY REPORT

CLIENT : *a*

MONTH : *X*

INCOME	£	
Fees (or commission)	25,000	
Handling (mark-up)	5,000	
Total income		30,000
COSTS		
Professional staff time (from time-sheets)	15,000	
Direct costs (identified by client)	5,000	
Allocated overhead (general to the firm)	5,000	
Total costs		20,000
CONTRIBUTION (= Client profit)		**10,000**
Contribution as % of income		33%

The profit contribution of individual clients must be calculated if the firm is to manage its resources and maximize the overall profits of the firm.

Figure 1.18

those over which the client service professionals have some control and which are incurred to different degrees depending on amount of activity involved in serving the client.

The problems come when a particular client proves costly to administer. Typical difficulties might be consistently late payers (costly because of the need to finance the missing cash flow) or clients who demand an exceptionally high level of documentation and cost analysis of their bills. Badly-managed firms simply regard these clients as difficult, well-managed firms will seek to charge them more to reflect the extra work.

The issue of client profitability is covered in part II.

CLIENT RELATIONSHIP AUDITS

The output of the service firm is intangible and perishable, and thus one of the only satisfactory measures of the firms performance is the nature of the client relationship. Is the client satisfied? A key part of the role of the director on a client's business should be to test this relationship frequently. Some form of regular, formalized assessment of the client's state of mind should be undertaken.

Figure 1.19 is an example of a typical quarterly assessment for a PR programme. Normally this would be completed by the most senior executive from the client company involved with the

---

CLIENT FEEDBACK REPORT

CONFIDENTIAL

CLIENT : __X__   Period of assessment : _____ to _____

Completed by : __Z__

Please circle appropriate figure with your assessment of our performance working on your account

	Poor	Satisfactory	Outstanding
Impact of programme	1	2	3
Application of strategy	1	2	3
Ability of team	1	2	3
Efficiency of team	1	2	3
Attitude of team	1	2	3
Performance of managers	1	2	3
Performance of execution	1	2	3
Overall assessment	1	2	3

A typical client feedback report which should be completed at least twice a year or at the end of a project. It provides a safety valve and a way for the firm to judge the quality of its services.

Figure 1.19

account and then discussed with a director of the PR firm. The form is mainly a safety valve to give early warning of problems and to form the basis of a discussion about the conduct of the account. Client relationship audits and other client relationship issues are discussed in part IV.

INTERNAL QUALITY CONTROL

The client's opinion of the firm's performance is rather subjective from an external view-point. Quality control and what constitutes quality is also a subjective assessment but from an internal view point.

As was explained earlier the intangible nature of a professional service firm's output and the fact that it is created by the firm's professionals themselves (who are often working in remote locations on client premises away from the direct supervision of senior firm staff) means that quality control is hard to achieve. In manufacturing companies standards are laid down and samples are tested. Professional firms have to find equivalent methods. Much of the control comes from the personal, professional standards of the directors and managers. These standards need to be clearly set in internal training sessions and closely adhered to by the senior people themselves when engaged in client projects. In some businesses a formal internal review of work is appropriate. Team members may present advertising strategy or PR plans or consulting solutions to other members of the firm. It is usually the case that professionals value the approval of their peers above all other accolades.

Managers of professional firms need to develop and use specific quality control tools and techniques, such as internal reviews, to keep standards high. Chapter 29 'Quality Control' suggests some actual standards of performance and discusses ways of monitoring quality inside the firm.

PART II

LEVERS OF PROFITABILITY

What can managers of professional service firms do to make their business more profitable?

There are usually a few things which can be done really easily, really quickly to improve the bottom line. I'm often amazed that people don't do it for themselves and they wait to get taken over.
Director, marketing services group

There are specific actions that can be taken by managers in professional firms to maximize profitability. Part II of the book identifies those levers that can be used to maximize profits.

In publicly owned companies profit is easily measured as the surplus after operating costs. In private companies (the majority of professional service firms) profit might be defined as the surplus available for payment to the partners, who are often the owners. Central to the issue of maximizing profit (however defined) in professional firms are the following levers of profitability:

- How profitable are the individual *clients* that the business serves? Are any clients subsidizing others? Are any clients being given more than they are paying for?

- How profitable are individual service *products* – in those firms where clear products such as house conveyancing or designing an annual report can be identified are some better profit earners for the firm than others?

- How *well balanced* is the firm in terms of the ratio of junior staff to partners? Are highly paid senior people doing simple work that could be done more profitably by less costly staff?

- How well does the firm recover its costs from clients – what is the effective *billing rate* for its professional staff? In other words has the firm got its pricing right?

- How well *utilized* are the staff – is everybody being kept busy on the right sort of work? How many hours are being billed to clients and how many to non-income generating, but important, activities like training and marketing?

- How well is the business managing its *working capital* – is it letting clients have free credit? Is it paying suppliers too quickly? Is it leaving money lying around?

- How good is the *housekeeping* – how well controlled are the overheads of running the firm? Is money that is spent on costs not directly associated with client service being wasted? Is the firm spending too much on rent, telephones, etc?

One of the critical aspects of profitability is the recognition that in professional service firms profitable trading is not something that can be left to the accounts department or the managing director but must involve *all* members of the firm.

This attitude is variously described as a 'total service culture' or a 'one firm approach' but the reality is that no amount of systems and incentives will induce profitability without the right attitude. In this respect profitability becomes inextricably linked with quality control and staff morale.

Improving a firm's profits has short-term and long-term elements. If a firm is making losses, or is close to it, the emergency solutions are almost certainly to be found in improving utilization and reducing housekeeping costs. These two initiatives should help prevent further losses. For the long term to help the firm equal, or better, industry profit averages the focus must be on improving the firm's balance to achieve the right mix of senior and junior staff; increasing the firm's billing rates to maximize the gap between total employee compensation and total income per employee; and improving client and product profitability. Attempting to change the firm's balance or client profitability over a very short period is almost impossible. The solution is, usually, to set targets for the firm to reach over a period of time.

8

WHAT IS PROFITABLE?

What is meant by profitable?

For me profit is what I have taken home at the end of the year
Partner, accounting firm

The profitability of one professional firm compared to another should not matter in absolute terms. It is pointless to compare profits because the profit figure is simply an accounting exercise that can be manipulated. A small, private firm can choose to pay high wages and to show a small profit or it can pay low wages and look profitable. It is often a decision to do with personal versus corporate tax rates and the public image the firm wishes to give rather than any real, underlying, measure of performance.

If profit is defined as the surplus available for distribution to partners (i.e. owners) then private firms would always appear to be more profitable than public companies. In public companies the owners and managers are distinct groups. The directors will be paid salaries which are defined as operating costs before the calculation of operating profit. Profitability is often taken as the profit margin in other words the operating profit divided by the turnover. In some firms such as advertising agencies this would be grossly misleading as the turnover includes vast sums of money spent on behalf of clients which simply pass through the agencies' books. The most useful definition of profitability in professional firms is operating profit divided by gross income where operating profit is calculated after a reasonable salary payment to partners or directors.

The main terms are set out below:

TURNOVER (money coming in)
— Cost of sales (money paid to suppliers)

= GROSS INCOME (money left for the firm)
— Operating costs (salaries, overheads etc.)

= OPERATING PROFIT (for distribution to owners before taxes)

PROFITABILITY or operating profit margin =

$$\frac{\text{OPERATING PROFIT}}{\text{GROSS INCOME}}$$

Figure 2.1 gives an estimate of the relative profitability of different British professional service firms over the five years from 1985 to 1990. These estimates are based on conversations with senior managers of typical firms and analyses of data from trade publications. The main assumption is that a typical partner or director is paid £50,000 as a salary *before* receiving any profit sharing. The £50,000 is an arbitrary figure roughly equivalent to a senior manager in industry. In a private partnership all of the profit margin might be distributed in profit shares. The £50,000

ESTIMATED PROFIT MARGINS

BUSINESS	OPERATING* PROFIT MARGIN
Advertising	20%
Accounting	35%
Architecture	30%
Consulting engineering	25%
Law	45%
Management consultancy	40%
Public relations	25%

* Defined as operating profit/gross income. Assumes a partner or director is paid £50,000 *before* profit sharing

Some types of professional firm are more profitable than others — partly because of definitions and partly because of the nature of the particular industry.

Figure 2.1

figure, though, bears little relation to reality in some of the professional areas. The *Financial Times* (9 April 1990) estimates a typical partner of a large law firm will be paid £120,000 and a typical assistant solicitor (executive) will make £45,000 per year.

A number of points are raised by figure 2.1:

- The profitability of law and management consulting firms looks very high as, by and large, their partners take home much more than the standard £50,000. Also their markets are relatively predictable and have been growing, thus they can manage capacity and utilization quite well. In addition the pricing of their services is still relatively hard for clients to compare in the marketplace. As market growth slows these high levels may well fall. It is likely that for 1991 the profitability of management consultants will have fallen

- The profitability of advertising would have been much higher ten years ago when most clients paid a standard 15 per cent commission on the media time and space purchased for them by the agency. This often left the agency with a large surplus over operating costs. During the 1980s many clients refused to pay a fixed 15 per cent and negotiated the agencies' percentage down thus greatly reducing agency income. Agencies only started coming to grips with the need to cut costs in the late 1980s

- Accountancy tends to be slightly less profitable because of the large amount of basic work done. Clients can shop around different firms and negotiate low fees. In the early 1990s profitability will have declined further as the basic audit work, for example, of accountants has become more and more subject to price competition

- Consulting engineering and architecture tend to be relatively low because clients put jobs out to competitive tender and can compare charges. In addition both are constrained by the slow growth of the construction sector

- Public relations has a relatively low operating profit margin because clients are very fee-sensitive and the very low barriers to entry make it easy for new firms to spring up, offering clients low-cost services. However the 25 per cent margin suggested is much nearer to what many of these firms may actually report in their accounts, as their directors and partners tend to be less well paid than in the other professional areas. Thus they are not taking large amount of profit out of the firm by way of bonus payments or partners drawings

The profitability of any individual firm will, of course, vary greatly depending on its particular trading conditions. The profitability of an industry will change over time reflecting the level of demand from clients and the industry's own structure. For example it is likely that law firms will become less profitable as the various restrictive practices of lawyers are removed and management consultants will suffer if clients become more price sensitive and more firms enter the industry.

Firms must always strive to be among the most profitable in their industry as this will help to attract and retain the best people to the firm which, in the long run, is the basis for success.

At the aggregate level (i.e. for the whole firm) the most useful measure, and control, of profitability is to monitor actual performance against the budget. This analysis of comparative performance should be undertaken monthly and should also reflect the cumulative position for year to date. Figure 2.2 is a typical top-line profitability analysis. It shows a month where client activity (fees and handling) has fallen below budget by a total of £30,000 or 19 per cent. The drop in handling income suggests some client project may have been cancelled. At the same time the firm has managed to keep down its overheads but has not reduced payroll costs. The net result is a significant drop in

TYPICAL BUSINESS PROFITABILITY REPORT — MONTH : X

	ACTUAL £	BUDGET £	VARIANCE %
INCOME			
Fees	100,000	110,000	-9
Handling	30,000	50,000	-40
	130,000	160,000	**-19**
COSTS			
Payroll	75,000	75,000	0
Business overheads	15,000	20,000	-25
Premises overheads	20,000	25,000	-20
	110,000	120,000	**-8**
OPERATING PROFIT	20,000	40,000	**-50**
Profit as % income	15%	25%	

The regular analysis highlights the variance from the budget plan which warns managers where to look for potential trouble.

Figure 2.2

operating profits. Faced with this information management should look hard at projected revenues to decide if the month was a one-off aberration or if it is a warning of a business downturn.

The example shows how close the link is between the firm's profits and its payroll costs. A ten per cent reduction in the £75,000 payroll would lift the operating margin from £20,000 to £27,500 – a full six percentage points increase from 15 to 21 per cent. It highlights the importance of getting the firm's capacity right.

9

CLIENT PROFITABILITY

Which clients are making you money? What can be done to convert unprofitable clients into valuable ones?

We acquired a small consultancy with about 40 clients which was making some money but not much. When we investigated we found only five of the clients were really profitable. All the others represented a loss. It wasn't a business as much as a charity.

Director, public relations group

All professional service firms, by definition, have clients to whom they provide some service. The main element of that service is the time worked by the firm's professional staff on the clients' behalf.

The basis upon which clients are charged varies greatly from business to business. For example a stockbroker or estate agent may charge a fixed percentage commission for executing the sale of some shares or a house. A PR consultant may charge £500 per week for being available and handling press enquiries. A solicitor may charge £100 an hour for work done in drawing up a contract. An advertising agency may charge 15 per cent of the total advertising budget for the creation of some advertisements. In all cases there is an implied relationship between the value received by the client, the level of services provided by the firm and the costs incurred by the firm in the provision of the service. The task of management is to ensure that all work done on behalf of all clients is profitable. Simply because the firm, the aggregate of all the client work, is profitable it does not mean that each individual client relationship is equally profitable.

ASSESSING CLIENT PROFITABILITY

All firms should put in place mechanisms for collecting and analysing the data which will enable them to calculate the profitability of each client.

Profitable – over what period?

In deciding whether a particular client is profitable the first decision is over what period – weekly, monthly, quarterly or yearly – should profits be assessed. The decision depends a great deal on the specific business and the nature of its cash flows. At one extreme to do it daily would involve a very high cost of capturing and processing data and, in most cases would provide a meaningless analysis. At the other extreme to do it annually would make it difficult to identify problems and rectify them in time. The best solution is probably to capture all the necessary data weekly and to do the analysis every month.

Client related costs

There are three items which must be included when calculating client related costs:

- Professional time – calculated at its total cost to the firm
- Directly related business overheads
- External costs not passed on to the client

Professional time

Professional time should be logged for each client and all other business activities by recording it on time-sheets. The total cost of each professional (salary, national insurance, car, health insurance etc.) can then be expressed as an hourly *cost*. Remember that this is very different from the hourly *billing rate* which must be high enough to cover the overheads of the business and to provide a profit. At the end of any selected period the total cost of the time of those professionals working on any account can be calculated. The management information system to collect this data is discussed in more detail in chapter 28.

Directly related overheads

Directly related business overheads include telephone, fax, photo-copies, taxis, travel, hotels etc., which can be directly identified as costs associated with serving a particular client but which are not, for reasons of policy or oversight, passed on to the client for direct payment.

In many businesses great store is placed in ensuring that all these overheads are charged directly to the client. However many clients find this irritating and will argue at great lengths about small sums. In addition a sophisticated client will consider the total cost of using a professional firm by adding together fees and overheads and balancing this total against the value being created by the firm.

External costs

External costs include printing, specialist consultancy, legal work etc. In most cases these will be billed directly to clients with the firm often charging a small mark-up or handling charge. In those cases where they are not – such as the manufacture of 35 mm slides for presentations to the client – the cost must be added in as part of the overall service charge.

Client related income

The income side of the equation will include the number of professional hours billed to the client and the income from any handling charges or mark-up on goods or services purchased on the client's behalf. In the case of an advertising agency this mark

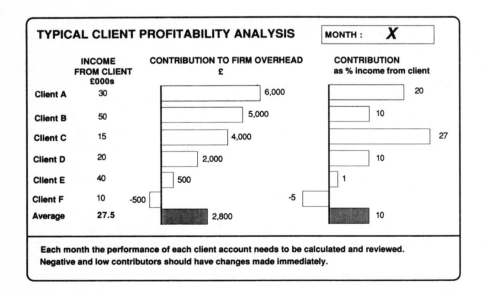

Figure 2.3

up will probably represent the vast bulk of the client income as most agencies are paid on a commission rather than a fee basis.

CLIENT PROFITABILITY REPORT

Having established the costs and income associated with each client you can calculate the profitability of the client account. This can be done for periods of the past month, the past year and since the relationship first started. Figure 2.3 shows the profitability (in terms of contribution) for a firm with six clients. The analysis is only for the past month but managers should also look at longer periods.

The main points from figure 2.3 are:

1   The average contribution from all the clients is *not* the profitability of the overall business. It is, more correctly, the contribution made to the non-allocated overheads which come from the excess of client income over client service costs. The size of the contribution percentage will vary greatly from company to company depending on the nature of its work and the nature of its industry. Firms which have a very high central fixed cost will need a much higher contribution per client than those with low central overheads.

2   The correct response to the losses being made by client F (or the very low contribution of client E) is not simply to resign the business but first to seek ways of improving the performance. In broad terms there are three possible reactions:

- Renegotiate the levels of fee with the client. This means, in effect, putting up the price to reflect value added by the firm. This will increase the income side of the equation. This can only be done, of course, if the firm really is delivering value which is not being paid for

- Reduce the level of resource serving the client and thus reduce the cost side. Again cuts cannot be made to the extent that the client's perceptions of value received will suffer

- Accept the loss as being strategically desirable – perhaps a client whose appearance on the client roster helps the firm – such as a charity account which will enhance the firm's image or an account with growth potential.

    A loss in one month may be a case of an abnormal time period throwing up an erroneous result. In figure 2.3, for example the results of client F may reflect that the annual conference has just been held with all the associated costs while the monthly fee remains the same throughout the year. As another example client F may be in the start-up phase of the relationship

3   There is no such thing as an *acceptable* level of individual client profitability, as one client can vary greatly from another in the nature of the work and the industry. There is certainly an acceptable aggregate level, though, at which the firm becomes profitable by combining the individual profits and losses. The value of knowing the individual figures is that it provides guidance for finding solutions to overall profit levels by highlighting the individual problems.

4   Client C is potentially highly profitable but if that very high profitability results from a level of service way below the level of fee, the client could become very dissatisfied and fire the firm.

Some service firms, shortsightedly, try to achieve these very high levels of profit – regarding such clients as golden geese and being prepared to lose them if they catch on to the effective overcharging. This fails to account accurately for the cost of lost reputation and the high cost of finding replacement business.

CLEAR RESPONSIBILITY

Ideally the manager in charge of each account should be held responsible for its profit performance. The account director or partner in charge has control of all the key elements of both cost and income and should be made to answer to his or her colleagues for an account that is constantly unprofitable.

It is usually good practice to review account profitability regularly at management meetings so that decisions can be taken about individual under-performers. Since each account is potentially a special case it is important that the profitability levels are openly discussed in such a way that managers of poor contributors are not made to feel guilty or at risk. Instead they should feel able to get their colleagues' advice on ways of improving performance.

Many firms pay account directors bonuses that are directly related to the profit performance of their accounts. This works well provided the period related to the bonus is a long one to prevent directors seeking to achieve artificially high profits by under-servicing clients. Managing partners and directors must monitor this as carefully as they monitor loss makers.

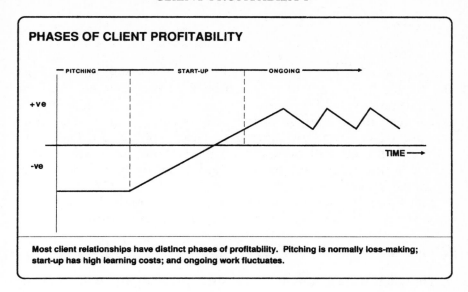

PHASES OF CLIENT PROFITABILITY

Most client relationships have distinct phases of profitability. Pitching is normally loss-making; start-up has high learning costs; and ongoing work fluctuates.

Figure 2.4

PHASES OF PROFITABILITY

Individual client profitability will vary at different stages of the relationship with any one client and the firm as illustrated by figure 2.4.

Pitching

Advertising agencies, designers and consultants are frequently asked to appear in 'beauty contests'. Lawyers might pretend they do not have to but they too are increasingly asked to participate in competitive pitches.

Pitching is an expensive activity. The firm must invest management time in understanding the client and the business problem and may have to buy in services, at the firm's own risk, for things such as research and presentations. Many firms seem reluctant to identify all the costs of seeking new business as many executives find the process very enjoyable. Pitch fees are sometimes paid by clients but even then they will only cover part of the cost. The firms must risk an investment on this first stage of a client relationship and the profitability must, therefore, be negative. The issue of new business costs is covered in detail in chapter 39.

Start-up

The 'getting to know you' phase can be especially expensive. The proportion of senior time required by the client will be very high during the early days of the relationship. Promises made to the client about levels of service and speed of results, which would be quite realistic a year into the relationship, require far more resources from the firm during this early phase. An enormous amount of time will be spent learning about the client and its business, meetings will be long and their productivity low as relationships are built.

The faster the service business can get through this phase the more rapidly the account will achieve acceptable profitability.

Ongoing

Even when an account is established profitability will fluctuate considerably as the level of resource required to to meet the client's needs will vary over time. However in many cases the flow of income may stay fixed where, for example, a regular montly fee has been agreed. In advertising, for example, there may be many months where work is done without any immediate income being generated – until, say, Christmas when the actual media spending generates a commission.

An investment bank may do a whole range of tasks for a client on a small monthly retainer but it will only be when it becomes involved in a big deal, and receives a large deal-related fee, that the overall account becomes profitable.

When considering the question of client profitability the total income and costs for the whole life of the relationship must be considered. Taking a snapshot of profitability will be most misleading. The high costs of the pitching and start up phases are powerful arguments for trying to sell additional services to existing clients rather than constantly seeking new ones. The firm that grows with its clients is likely to be far more profitable than, although not always as large as, a competitor which has a very successful new business record.

LOSS MAKING NEW BUSINESS

A Paris-based advertising agency was encouraged by its foreign parent company to invest in an aggressive new business drive. Expensive creative people were hired, a successful public relations effort helped the agency to get invited to pitch for many new accounts, considerable resources were invested in research, very professional presentations and sample creative work. The agency had phenomenal success at converting new business leads into account wins.

Unfortunately, despite nearly doubling its turnover, the agency made significant losses because of the high cost of the new business effort and the low profitability in the start-up phase. With the relatively low profitability of advertising accounts it is unlikely that the company will show a net profit for five years.

10

PRODUCT PROFITABILITY

How do you create profitable products in service firms?

When we find things we are good at – services which client's want time and time again – we try to focus on doing these things well and learning from our experience. One-off projects are fun but it's difficult to start from scratch each time.

Director, marketing consultancy

In a service firm a product is a standard set of services which is required by clients on a regular basis and which produces a clearly defined end-product which the client needs. Typical product examples in service firms are:

- A house conveyance done by a solicitor
- A five day course from a language school
- A brand valuation from an accountant
- Annual results tombstone advertisement placed by an agency
- Communications audit done by PR firm
- Company annual report from designer
- Overhead cost reduction project from management consultant

Although many professional firms do not like to think that they make products the fact is that they usually do. Firms often create manuals describing how to carry out a particular type of client assignment which is, in effect, creating a product. If in structuring some work for a new client the work-plan is largely based on the way the firm approached similar tasks in the past then the firm is creating and using a product.

Clearly each time a product is made it will be slightly different from client to client but the basic elements will remain the same. The analogy is with buying a bespoke suit (a one-off solution) as opposed to an off-the-peg alternative. Service firms are unlikely to be able to sell in a way that looks too off the peg as clients will feel the service provided is not specific enough to their needs. However, clients will be happy with a service product that is customized to their needs.

A product does not have to have a physical, tangible, end result like a standard document (e.g. a will or an annual report) but it must be something that can be described as having a clear purpose and which the client will recognize as serving a specific need. The client may even feel able to put a specific monetary value on having the product delivered.

PRODUCT VALUE

A typical product offered by many management consultants is some form of cost-cutting exercise based on a thorough analysis of what all the executives in a client company actually do all day and what value they create for their organization. The cost-cutting analysis is carried out using standard forms and questionnaires and the aim is often a 20 per cent cut in overhead costs. Assuming this target is met the client can easily calculate the value of the cost cutting product if it really saves him or her 20 per cent of annual costs without damaging the quality of the work done by his or her organization.

ADVANTAGES OF OFFERING PRODUCTS

Developing products has a number of advantages.

Easy to sell

A well-defined product is relatively easy to sell to clients; it is straightforward to explain exactly what the client is getting and the client can see the value in something which is described in end-product terms rather than in terms of being a service process. The products can also be described by using examples of previous work.

In a manufacturing or retailing business with a tangible product it is, of course, possible to say to a customer 'you can have one of these.' Service firms cannot do that but they could bring along a satisfied past client to attest to the value that the service product provided for them.

A product can often be offered at a fixed price (and with a fixed timetable) as past experience will allow the firm to predict accurately what needs doing. This helps overcome the client aversion to the feeling that it is signing a blank cheque when it takes on a professional firm.

A potential problem with selling products is that they are easily costed by the client by comparing the offering of various competing firms. Given the client pressure to charge the minimum for an identifiable product on a competitive basis it is in the interest of firms to have a very clear idea of what any product will cost them to make.

Easy to do

If the tasks required to produce a service product are well defined and based on past experience, relatively junior members of the team will be able to do them with the minimum of supervision. The product is a good way of leveraging the experience of senior staff. In a communications audit, for example, a PR firm might need to discover how many telephone calls the client receives each week from the media. This is a clearly defined, straightforward task, which can be carried out by a very junior firm member. If the whole audit process is composed of similar tasks (which it usually is) then most of the work can be done at a low cost in terms of staff involvement.

Past experience

Offering a similar product on many occasions allows the firm to give the client the value and benefit of past experience. In the example above of auditing the telephone calls the firm would be able to compare the client's performance with other firms previously audited.

Continuing with the same example, a communications audit is trying to answer the question: how well do we do in getting our message across? If this question were addressed from basics each time, by a PR firm, then the process of finding answers would be more haphazard and more expensive than it is to apply the techniques of a tried and tested audit product. The firm can give the client the benefit of past experience for example by knowing which are the best questions to ask to get the necessary information.

Easy to cost

Assessing the costs associated with a product is a process of identifying all its inputs. As with client profitability these will be:

- Professional time – calculated at its total cost
- Directly related business overheads
- External costs not passed on to the client

With products, however, costs such as specific product related advertising, insurance and support staff time can often be calculated and included in directly related costs. In this respect products can be more accurately costed than general services.

Easy to manage

Because a product has been made before, it is much simpler to assess the right level of staff and other costs and to see at an early stage if resources are being wasted. Like all service tasks the creation of the product will involve the client's own staff. Senior firm managers who have seen the product in use before will be able to identify very quickly do's and dont's to help client people work more effectively.

Product engineering

Having identified a service product which seems attractive to clients, firms should constantly keep it under examination to see if they are doing it in the best way and if the same value can be provided to the client at a lower cost to the firm. The idea of product engineering comes from manufacturing, but the concept also applies in a service context. The essential question is how to achieve the same result for a client but more cost effectively.

A classic example would be to create a self-administered computer programme to capture answers to a questionnaire. Using this approach the client's own staff directly input the information rather than having an expensive consultant asking basic questions. This saves time and cost on behalf of the firm but provides the client with the same data for analysis.

PRODUCT PROFITABILITY REPORT

The cost of any products produced by a firm can be calculated very simply by identifying what constitutes a product and then collecting all the costs and comparing these with the income.

A key difference between product profitability and client profitability is that while client profitability is only a valid idea during the period of the client relationship, product profitability can be monitored year after year for as long as the product is in existence.

An analysis of relative product profitability can help in deciding whether to discontinue a certain product or to try to expand its sales. It can also give guidelines in respect of product construction as, quite often, costs can be trimmed to turn a money loser into a winner.

Senior management should assess the profit performance of all products regularly to identify any which are not doing well either because the market has changed (intense competition for example) or because the firm's own cost structure has changed and is now making certain products uneconomic.

THE RIGHT PRODUCTS

Some firms may find it impossible to offer certain products because of their own cost structure or skills base. Even though clients may be demanding a certain product it would be foolish for a firm to offer it if it would never make a profit. For example a high cost/high price city centre law firm is unlikely to be able to carry out domestic house conveyancing as cheaply (or as profitably) as a small suburban practice. In some cases the firm will continue to offer a product because of client demand, but will contract out certain elements of making the product to low cost suppliers to make the business profitable.

CONTRACT OUT ELEMENTS

A graphic design firm offered the product of the turn-key management of company annual reports. One of the main elements of cost is the typesetting. The firm found that it would not make economic sense for it to have its own, in-house typesetting as the relatively small size of the firm meant that it could never handle enough report projects to cover the fixed costs. To create the product but keep the

76

costs down it contracted out the typesetting work on each report but still presented the report creation process to their clients as a single product.

Another approach might be to demonstrate to clients that it would be cheaper for them to make the product for themselves. Some lawyers are looking at providing private clients with conveyancing kits to help a house purchase to be done cheaply while keeping client goodwill.

SELF SERVICE

A London based PR company issued regular press packs about new products on behalf of a client in the West of England. Most of the press packs contained literature and product samples. It was expensive for the agency (with central London salaries and costs) to fill and process the envelopes. They suggested the client used its own office staff, which also cut the cost of shipping samples and literature to London. The net result was a reduced fee for the agency (but more profits as the remaining work was higher added value) and the client was happy as it felt the fee reduction was more than the work cost them to do.

Firms will prosper if they can identify what they do well and which offer them the highest profit margin. They must ensure that their management information systems give them the data to do this analysis. The design of such a system is covered in chapter 28.

11

BALANCE OF STAFF NUMBERS

How many people should you have at each level in the firm? What is the right shape of the staff pyramid?

In the past I was able to run five teams of three or four bright graduates and we made a lot of money. Now we have four senior directors – bright graduates who've grown up – and there just isn't enough work to justify each of them having five teams of their own. Our payroll has gone up and our profits have gone down.

Managing Director, marketing consultancy

Managers need to design their firms to ensure that work of acceptable quality can be done by relatively junior teams. This is the idea of leverage. The skills and experience of expensive, senior people are spread across a number of clients.

JUNIOR STAFF ARE PROFITABLE

As the pyramid structure shown in figure 1.9 (p. 38) shows, firms will be more profitable the greater the ratio of junior to senior staff. Most junior staff are highly profitable in that their billing rates are far higher than their cost per hour; and, in a well run firm, they work on fee-earning client business for a high percentage of their time.

Clients are paying for quality of work and insight into their problems. Well-supervised junior staff can do outstanding work for clients as long as senior staff are available to manage the client relationship and support the efforts of the juniors.

SENIOR STAFF MUST DELEGATE

Senior people should involve themselves, primarily, with winning new business, training and cementing client relationships rather than doing day-to-day work.

A major disincentive to effective delegation (and thus to higher profitability) is often the culture of professional firms which expect all staff to be fee earners. Some senior people get worried if they are spending a lot of time on training, recruitment and administration and if their total billing income and billable hours worked is seen to decrease. Some senior managers or even partners seem happier when they are billing very high number of hours on client work. They find it easier to face their colleagues with a very high, apparent, personal profitability. The reality, however, is that, in many cases, the client would have been just as happy with well supervised juniors doing the work. This would have made the firm even more profitable while the senior person could have been engaged in more useful activities.

The use of high cost resources (partners or directors) to do routine work (normally done by associates or executives) is analogous to using the company limousine to do the work of a dispatch rider. Merely because it can be used to deliver mail does not mean it shall be.

In terms of profit-levers, top management must insist that partners or directors run all their accounts at the same ratios (or leverage) that have been agreed for the firm as a whole. Persistent refusals to delegate work by one or two senior people not only de-motivates junior members of the team but squanders the firm's resources.

False economies

The idea that it is better for senior managers in service firms simply to do the job themselves rather than coach juniors is a false economy. In the April 1990 supplement to his book, *Professional Service Firm Management*, Dr David Maister identifies systematic underdelegation as a major problem in professional firms and says:

> *A (second) reason for underdelegation to develop is that there is a reluctance to invest in the coaching and supervision time necessary to achieve successful delegation. On any single engagement it will always be MORE costly, not less, to spend the time to get a junior involved: it will take them longer to do it than doing it yourself and you'll have to spend the time supervising. Consequently, even though more supervised delegation and coaching will reduce costs over time, they increase costs in the short run. This is the old Catch 22. Using the junior on this one is more costly because we haven't previously trained him or her, so we make a short term economic decision not to train him or her. Because of this reasoning firms*

tend to under-invest in good coaching, even though they preach it fervently.

It is certainly my experience that every professional firm which I have worked in or studied has this problem, and many fall victim to the vicious circle which dictates that when profits dip senior people spend even more time chasing billable hours (to look like valuable firm resources) and even less time building intellectual capital or seeking new business for a more profitable future.

DEFINING THE BALANCE

Professional firms can choose either to be high leverage with a large number of juniors doing work that lends itself to delegation, or low leverage with a large number of senior people doing high level counselling work that generates consistently high fees. The problem comes when there is a mixture of the two because of the preferences of individual senior managers. As a broad generalization the more profitable firms will have flat staff pyramids and, therefore, a greater degree of leverage of a small number of senior staff. However the degree to which a firm can have a flat structure will be dictated by the needs of its clients. The matching of the firm's structure with the needs of clients and the state of the market is covered in detail in chapter 26.

MAINTAINING THE BALANCE

Having identified a profitable structure, one of the greatest challenges is to keep it in place as the firm grows. As the business expands maintaining the staff balance is a key lever of profit. If this is not done firms become top heavy as people get promoted in greater relative numbers than new client income is generated and faster than junior staff are recruited.

In this respect, growth can be a profit lever in itself. In firms which are rather top-heavy, new business can be serviced by hiring a disproportionate number of junior people to improve the staff ratios and improve leverage.

Unless a firm is growing at enormous speed it is unlikely that recruitment at a senior level will ever be required except where, as a strategic decision, a firm wants to start up a new area of professional practice based upon one or two key individuals.

The ways of growing profitably by planning ahead are covered in more detail in chapters 34 and 37.

Balance can also be achieved, and maintained, by using part-time or para-professionals – people with the skills to do many of the more routine jobs but who do not have the experience or training to follow the normal professional career path or to handle all aspects of the client relationship. The use of these types of staff – who form a special group in addition to professionals and support staff – is discussed in chapter 23.

12

BILLING RATES

How much should you charge for the firm's services?

For me the secret of profit growth is simple – put up the prices!
Director, design consultancy

Billing rates (or commission levels, or mark-up percentages and other elements of income) are the price the firm charges for its services. A firm will set its rates partly to reflect its own cost structure and partly to reflect what the market will accept. Assuming the senior members of the firm (who are often also the shareholders) want to increase their own wealth, and take increasing sums of money out of the firm, they will almost certainly have to try to raise the firm's charges for the services offered by themselves and more junior staff. Finding ways to increase the billing rate is, clearly, a method of increasing profits. The ending of the professional services boom of the 1980s will put far more downward pressure on billing rates/prices as firms compete more on price and less on quality.

PROVIDE MORE VALUE

Over the long term the best way to increase the billing rate is by finding ways of providing clients with services which they find more valuable and will pay more for. Doing this will increase the overall income to the firm which will, in turn, enable the firm to reward those individuals creating these higher value products more generously.

In professional firms the most direct way to increase the value of individuals' efforts is through training. This is covered in more detail in chapter 22. An advertising agency, for example, might teach its account managers about the operations of the financial markets to make them more effective in helping clients with corporate advertising campaigns; a PR consultancy might train its staff in the use of local radio stations to help clients get more and better coverage from this growing medium; a management consultancy might give its associates tuition in the application of personal computers to administrative tasks to help clients save money in the implementation of new business systems. Training can actually help improve profits in the long run by helping to push up billing rates and fee income as well as helping staff morale and improving retention rates.

Services of more value can also be found by addressing issues of greater concern to clients.

MORE VALUABLE SERVICES

A very small PR consultancy employed eight staff who were all experienced in dealing with the press and who offered clients a range of services such as sending out press releases and answering questions. The consultancy decided to specialize in environmental issues and trained its small staff to be up to date on the latest green concerns.

It started to hold seminars for clients on green issues as they affected business. The consultancy resigned much of its general PR work and worked only with clients on environmental projects. By being in the right place at the right time and helping with a key issue they were able to increase their daily rates significantly and they became far more profitable as there was not a comparable rise in their cost base.

DO NOT UNDERCHARGE

The skill of setting the price for professional services is covered in chapter 43. The main objective for managers is to ensure that they understand the value that they are really giving to clients and fight hard to have that fully reflected in the income from the client.

Cost-plus pricing

Some firms operate a simple cost-plus approach in which billing rates will be a multiple (often three times or more) of the salary of an individual. Thus if an account executive's annual salary was £25,000 this method would assign an annual billings target of £75,000 (3 x £25,000); and assuming 2,000 billable hours this would produce £37.50 per hour or £262.50 per seven-hour day.

This approach assumes the resulting billing rate will cover costs and yield a profit. There are two main problems with this mechanism:

- It fails to take into account the market conditions
- It makes an assumption that the value provided to the client is directly linked to the cost of the individual to the firm

It is quite possible that firms will underprice their services if they simply seek to recover costs and add a mark-up.

Market rate

In those circumstances where professional jobs are put out to competitive tender, firms will be able to judge what the market is prepared to pay for a service or at least what competitors are prepared to do it for. The main difficulty in service firms is that no two service solutions to a problem are identical, so it is hard to compare market prices accurately. Firms should, however, understand the market and should monitor it to get a picture of the market rate. Useful information can come from clients and from newly recruited staff as well as from trade organizations and even the trade press.

Those firms which work on commission are, in effect, basing their prices on market rates where the market will choose between firms on the basis of the size of the percentage charged compared to the level of service received.

Umbrella pricing

Any firm, particularly a market leader, must be cautious about charging so much that it creates a price umbrella. A firm with a high cost base may charge premium prices for its service. Other firms (or even break-away groups of people from the market leader) can set up and make very good profits by offering the same services from a lower cost base. Clearly the more you can charge for a service the greater will be the profit if the costs remain the same. Superprofits which result from high charging and a low cost base can only be sustained for a short time until clients get wise or competitors move in.

Value billing

Under this approach firms will ask to be paid in relation to the value they have generated for the client. The most obvious example is the contingency system of American lawyers who get a share of any damages awarded. The success fees of investment banks involved in a takeover are also examples.

There are other cases where value can be achieved without being in some sort of win or lose contest. There will be many occasions when the firm's service is worth more to the client than the normal billing rate because of special circumstances. A typical example might be a legal or PR firm working over the weekend to meet a client deadline. Even if the firm's people are not paid overtime or special week-end rates the fact that the work will not be delayed until the Monday means it is worth more and thus the client would pay more.

A firm should agree with a client the basis of assessing the value added by the firm and seek to have this reflected in the price of the services. For example a management consultant with an account team that already has wide experience in the marketing of grocery products would be of great value to a food manufacturer seeking advice in this area. The members of that same team might equally be called upon to work on a problem to do with manufacturing costs in the car industry where they would be competent but far less valuable than in the grocery area.

A cocktail of charges

A very successful approach which is becoming more popular is to agree a basic charging structure with an agreed mechanism for the client to pay more if additional value is created. As a basis a minimum billing rate (or commission rate, etc.) is set. Account directors (or partners) will then negotiate with clients to achieve additional income reflecting the value the firm is providing. In some cases this will mean the account director quoting higher daily rates than the minimum (reflecting, perhaps, the skill base of the team and the nature of the client job); in other examples some sort of success fee or performance-related bonus may be agreed.

13

STAFF UTILIZATION

How do you make the best use of people's time?

The worst thing in the firm is when people have no fee-earning work to do. People know if you haven't got a client, others resent you. It makes you feel vulnerable.

Architect

Utilization is the number of billable hours actually worked for clients by professional staff. These hours are expressed as a percentage of the total number of, potentially billable, hours worked by each individual in a given period. Having high utilization will naturally make an individual more profitable as it brings in more income without increasing professional staff costs. However, simply having everyone in the firm spending all their time on billable client work would be counterproductive, as it would place the individuals under great strain and would leave the firm without adequate management.

HIGH OR LOW UTILIZATION

A typical firm might expect a professional actually to work about 2,000 potentially billable hours a year – something over 40 hours a week taking into account annual vacations and public holidays. Just how many of those 2,000 hours are billed to clients and how many are spent on administration, training, practice development or simply unassigned (what many firms call 'on the beach') will depend on the individual's seniority, firm policy and the amount of work available.

Typical utilization rates for a firm with a 2,000-hour annual target are suggested below:

Grade	Utilization rate	Hours billed per year
Director	50%	1,000
Manager	70%	1,400
Executive	85%	1,700
Trainee	50%	1,000

The low number of hours billed by the more senior people reflects the amount of time they need to spend on business development and firm management. Managers and junior staff have fewer non-client responsibilities. Trainees will spend a lot of time on courses and so on.

It is, of course, possible (and often the case) for people to have a utilization rate in excess of 100 per cent by simply working and billing more hours than the target. Such people are usually highly motivated and talented and do outstanding work. The problem comes when those individuals (if they are rational) demand to be paid more to reflect their contribution. If the marginal extra pay is at a higher rate than their normal salary then the *extra hours will be less profitable* to the firm as the firm's costs per hour have gone up while the income per hour remains the same. Also people who spend all their time on client work will have little time to train others or to seek new business. They will not, therefore, be making a contribution to the development of the firm itself.

PLANNED UTILIZATION = PROFIT

As a profit lever, utilization needs to be kept as high as possible without turning the firm into a sweatshop. Individuals with very low utilization must be identified so that they can be refocused on to fee earning activities. Most firms have some people who shy away from client work and will spend far too much time on administrative and practice development matters. Top managers must look hard at the real value these people are giving to the firm. Maximizing utilization is one of the objectives of the assignment process which is described in detail in chapter 21 (see figure 3.4, p. 127).

From a profit point of view it is desirable to match individuals with work which makes maximum use of their skills and past experience. A client may be happy to pay a manager's billing rates for an executive or associate who has a detailed knowledge of a particular industry or type of problem. In this sense the firm is realizing the greatest market value of the professional. This can, however, conflict with the individual's desire to get experience of new industries and problems.

The manager in charge of the assignment process must be senior enough to be able to balance the firm's need for profit from the client with the client's own requirements and the desires of the individual professionals.

It is very important from a profit point of view to plan future utilization. Managers should anticipate what the workload will be in three to six months and then look at how this will translate into projected utilization of professional staff. They might realize that the mix of client locations and skills required will mean that certain individuals will be overstretched while others will be down to 25 per cent utilization. It seems obvious that firms should plan this way, but in many cases senior professionals argue that they are too busy serving clients to devote time to planning. Because of the nature of the economics of a professional firm, however, allowing utilization to drop by 10 percentage points through bad forecasting will cost far more than the loss of a few hours per week of billable time devoted by a senior manager to planning.

VALUE OF UTILIZATION

A firm with 10 professionals might have a total billable hour capacity of 20,000 hours per year. At 60 per cent utilization with an average hourly billing rate of £50 this produces an income of £600,000 (20,000 x 0.6 x £50). If the firm's costs are £400,000 this produces a £200,000 profit.

If utilization goes up by just ten per cent (equal to six percentage points) to 66 per cent of hours then the income becomes £660,000 (20,000 x 0.66 x £50). Costs remain the same so profits go up to £260,000, an increase of 18 per cent. Underused staff are an expensive wasted asset.

In a perfect world an individual would move straight from one client assignment to another, avoiding a period of down-time. There is a temptation to suggest to people that they take vacation time in the gaps between clients but this can create great resentment. A more successful approach is to schedule training and practice development work during the unassigned periods. One common error in many professional firms is to assign a relatively senior individual to do the work of a more junior staff member at the latter's lower billing rate on the grounds that any fee earning work is better than none. A danger of this is the lost opportunity of getting the individuals full billing in the event of more appropriate work coming along. A more serious problem, however, is that it devalues that individual in the eyes of the client (and other firm members) and it gives the client an unrealistic idea of the quality of individual available for that level of fee.

14

WORKING CAPITAL

How do you keep down the amount of money required to run the firm?

The only thing you have to worry about is cash. Watch the cash balances and the monthly report on aged debtors and you know exactly how well the business is doing.

Chairman, PR group

The amount of working capital in a professional firm reflects the level of unpaid debts.

Service firms do not build stocks of finished product which must be financed prior to sale but they do have work in progress in the sense that there is a time-lag between the completion of a piece of work and getting paid for it. As the vast majority of staff (the main cost element) are paid monthly in arrears any firm which gets its money from clients more than 30 days after the work is done will need to find cash (often from reserves or borrowings) to pay its staff until the client's money is received. Although the ultimate threat of legal action is available to professional firms to enforce payment they face much greater problems than manufacturing businesses. In the event of court action clients will often claim the quality of service was unacceptable and it is not unknown for the firm to find itself facing embarrassing criticism in open court of its professional standards when a client is forced to defend late or non-payment on the grounds of disputed service quality.

PROMPT PAYMENT IS PART OF THE CLIENT RELATIONSHIP

Managing working capital in a professional firm has as much to do with managing the client relationship as it has to do with a well run accounts department. To minimize the late payment of accounts and bad debts the responsibility for managing the debtors days of each account must be placed clearly with the account director. Achieving prompt payment is very much part of the client relationship although many professionals prefer to leave this task to their accounts department and some refuse to get involved in chasing debts at all.

Each firm should have a very clear policy on its terms of trade – usually dictated by the norms in its industry – and all account directors and clients must be made aware of them. The account directors, in their turn, must ensure their clients understand *and agree with* the basis of charging. To reduce misunderstanding there is merit in having a member of the firm's accounts department brief the executives in the client accounts department to ensure there is an understanding of how the firm's charging system operates. Some firms create a dummy invoice with annotations to describe how it works.

When it comes to chasing unpaid invoices a common mistake is to assume that regular, computer-generated reminders with increasing amounts of red ink and increasing hostility of language will actually speed things up. Winning the support of senior client executives who will instruct prompt payment is the best way to achieve rapid results.

INVOICING SYSTEM

All professional firms need a simple system to issue invoices promptly and to flag up any that are late in being paid. Late payment is often the first sign of a potential bad debt and the earlier these are spotted the better the chance of recovering the money.

Some firms charge interest on unpaid accounts. While this can make economic sense it can create client relationship problems. Some firms invoice clients for work done in advance, hoping that if payment is received within 30 days then the lag between receiving the cash and paying the firm's staff will be minimized.

Firms which buy substantial amounts of goods or services on behalf of clients (such as advertising agencies or design companies) will have to decide whether they will seek to be paid by the clients at the time, or even before the firm pays the ultimate supplier, or whether the firm will act as a bank by paying the client's bills for it and will charge interest to the client accordingly. These firms can actually benefit from having other people's cash in their bank during the period between being paid by the client and waiting to pay the supplier. This can create *negative* working capital, that is, the firm can benefit from interest earned on cash balances.

Historically advertising agencies were paid by their clients before the agencies had to pay the media owners for advertising time and space. This allowed the agencies to earn interest on the client's money for as long as 30 days. As clients have become more sophisticated they have recognized this practice as a hidden subsidy.

In terms of systems the data inputs and management information outputs are discussed in chapter 28.

MONITORING SYSTEM

Each month the firm's executive committee should examine the business profile of aged debtors so they can identify any trends in the way the firm is collecting payment from its clients. It is useful to see how much of the total unpaid debt falls into the various bands. If most of the debts have only been outstanding for 30 days there is a strong likelihood of receiving payment soon. If, however, debts are still unpaid after 90 days the firm should be concerned about possible default. An example of the analysis of aged debtors is given in chapter 28 (see figure 4.14, p. 188).

The executive committee should also see a debtor days analysis for every client or account. This expresses the amount of money currently outstanding as a proportion of the total annual budgeted income for the account. Thus a client who was expected to produce income of £100,000 and had been invoiced for, but had not paid £20,000 would be said to have debtor days of £20,000/£100,000 (i.e. 0.2) times 365 days, i.e. 73 debtor days. What is important is not so much the size of the debt but its size in relation to the overall size of the client.

The cost of carrying unpaid debts (working capital) can be very considerable and in a sophisticated accounting system the interest charges associated with funding late debts should be deducted from account profitability. This will further focus the attention of account directors on managing unpaid debts. It is certainly possible for large, and apparently profitable, accounts actually to be loss makers if the clients are chronic late payers and the firm does not charge them interest on overdue accounts.

AVOID UNNECESSARY DELAYS

Many firms run into problems over expenses which the client does not understand or objects to. Frequently an invoice for tens of thousands of pounds of undisputed fees can be held up because of a few hundred pounds of expenses.

DISPUTED EXPENSES

A well-respected international design company had completed a project with fees of US$80,000. An invoice was submitted for payment in 30 days and included US$6,000 of expenses. Amongst the expenses was a hotel bill for one of the design team which included the cost of a manicure for US$30. The design firm's accounts department had requested accelerated payment of the bill so it went to a senior client executive for approval. The executive was sufficiently irritated by the manicure charges (which had, obviously not been discussed in advance as they were so trivial) that he started a correspondence to seek justification of the charge. In the end it took 90 days to pay the invoice (less manicure charges) which cost the design firm more than US$1,000 in interest charges.

Most professional services are intangible and there is always a tendency for clients to resent the bill when it comes and to question certain aspects of the invoice. Many professional firms exacerbate this by presenting their accounts in a crass and incomprehensible fashion.

BAD INVOICES

An advertising agency took great pains to build client relations. The managing director would buy an expensive lunch for senior clients at least once a year, corporate hospitality was generous and the agency culture was to get close to clients and understand their concerns. Unfortunately the monthly account of fees, and so on, was produced on the nearly illegible third carbon copy of a computer system and contained so little detail and so much accounting jargon as to be incomprehensible. When clients' accounts departments did not understand the invoice it would be referred up to the senior client executives who would, nearly always, be frustrated and angry at being unable to read, let alone understand it. It would be sent back to the agency for explanation, thus slowing down payment. The agency was averaging unpaid debtors of more than 100 days – more than twice the industry norm.

AUDITING LAWYERS

In a long article on the problems understanding legal bills the *Wall Street Journal* (18 January 1991) described the development of specialized auditors:

Executives frustrated with paying huge legal bills – no questions asked – are increasingly turning to professional auditors to ask questions for them . . . Legal bills can be incomprehensible – some would say purposely so. Lawyers often bill their time in 15 minute segments and provide minimal description of their work. Auditors reshuffle entries so bills can be itemized by task.

There is little doubt that professional firms can do a lot to help their clients pay more promptly simply by making clear how much is owed.

15

HOUSEKEEPING

How do you control the firm's own overheads?

I watch the way people use our resources – paper, copiers, even the coffee machine. It must make me sound mean but I do worry about how much we are wasting.

Managing Director, PR consultancy

The housekeeping costs – or business overheads – will vary between about 10 per cent and 30 per cent of a professional firm's total costs depending on the particular business the firm is in and the definition of business overheads. The broadest definition will include all administrative staff salaries (i.e. the costs of all those people not *directly* involved in client service), all business–related overheads (i.e. telephones, stationery, copying machines etc.) and all building overheads (rent, heat, light, power). These are the basic components shown in figure 1.5 (p. 25).

DON'T SUBSIDIZE CLIENTS

The first key lesson, in profit terms, is not to subsidize clients by doing administrative tasks for them without charge. Servicing some clients will prove far more costly than others in terms of photocopying, telephone bills, fax and mail charges. The business must put in place simple systems (such as coded loggers on the telephone and copying machines) which record costs incurred on behalf of clients and ensure that those costs are passed on to the client for payment.

There is nothing wrong with the idea that clients should be charged for housekeeping costs. If the firm employed a translator or graphic designer on the client's behalf there would be no issue about the costs being passed on. Equally if the firm does bulk photocopying which the client could have done for itself it makes sense to charge it. Firms must, however, be careful not to irritate clients by apparently seeking to make huge profits on these charges by, for example, charging 50p for sending a letter when clients know the cost of the post is only 25p. It may well be true that the actual cost of a fax sent on the client's behalf should include the depreciation charges on the fax machine and the salary costs of the sender but clients will rebel if they feel they are being asked to pay too much.

The final decision of which of the firm's costs to pass on to the client and which to absorb – to be covered by the income from fees – is a matter of policy and the individual judgement of the senior person (partner or director) in charge of the client relationship. Having identified and passed on those housekeeping costs directly attributable to clients the firm can then focus on the other costs which are incurred in the course of keeping the firm running.

PREMISES

How much to spend on accommodation will depend on the firm's view of how important comfortable and prestigious offices are in recruiting and motivating staff and in giving confidence to clients. As a broad rule of thumb the more intangible the firm's services the greater the need for offices that inspire confidence. Trying to cut costs by adopting a low standard of accommodation is almost always a false economy in professional firms. The issues of premises are covered in more detail in chapter 32.

Future planning

The most complex accommodation task is planning for the future. It is important to try to keep the space available in line with the growth of the number of people in the business. Moving to premises which are too large on the assumption of growth which may not happen will hit the bottom line hard as accommodation costs will rise dramatically as a proportion of overheads.

No professional firm will ever get the balance exactly right but it is always better to be a little overcrowded than to have the embarrassment of excess space. Firms needing to expand should consider looking for partners to sub-let space to on a temporary basis while the main firm is growing into a new building.

A COST-CONSCIOUS CULTURE

An image of being mean will damage a professional firm but within the context of a generous housekeeping budget it is possible (and desirable) to foster a culture of economy.

Housekeeping incentives

One simple measure is to establish a budget for consumable items such as stationery and to create a bonus system for secretaries which will provide them a Christmas gift if the budget is met or not spent. At its most literal this will lead to the re-use of paper clips but far more importantly it will engender an attitude that the firm's resources are limited and while facilities and equipment may be of top quality waste is to be avoided.

The client's money

Good use of the client's housekeeping money is another important message which needs to be got across to all staff. Just because a cost is being passed on and not borne by the firm does not mean they should not be prudent. Endless use of dispatch riders or huge investments in research to 'help' the client can backfire on the firm if the client starts to feel the overall relationship with the firm is becoming rather expensive.

Resources of the firm

In terms of preventing abuse of the firm's own resources (such as personal international telephone calls, theft of stationery, private use of taxi services) the firm must first make quite clear what is allowed and what is not. Many companies will pay for *local* personal telephone calls but not for international ones. Having established the rules it is necessary to be very tough about the penalties for abuse – usually firing the individual.

Expenses

With professional staff, entertainment expenses can become a problem. The very successful new business winner may run up huge bills with justification. In the end it is a matter of subtle judgement by senior management as to what is acceptable. But as with the case of all firm resources, clear guidelines must be laid out, in advance, and those who persistently breach them must be restrained.

In some firms – particularly advertising agencies – the ability to incur huge expenses has, in the past, almost been seen as a badge of honour and a matter of status.

Keep a perspective

There is a danger with business costs like free coffee, free lunches, office artwork, potted plants, and so on, that managers can develop a mean streak which saves a few pounds but demotivates and irritates the professionals and support staff. As a general observation the cost of new carpets or top-of-the-range office chairs is tiny compared to an improvement in professional utilization rates of five per cent. If firms want to attract and keep good people they need to provide them with a good office environment.

CONTRACTING OUT

All businesses need support services such as cleaning, catering, security and building maintenance. What management must decide is whether to employ people to do these services in-house or contract them out.

The first consideration is scale. Small firms are unlikely to be able to justify internal catering as the amount of work would not provide full-time employment for even one person. Big firms are more likely to be able to employ full-time staff but need to consider the question of management of those individuals.

Professional firms tend to be geared towards the employment of professional people. The personnel systems and attitudes are all designed to deal with a certain type of employee. It is often the case that the managers used to managing professionals are far less competent when it comes to managing non-professionals.

In most cases the right decision is to contract out as many of the support services as possible. Doing this will ensure that a budget is agreed at the beginning of the year and that this budget will be met. All that is required from the firm is for one of the senior managers to deal with the contractor's own management. As with so many other aspects of running professional firms the hidden cost of senior managers' time is avoided by contracting out.

16

PROFITABILITY – THE RIGHT ATTITUDE

How do you make all members of the firm profit conscious?

We are successful because everyone here is concerned about the bottom line. I don't just mean they watch the pennies, I mean they think about how every action will affect the firm's performance.
Accountant, small firm

A clear understanding of what makes a firm profitable and a commitment to achieving profit should be a basic requirement of becoming a member of the top management group but it must be supported by a profit-driven attitude held by all firm members. As many people as possible should be motivated to act profitably. This necessitates being able to:

- Identify the contribution of each firm member

- Provide financial reward for profitable behaviour

IDENTIFY PROFIT CONTRIBUTION

Making profit means increasing income and decreasing costs. All members of a professional firm will, to varying degrees, have some control over one or both of these elements. Wherever possible management should clearly identify what people can control and reward them for controlling it in such a way as to maximize profit. Account directors can influence income from clients and the use of professional staff time. The head of the accounts department or the chief administrator can be rewarded for keeping his or her departmental costs within budget

All professional staff members should be reminded that they are each a profit centre. Each is responsible for income and each incurs costs. It is quite possible to devise an accounting system which provides printouts of the profitability of every professional member of staff but in most firms this would be meaningless as the majority of the junior staff can do little to control their overall profit contribution. Senior managers should spend some time talking with every member of staff about what he or she feels able to do to improve the firm's profits.

PROVIDE INCENTIVES

All members of staff must be allowed to share in their own success if they are to behave in a profit conscious fashion. In the previous chapter the example was given of a bonus scheme for secretaries to reward them for prudent management of the stationery budget. Account directors can be motivated by bonuses linked to the overall profitability of their accounts. Account teams can be rewarded for bringing in new businesses. As a fundamental principle people should only be given incentives for those things over which they can have, and *feel they have*, direct control.

It is almost certain that all professional firms would benefit from some form of profit-sharing system which pays out a proportion of operating profits to *all* staff at the end of each year. Everyone is aware the firm exists to make profits and it is reasonable for juniors as well as seniors to share in success. In professional firms, more than in most businesses, high profits (as opposed to high sales) will be directly related to how hard, and how efficiently, all the firm members have worked.

The firm's leaders must set an example in terms of personal lifestyle and conduct as their actions will affect all the firm's staff and be reflected in profitability. A flamboyant use of private cars and expensive lunches by the managing director will make it difficult to argue the case for restraint with a junior associate.

PROVIDE INFORMATION

Information is a sound basis for creating a profit conscious firm. The most useful data for individuals relates to those things over which they have direct control.

- Account directors should have monthly information about the profitability (past and forecast) of their own accounts and should be held responsible for poor performance

- The office manager or a senior secretary should be given all details of the stationery budget and actual spending and should communicate this to the other secretaries

- Junior executives should be told about their utilization rate and encouraged to seek additional, billable work if they feel they are falling behind.

NON-FINANCIAL INCENTIVES

Rather like the employee of the month awards given in many hotel and restaurant chains, top management should adopt a policy of sending 'herograms' – notes of congratulation – to those people who bring in profitable new business and who are involved in profitable accounts. Professional employees seek status and career advancement. Being sent on special training courses or given the opportunity to spend a few weeks in an overseas office can be a powerful incentive.

As with the financial incentives, though, the reward must be given for doing something profitable, *not* just doing something to save money. The members of the accounts department might be given a day off if they manage to bring the debtor days down by 20 per cent but it is less clear if they should be rewarded for cutting their telephone costs or postage charges if this resulted in less efficient debt collection.

PROFIT IS DESIRABLE

Top managers must be prepared to defend high profits to clients and staff alike as being desirable for the long-term good of the firm. Improved financial stability will help a firm ensure future success by being able to pay well and by being able, when required, to re-invest in training and facilities. Firms must actively promote the idea that a well-run and profitable business makes a better professional partner than a less successful company.

A COMMON GOAL

Managing a professional firm is all about getting a group of people to adopt common norms and working practices. The most effective profit lever is to get everyone in the firm enthusiastic about being profitable – not just big or famous or prestigious but *profitable*.

Top management should devote a great deal of time and effort to winning this cultural battle and many of the tactical points highlighted in part II will then follow of their own accord.

PART III

PUTTING PEOPLE FIRST

What methods are best for managing the people in professional firms?

I suppose it goes without saying that dealing with the people who work here, and I do NOT mean personnel management, is by far the most important skill in making the business successful.

Managing Director, executive search firm

The most successful firms are those which manage their people well. The most valuable assets and also the principal costs of professional services firms are its people. Managing people well does not mean running a sweatshop to create profits by exploiting employees but it does imply making the best possible use of their time. The management of a service firm should give consideration to its people in the same way that the managers of a chemical plant will devote considerable time and effort to the care of their plant.

This part of the book is about people management as it directly relates to the success and profitability of professional firms. It is not intended to give guidance on personnel policies or employment law.

People management does not come naturally

Unfortunately people management is often regarded as being an intuitive skill and is simply assumed to be going on in a satisfactory fashion. Good people management is often not formally recognized or rewarded as part of a senior professional's job. In fact the problem goes deeper than that: in many professional firms management of the firm itself ranks as being less important than the professional work carried out by that firm, and is often forced upon somewhat reluctant seniors. Yet paradoxically it is effective people management that is a key *strategic* area for the long-term success of the firm, based upon the recruitment, management and retention of qualified and moti-vated people who otherwise might work for a competitor, a client or other types of professional firm.

As the potential to move between firms and even between different professional disciplines increases there can be little doubt that those firms that manage their professional staff best and attract and keep the stars will be the winners.

Personnel experts

In most professional firms the full-time personnel function or department will usually be very small or non-existent despite the fact that people issues are critical to the business. Keeping it small is often the right thing to do as most of the key personnel roles have to be managed by the professional staff themselves. Like the cliché about war and the generals people management in professional firms is too important to be left to the experts!

The right approach is to make people management a valued part of the skills profile of everyone's job.

The personnel department (if there is one) should manage 'housekeeping' items such as holiday, sick pay and pensions. It should be involved in the mechanical aspects of recruitment and assignment but all recruitment interviews and assignment deci-sions must involve professional staff. The personnel function should usually act as the line managers for all the non-professional staff to ensure that their needs are met and that they have people other than the professional staff with whom to discuss their problems. The non-professional employees in profes-sional firms are sometimes called support staff or non-career staff. These are the secretaries, computer operators, accounts staff, receptionists and so on. They tend not to be directly involved in client service but are nevertheless important members of the team whose efforts will affect the firm's profits. In some businesses the personnel function takes over all the tasks under the general heading of office management.

Measuring success

In the same way that the success or failure of asset management can be assessed in an industrial company such tests can be applied to professional firms. Staff productivity in terms of levels of utilization and profitability were covered in part II. This part of the book considers other objective measures such as cost of recruitment, staff turnover, training costs and wage inflation.

17

RECRUITMENT

How do you get the right people to work for the firm?

---

*The only thing that holds back our growth is finding talented
people. Getting new professionals is probably the most important
thing we do.*

Director, management consultancy

A firm based on people needs to recruit in order to grow and to
replace those who leave. Ideally recruitment would be at the most
junior level as most senior posts would be filled by internal
promotion. This ideal allows the firm the maximum amount of
quality control and tends to build a very strong culture and a
consistent and relevant set of skills. Recruitment of juniors also
helps keep the firm's pyramid structure (and hence profitability)
in place by ensuring that new people come in at junior levels.

However, there will always be some need for very senior
recruits. A leader of the firm may leave at a time when no internal
candidate is ready to replace him or her. The firm may win major
accounts which immediately require senior people to service them.
The firm may want to make changes to reflect a new strategic
direction – if these changes require new skills at a senior level they
may only be found externally.

SENIOR APPOINTMENTS

One of the major international accounting firms based in
London wanted to set up a strategy consulting practice to
allow it to be active in a rapidly growing market. At first
attempt the new unit was run by existing accounting
partners with consulting skills and only junior recruits were
drawn from business schools and other consulting firms.
This was consistent with the firm's philosophy of only
making senior appointments from within.

After a few months it became clear that the new unit was in trouble. The best junior staff were leaving and the firm had a very poor new business record. Although it went against the firm's culture, three partners of other consulting firms were recruited to be in charge. They brought with them the skills and attitudes which after a year made the consultancy a success.

SOURCES OF RECRUITS

Whether they be at a junior or senior level recruits come in three main ways:

- They seek you out
- You find them through advertising
- You find them via 'headhunters' or contacts

Self-selected

This option clearly has advantages from a cost point of view as candidates approach the firm leaving only the problem of selection. For very high profile firms with good reputations this will happen in respect of new graduates and a few more senior people. The main problem with these self-selected candidates is that, while they know about the firm, they may not understand the skills it is looking for and the opportunities it offers.

Advertising

Advertising has the advantage of stimulating interest at the actual time the firm is seeking recruits and gives the prospective candidates a better idea of exactly what the firm offers and what sort of people it is looking for.

Advertising has the additional, secondary benefit of raising the profile of the firm with potential clients as well as potential staff; the appointments pages are among the most read in a newspaper and a well-positioned, well-presented advertisement which clearly states the firm's values and achievements can be a strong influence on clients as well as attracting candidates.

Headhunters

The use of search consultants or 'headhunters' is almost the only way of finding very senior staff as in many cases they will already be happily employed elsewhere.

This method is costly as executive search firms frequently charge up to 35 per cent of the first year's salary of the candidate. There is, however a saving in the time of the firm's own executives as the search firms will do their own screening to produce a short-list. Problems may arise if people are recruited from companies who are clients of the firm and who may feel their staff have been poached.

RECRUITMENT OBJECTIVES

Broadly speaking recruitment can either be strategic or tactical.

Strategic recruiting

Strategic recruitment reflects the firm's plans for growth and diversification. Clear guidelines can be prepared about skills and likely career paths.

STRATEGIC RECRUITMENT

A medium-sized London advertising agency decided in the early 1980s to build its skills in the area of government and commercial advertising linked to the de-nationalization or privatization of industries. At a senior level it recruited, over several years, people from the financial and political world to provide client handling and financial marketing ability. At a junior level it sought candidates who had or wanted to build financial skills.

When it came to bid for government work it was successful because it was able to field a team of people who had the reputation and skills to impress those who were appointing agencies to this sensitive and specialized area.

At a junior level strategic recruitment is likely to be continuous. Certainly some firms have a policy of *always* recruiting a good candidate, irrespective of current workloads, on the grounds that after a period good people will usually pay their way.

A well-managed firm should always have a strategic recruitment policy in place reflecting the firm's clear sense of direction in terms of growth and development. The key recruitment criteria should be developed from a model of what the firm will look like one, two and even five years into the future.

Tactical recruiting

In the normal course of events people will leave and jobs will become vacant. The annual milk-round of graduates is, in many ways, tactical recruiting as the objective is to find general trainees rather than change the firm's direction. Replacing support staff is nearly always a tactical recruitment task as the job to be filled is well-defined and consistent with overall policy.

RECRUITMENT OF GRADUATES

This is a special type of recruitment process. Graduates, by virtue of their age and experience, will almost always come into firms as trainees. Firms are competing against a wide range of alternative career options when seeking graduate recruits, and decisions have to be made on the basis of academic record and personality rather than on proven professional achievements. It is certainly not the case that all professional firms will seek to recruit graduates directly. There is intense wage competition to get the best and some firms find them expensive to train and difficult to integrate.

Initial interviews are usually held in the spring with candidates potentially starting in late summer after graduation. Although many of the large employers participate in the milk-round of interviews on campus, arranged in conjunction with the university or polytechnic, this is not necessary and potential applicants can be invited to see the business – usually with their expenses paid.

For those contemplating graduate recruitment it must be tied to a comprehensive training programme. This will be a major attraction to recruits. It is generally considered that most graduates cannot immediately add value to the business. Clearly a balance of work and training must be achieved but simply to expect people to work from day one is counterproductive.

If a business is serious about graduate recruitment it must remember its most powerful communication tool to reach into universities and colleges is almost certainly its own graduate recruits one year on. Keep them happy and they will help recruit their juniors.

Some firms operate systems such as having summer associates or internships to allow students (particularly post-graduate students) to spend a long vacation working in the firm to get a better idea of whether it would be the right place for them in the future. As long as these temporary jobs involve real work and provide candidates with an exposure to the typical aspects of working with a firm they can provide an excellent introduction.

FIT – THE RIGHT PERSON FOR THE JOB

Whatever the source of people the desired end product of the recruitment process should be to achieve a good *fit* between the person and the firm. Successful recruitment is based upon finding a happy marriage between the needs of the business and the needs of the potential recruits –this is true at all levels in the firm.

An honest picture

A key aspect of achieving this fit is for the potential recruits to get a *genuine* picture of the business right from the start of the recruitment process. The somewhat bullish presentation that may be given to potential clients or shareholders describing the firm in world-beating terms may mislead candidates and can result in expensive, and pointless, recruitment mistakes if the truth is far from the image.

In presenting the overall image of the business the attitude of the firm to potential recruits must be described, not just the immediate salary package and job prospects. Recruiting brochures should also always try to convey the *real* truth about a company in terms of its values, ways of working and future prospects.

Given the inevitably high job mobility, recruits must feel that employment with the firm will be an enhancement to their CV as well as being a well-rewarded and enjoyable place to work.

SCREENING

Recruiting is very expensive in terms of management time and thus some form of pre-screening is crucial. This may be on the basis of paper qualifications and/or by the use of search consultants who will suggest interviews only with candidates who look likely.

Most firms set certain minimum qualifications such as A-levels or a university degree. Some set aptitude tests or invite candidates to take part in selection games even before starting on the detailed interviewing process. Some firms use psychologists to assess the personality make-up of candidates to report on the degree of fit between the individual and the firm. Some even resort to graphology.

An honest presentation of the truth about the firm is important in the screening process as candidates who do not fit will be more likely to rule themselves out.

Creating a recruiting team within the firm will help focus on what the firm is looking for and will make screening a more effective process.

INTERVIEWS

The interview is the most important part of the recruitment process in establishing the degree of fit between the person and the firm and will provide the final information upon which decisions are made.

There should be a series of interviews with professionals at various levels in the firm. This should not be done with a view to winnowing out the weak or to cut down on the numbers seen by the managing director, but to allow as much dialogue as possible with the candidates. Each interviewer should complete a set of notes on each candidate and should suggest areas for discussion in subsequent interviews. Firm members who see candidates early in the process should ensure they spend a good proportion of the time describing the firm, its clients, its operating methods and its value system. There is certainly an argument that the views and instincts of junior firm staff are more valid when it comes to junior recruits as they are more likely to judge how well a person will fit in.

A dialogue not an interrogation

A selection interview should be a dialogue during which the candidate learns about the firm and the firm learns about the candidate. Under no circumstances should an interview be an interrogation. If candidates are going to be given ability tests that should be made clear to them and should be done quite separately from the interview. Naturally the interviewer will form a view as to the candidate's ability but this is far from being the sole object of the meeting. The use of case studies to give the candidate a chance to discuss the sort of business problems relevant to the firm are very useful but again should not be presented as a pass or fail test but simply as a subject for discussion.

Figure 3.1 Typical candidate assessment form

Full details of the candidate's background and records of previous interview with members of the firm are attached.

Candidate name:---

Interviewed by:---

Date:---

Has the candidate been interviewed by other firm members: yes/no?

ASSESSMENTS

Please insert number by each criteria: 1= unacceptable; 2=average; 3=high

APPEARANCE

Dress ....
Presentation............................
Manner ....

SKILLS

Verbal communication...............
Knowledge of marketing ....
Numeracy...............................
Interpersonal skills ....

SUITABILITY FOR US

Attitude..................................
Expectations............................
Enthusiasm:.............................

OVERALL ASSESSMENT OF CANDIDATE...................

Case study discussed: yes/no. If so which:

Areas for questions in future interviews

Do you recommend candidate employment: yes/no
Would you have this person on your team: yes/no

Figure 3.1 shows a typical candidate interview form used by a marketing consultancy. These forms are simply a discipline for the interviewer. If time permits all the interviewers should meet to discuss candidates before job offers are made.

RECRUITMENT SUCCESS

The firm should monitor its own recruitment efforts in order to assess its success and to highlight the possible need to make changes.

The total cost of recruitment in terms of advertising, fees, brochure printing and *professional time* (recorded on time sheets) should be noted and the average cost per successful recruit monitored from year to year. Given the importance of recruiting to professional firms they should not stint on the budget but equally it should not get out of hand. It would not be outrageous if five per cent of overheads and up to five per cent of professional time was devoted to recruitment. A measure of success is the number of candidates who accept job offers. If the firm gets only a small proportion of those people it wants it will need to reassess its salary structure, perhaps reconsider the type of people it is looking for and look more closely at its recruitment process in general.

18

EVALUATION

How can you assess the contribution of your professional staff?

We make a point of letting people know how they are doing. We tell them their strengths and weaknesses. We help them try to get better at what they do. Better people are what clients want.

Director, management consultancy

Having successfully recruited people to a professional service firm you must be able to monitor their progress and communicate it to them. Monitoring performance is important for staff as it gives them feedback on how they are doing, and important for the firm as it indicates where the firm is strong and weak and may highlight certain skill shortages.

As evaluation is the basis for the future success of an individual in the firm it is important that it is both effective (to ensure the right people get on) and transparent (to ensure that people feel it is fair and know where they stand).

ACCEPTABLE PERFORMANCE LEVELS

The first key issue of evaluation is some system of defining what constitutes acceptable *levels of performance* in a job and then measuring each individual against those criteria. Thus the job description and job evaluation go together. This means that an analysis of each level of work in the firm needs to be undertaken and an assessment made of what skills are required to do the job and what proficiency in those skills is expected of employees. For example it would be unreasonable to require new executives to show great abilities in winning new business, but they might reasonably be expected to communicate well in writing.

Having established the appropriate performance standards management must ensure these are communicated clearly to all members of staff.

CLEAR CAREER TRACK

The second key issue for successful evaluation is progress against some form of career track within the firm. Figure 3.2 shows a typical career track for a management consultancy, but something very similar should be in place for any professional firm. The titles of the grades will differ but the underlying ideas of progression will not. Members of the firm should always know where they are on the track. It sets achievement goals for them and manages their expectations about bonuses and promotions.

In the figure a typical successful executive will follow the career track staying in each grade for the target number of years and being made a manager at the end of year four, elected a junior partner in year seven and a senior partner in year twelve.

A fast track individual might remain in the executive and manager grade for only two years each making junior partner after only five years and then spending only three years before becoming a senior partner. People who do not get promoted and are forced to stay in a grade much longer than target, present a major problem to the firm as their level of compensation will fall below that of their peers and they will become dissatisfied.

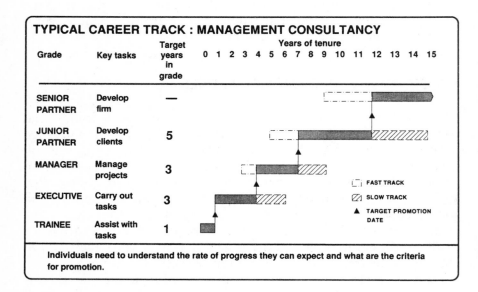

Figure 3.2

EVALUATION : ACCOUNT EXECUTIVE

Name : _____

Years in grade : _____   Target tenure for grade : _____

Rate the executive for their skills shown over the past year for each of the criteria shown.
For each skill indicate level as Outstanding (3), Good (2), or Standard (1) by circling number.

Managerial

Management of own time	3	2	1
Use of agency resources	3	2	1
Interpersonal skills	3	2	1
Budget management	3	2	1

Client management

Relationship	3	2	1
Client development	3	2	1
New business projects	3	2	1

Skills

Written communication	3	2	1
Presentation	3	2	1
Strategy development	3	2	1
Overall grading	3	2	1

Training courses completed :

_____

_____

Training recommended in past year :

_____

_____

Is the executive recommended for promotion :   YES/NO

Signed (Executive) _____

Signed (Assessor) _____

This sort of assessment should be completed at the end of each project or each half year and should be discussed with, and signed by, the executive.

Figure 3.3

BASIS OF EVALUATION

At each stage of an individual's career path it is necessary to establish an acceptable level of performance against a set of professional skills. This will enable the firm and the individual to know how he or she is doing. The degree of achievement of these levels of skills forms the objective basis of decisions such as promotion and salary level.

Figure 3.3 shows part of an evaluation for a typical advertising agency account executive. The executive's assessor, who is normally a senior person in the executive's department, will grade each skill from 1 to 3 and then provide an overall assessment. In reality most forms will be far more complex than this and will cover a wide range of skills. Such evaluations should always be discussed with the executive and the individual should be very clear about why he or she has been rated in that particular way.

In deciding what constitutes outstanding, good or standard performance a firm needs to bear in mind the quality of services offered by its competitors and its own future needs in terms of acceptable levels of performance. An outstanding executive will nearly always be a potential recruit for another firm or even a client. This is clearly a factor in determining compensation. In addition the outstanding people are those who might be expected to lead the firm (or its competitors) in the future.

113

Implications of grading

If a firm finds more than about 20 per cent of its people are in the outstanding grade it needs to look hard at its standards compared to competitors to ensure its quality control is acceptable. If it really does have a high percentage of such people it would normally expect to expand quickly as they will need to be part of a bigger enterprise if they are to enjoy the rewards of very senior positions.

If less than five per cent of the firm are rated as outstanding this must raise issues about where the future leaders will come from. Clearly recruitment from the outside is always an option but it is never as satisfactory as many of the people do not come onto the job market.

The annual (or more frequent) assessment marks the place of an individual on the career track. The level of skill achieved is *not* directly related to compensation. Salary matters should be discussed quite separately and should be decided by a senior manager or by a compensation committee. Naturally compensation will closely follow performance and promotion but will take into account other factors such as age and experience. Individuals must understand that the assessments are to help them identify areas to work on not simply to set their pay.

If members of the professional staff are not on track they must be offered advice and, possibly, additional training. If they seem likely not to achieve future promotion they must be told and offered help in finding work elsewhere. This is a critical aspect of running a successful professional firm, as people who are not going to progress are a major management problem.

Highlighting a bad fit

The lack of progress within any one firm is not necessarily a reflection of the professional abilities of an individual but simply a lack of fit between his or her skills and those needed by the business. If people are allowed continue for too long in relatively junior grades they will usually become discontented and, assuming that their pay packet reflects age and seniority, they will soon become too expensive to justify their position.

UP-OR-OUT POLICY

The leading international consultancy firm McKinsey like many top professional firms has an interesting up-or-out policy under which staff must constantly achieve promotion (which is based on objective skill achievement criteria). If they don't they are encouraged to leave. As the recruitment criteria of McKinsey are so high those who leave have little problem finding very good jobs. The impact of this policy actually helps retention of the right people as those who survive feel part of an élite group and do not feel, by and large, that they are carrying passengers.

HONEST ASSESSMENTS

Evaluation should be a transparent process in that it is important that individuals know what the firm thinks about them. Some problems such as specific skill deficiencies can be overcome with training. Personality clashes can also be dealt with. If people find that the firm's way of doing things is simply not right for them or if they find the ability levels needed for promotion are simply beyond them then the more quickly this becomes apparent the less harm will be done and the problems of finding alternative work will be reduced.

Professionals like to manage their own careers and are usually ambitious for themselves and their firms. A well-managed evaluation system which is felt to be fair will help to ensure that the firm has the right sort of people with the right sort of skills to meet its future needs. As firms grow and mature they should achieve a greater degree of fit between the skills demanded by clients and the skills present within the firm.

19

RETENTION

How can you get the best people to stay with the firm?

I think, at times, we are victims of our own success. Other partnerships are always trying to poach our best people and a lot of a senior guys do think about setting up for themselves. Keeping our stars is probably our biggest problem.

Architect

Once people have been recruited and regularly evaluated the next challenge is to make sure the firm manages to keep those it values and wants to stay.

ACHIEVING WEALTH

At its very simplest retaining staff is about ensuring that their long-term wealth potential with your business is greater than it would be elsewhere. If it is not then their particular set of skills is worth more to them somewhere else and they should leave. Long-term wealth potential means far more than simply what they are paid in salary. To be technical it should be thought of as the net present value of all their income and capital gains from employment for the rest of their working life.

More money

Being able to pay people more than a competitor implies that their skills are better used within their current firm than elsewhere. The fit between skills and the service the firm offers to clients is better than in another firm. For example a skilled acquisitions lawyer would be useful to a financial public relations business but would normally earn much higher fees in a legal practice because clients are prepared to pay more in that context. The danger with big salaries is that there will always be someone willing to pay more if they believe the candidate will bring clients with him or her or if the firm looking to expand is committed to building its skills in the area of the candidate's expertise.

Golden handcuffs

A classic retention device in professional firms is the so-called golden handcuffs, usually stock options or bonuses given if people stay with the firm beyond certain dates. These are often made available to individuals who have highly transportable, scarce skills and/or client contacts.

The main problem is that this tends to reduce the motivation package just to money, and can be very unsettling for those members of staff who are not granted this dubious privilege. There is also the danger of providing such strong financial motivation to stay that people remain when they are unhappy and unproductive. Tax may also be a problem for the individuals if all their rewards arrive at once rather than being spread to benefit, say, from capital gains allowances.

Pensions

In the past the pension scheme tended to be a great inducement to job inertia and to people staying put, but with new legislation the portability of pensions is much greater. As a retention device the pension really falls into the general category of tax-efficient benefits which all firms will tend to give and which, as a minimum, must be comparable with those offered by competitors. The example of the old style non-portable pensions which are felt to have kept people stuck in firms long after they should have left for pure career reasons is another reminder that techniques to encourage staff to stay must, where possible, be selective and relate to performance.

Perks

The company car, health insurance, incentive travel and even free schooling and cheap housing are all used to make people want to stay with firms. The status-seeking nature of professionals means that for certain individuals in certain types of business these rewards will be very attractive. It fits the stereotype of advertising that expensive cars are considered desirable. In his book on the Saatchi Brothers Ivan Fallon recalls that when Tim Bell was trying to lure a much wanted executive back into the firm he successfully won her over with the incentive of a red Ferrari! For some people there is no doubt that the promise of an improved grade of car or a corner office will keep them in the firm more effectively than a relatively large, but less visible, pay rise.

As with the golden handcuffs, indiscriminate stock options, pensions and perks will create a general job inertia which makes people much less willing to leave voluntarily when the fit between them and the business has ceased to be a good one. On balance, though, for those people who have strong client contacts and/or unique skills, some form of long-term financial or non-financial tie-in does make sense.

CAREER SATISFACTION

By definition professional staff should be seeking a career not just a job, and thus will see the firm in that context. This is true whether they see the firm as a stepping-stone or a permanent employer. Individuals need to see a clear career path ahead. They will need to understand the objective criteria for promotion and advancement – be clear as to what skills they have to develop to get on.

All firms *say* they are non-political and meritocratic but inevitably all firms *are* political. If staff get a strong feeling that politics is the principal basis of success they will be far more likely to leave if they do not believe themselves to be favoured. Far fewer people leave because they fear they cannot make the skill or commitment grade as human nature tells us all we are capable. Top management must stress at all times that merit and contribution are the key criteria for career advancement.

Becoming a specialist

Another attraction which can keep good people is the chance to follow a course of their own choosing. Some people are very attracted by developing very narrow but recognized skills. This can be achieved if their current firm also desires to specialize in the same area.

THE CHALLENGE OF CONVERGENCE

A particular challenge to the retention of key staff is the convergence of the service of professional firms. Lawyers, accountants, merchant banks, strategy consultants, public relations consultants and even advertising agencies are all offering closely related skills in areas such as mergers and acquisitions. It is easy for people to move from one firm to another and very quickly be contributing to profits.

The opportunity of jumping between professions means that firms must be even clearer in communicating to all staff the long-term objectives for their own firm so that people can see that their best opportunities lie inside rather than outside.

PARTNERSHIP

One of the main benefits of the partnership structure is that it locks in key employees. Partnership brings a share in the firm's profits but it also brings status, security and a feeling of being in control. For many people the goal of being elected (to partnership) becomes an end in itself and they will stay with the firm, even if the financial rewards are greater elsewhere.

Achieving partnership is often seen as the main pinnacle of achievement right from the first day of joining the firm. However for partnership to be a strong incentive to stay people must feel they have a real chance of success. Thus in very highly leveraged firms with a flat staff pyramid it is less likely that people will see partnership as a real option and thus will become more concerned with financial rewards.

Firms must be very clear in communicating exactly what level of skill and professional achievement is required of partners and must guard against giving the impression that the election process is highly politicized. In many firms which are not partnerships promotion to the board of directors carries similar status and attraction.

One risk firms must be aware of is that partners or directors are often seen as highly desirable recruits by other companies, often outside the profession, and that some individuals are very susceptible to offers having been elected because they feel they have achieved all they can within the firm.

SUCCESSFUL STAFF RETENTION

If a firm is not successful at keeping good people this will place a major strain on its recruitment and training programmes and will lead to dissatisfaction among clients and ultimately to poor profitability.

Among the professional staff some degree of turnover is

desirable to allow people who no longer have a close fit with the firm to move on. The problem is when turnover gets to be too high and therefore becomes expensive in recruitment costs. There is also the problem of not just how many leave but who they are – the firm must ensure it does not lose a disproportionate number of its most talented staff. All departures should be monitored and reported regularly to the board or management committee as a percentage of total professional staff numbers. The rate of departure from each grade should also be noted as an indicator of possible problems. Managers must also provide honest assessments of what happened when they lost people they really wanted to keep.

If the level of departures starts to rise the firm must look at its staff policies as poor retention levels may indicate greater problems on the horizon. A high rate of departure may mean the firm is not paying enough, or it could be that people despair of being promoted or achieving partnership because they feel the firm is too political. Or it could simply be poor morale or bad working conditions.

Retention rates among the support staff are also important as experienced support staff who really understand the firm's operating systems and approach have built up valuable knowledge. As with professional staff the rate of departures should be monitored and positive action taken if it gets too high.

Retention of staff is often overlooked by managers who are more concerned with recruitment and motivation. However losing staff has a definite financial cost and firms should certainly worry if they see an increase in the level of departures.

20

MOTIVATION

How do you keep people happy and productive?

We put great store behind keeping people keen. If people are excited by coming to work they will work better and clients will feel the benefit.

Partner, law firm.

Motivation of staff uses many of the same techniques as those devised to persuade them to stay (retention) but it has different objectives. Retention is about convincing people that the firm is a good place for them to be. Motivation is about helping them to want to do the work and to want to do it well. Motivation is about spurring people on to work better and more productively. It may also be about working harder but if the firm is well run more work will mean more pay reflecting the increased contribution of people. The extra contribution should be more to do with increased skills than with more hours worked.

At its simplest motivation splits into financial and non-financial incentives. The financial incentives are things like bonuses, stock options and performance-related perks. The non-financial are status, quality of assignments and quality of life.

FINANCIAL INCENTIVES

The most complex problem is, to misquote the Mikado, making the incentive fit the contribution. Giving people financial rewards for winning new business to increase the firm's turnover will backfire if they do so without regard to the money spent marketing the firm and on new business pitches or if they try to win new work by simply underpricing the firm to beat competitors.

At the other extreme using the firm's accounting profit as the basis for rewards can lead to damaging long-term effects if costs are cut too hard and investment is reduced to pump up profits. People may even issue invoices with little real prospect of payment (because of badly-managed client relations) in the knowledge that the *accounting* profit will look healthy although the debts outstanding (from late and non-payment) will start to rise.

An incentive package

The key tests of devising an incentive package for any employee should be:

- What aspect of the business performance can they affect most ?

- What levers of profit do they control?

Thus a secretary can be motivated to keep down stationery and courier costs by a simple bonus linked to meeting budget targets. An account director can receive a bonus linked to the profitability of his or her own accounts. A chief executive of a public, listed company can be given incentives linked to the growth in earnings per share on the assumption that he or she will ensure operating companies make the best use of shareholder's investments and that any acquisitions or disposals will increase the profits attributable to each share.

Having decided on the basis of the incentive the next decision is how should it be paid. Again in simple terms there are two methods – cash or shares.

Cash

The issue here is simply when and how much. As a general rule of thumb bonuses need to be about 15 per cent of basic salary before they really start to motivate.

BONUSES

A New York based economic research firm pays an annual bonus based on various assessments of the employees' contribution. The bonus varies from 10–30 per cent of basic pay depending on the evaluations. The key point is that the original basic salary and the year-end bonus becomes next year's basic salary: thus the bonus is a cash payment *and* a rise.

In effect this is like having a percentage of the salary deferred. The great advantage is that staff can see the tangible benefits of past efforts and are reluctant to slip from the fast track as the comparison with their peers over time depends on maintaining a high bonus.

At more senior levels bonuses can rise to being 100 per cent of basic salary which might be very apt for a new business director or a chief executive.

Share options

Under the vast majority of stock or share option schemes employees receive the legal option (for which they pay a nominal sum) to purchase shares in their company at a date in the future. What makes the option potentially valuable is that the price they will pay in the future to obtain the actual shares is the price of the shares at the time they are granted the option. Assuming the shares will rise in value they can, thus, enjoy a capital gain.

Writing in *The Independent on Sunday* (26 August 1990) Simon Rose quotes a manger of a firm with stock options as saying:

> *Our people identify more closely with the company and in addition we think that it probably improves productivity. People don't want to let the family down. Even though option holders are not yet shareholders we still want to treat them as part of the company so we send them much of the same information that shareholders receive. We've been rewarded by seeing a higher level of interest about the business in return.*

In the UK there are many variants of option scheme but three main models are the most used:

Approved executive schemes

Under these, which are approved by the Inland Revenue, options are exercisable between three and ten years after the date of grant. Capital gains tax is payable at the time of the disposal of any shares taken up and then sold.

The company has complete discretion over which employees receive options and over how many they get up to a certain level. The only constraint is that options cannot exceed a certain amount (usually ten per cent) of the company's total equity.

Non-approved schemes

Under these no approval is required from the tax authorities. Options can be exercised within one year of grant but income tax is payable on the gain in value at the time of exercise of the option whether or not the shares are sold and again on any gains made between the exercise of the option and the actual sale of the shares.

Save-as-you-earn-schemes

Under these all employees who meet certain criteria such as length of service must be allowed to take part in the scheme. Regular monthly sums are saved by the employee in a building society and after five or seven years the employee can use the accumulated funds to buy shares in the company at the price they were on the date that the scheme started.

Given the nature of professional service firms where the enthusiasm and goodwill of the staff is so crucial, it is hard to see any arguments against making stock options or their equivalent as widely available as possible.

Promotion

For people with their sights set on career development promotion is a key motivation. As discussed above promotion needs to be based on an objective evaluation of an individuals level of skill attainment against what should be expected on the typical career path. The real reason for promotion is to place people in more senior positions which enable them to sell their skills to clients at a higher rate in recognition of their increased experience and greater degree of managerial control.

One of the worst mistakes a professional firm can make is to promote people as an incentive or reward when they are not really up to the bigger job. Clients will pay more for their services but actually receive no more value. Junior staff will be demotivated by being led by someone they feel is inadequate.

SPURIOUS PROMOTION

A London PR agency employing 45 professionals kept promoting people to its board to motivate and retain them. In many cases the new title was not accompanied by any significant increase in salary although in all cases their nominal billing rate to clients was increased. At one point the consultancy had 16 people on the board – 35 per cent of the entire professional staff. For reasons of perceived status board directors were reluctant to do certain types of client work which resulted in freelance staff having to be employed. When the board was at its largest, utilization rates of directors dropped below 40 per cent and the business was losing money.

NON-FINANCIAL INCENTIVES

The existence of good morale, often demonstrated by a low level of complaints, can have financial benefits. It can be argued that well-motivated staff will enjoy themselves at work and be less concerned about straightforward hard cash in their pay packets. Firms should monitor their salary bill as a percentage of total costs and on a per capita basis. If salaries are growing much faster than inflation (and revenues are not keeping pace) it may indicate a motivation problem where money is substituting for other incentives.

Professionals feel good about their work for a variety of reasons:

- The firm has a good image and they enjoy the status of being part of it

- Their clients are interesting and well known

- They like their work colleagues and have fun

- They feel they are learning and making themselves more marketable

- They have good conditions of work and good facilities

The fact is that it will be a combination of all these and other factors. The task for top management is to be aware of this and to keep a dialogue going with members of the firm to detect any areas of discontent. If, for example, the firm is the subject of favourable press comment the relevant articles should be circulated to all members of staff. If the comment is bad a senior manager should write a note putting the criticism into context.

The spirit in professional firms is an important part of motivation and senior managers must regard improving it as a crucial part of their work.

21

ASSIGNMENT

How can you match the needs of the firm with those of its clients and staff?

I am guaranteed to make everyone unhappy. My colleagues never seem to get exactly the people they want, clients always want us to start the job sooner or later than we can, most of the associates would prefer to be on different projects to the ones I find for them.

Director (in charge of assignment), design consultancy

In any business which serves a number of clients the task of matching the available professional staff with the various client projects is complex and very important. The value received by any one client will depend very much on the skills and motivation of the people assigned to the team. The long-term career development and job satisfaction of the firm's professional staff will depend on what sort of projects they have done for which clients over the years.

ASSIGNMENT OBJECTIVES

Assignment is critical in any professional firm but becomes even more important in those which are not organized into teams or account groups but which have a pool of staff who are assigned to various projects and work with different directors.

The alternative models for organizing teams are discussed in chapter 26. Two types of team structure – fixed and flexible – are described and it is when the flexible project team model (see figure 4.4, p. 000) is being used that a good assignment process becomes of paramount importance.

Assignment tension

The assignment process is a political balancing act as is illustrated in figure 3.4. *Clients* want the best-qualified, best-motivated people they can have for the money. They also want continuity of professional teams. *The firm* wants to assign people who have low utilization rates and whose salary package is more than covered by the projected client income. Managers want to maximize profit. *Professional employees* want assignments which will help them develop any weak skills, allow them to work with important senior members of the firm and let them show abilities in those skills highlighted by their past evaluations. In addition people will look for assignments which are congenial to them in terms of location, nature of client's business and identities of other team members.

The increasingly aggressive stance of clients towards the make-up of their professional teams was illustrated in an article in *The Independent* (5 March 1991)

CLIENT REQUIREMENTS

Once a consulting firm has been chosen clients are insisting that senior people are assigned to the job. 'That has been a gradual pattern in recent years and is likely to continue into the 1990s', said Angus Hislop (a partner of Coopers & Lybrand Deloitte).

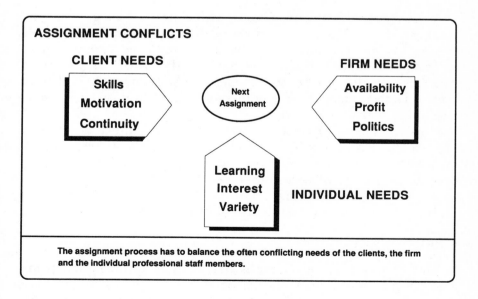

Figure 3.4

Fixed teams

Where a firm is organized into fixed teams the key decisions are which team an individual joins and when they should change teams. An individual becomes part of a fixed group for a period of time. This implies a certain required chemistry with the group's leader and other professional members of the team and will mean the individual will only get exposure to the clients of that group.

Very short assignments to a group will be disruptive and inefficient so it is likely that an individual will remain in a fixed team for at least 12 months. In many firms people only change teams when they are promoted and often those promotions are made possible by another team position becoming available.

In making the team choice regard must be given to people's strengths and weaknesses, to the professional skills they need to learn and develop and to the types of client they have worked with in the past.

Flexible teams

In the flexible matrix structure each assignment to a team requires a similar decision-making process to that of fixed teams but as most people will work for several different clients in a year there is less need to seek a perfect fit and there is a degree of swings and roundabouts. Some less than perfect assignments can be balanced against some very good ones.

A particular problem with flexible teams is getting the workload right. With the fixed teams the group leader will be able to set up his or her teams by balancing the various client assignments as he or she controls all the work of the team members. In the flexible model any one staff member will have several team leaders all of whom might want him or her to start and finish at particular times.

With flexible teams the assignment process must be able to resolve the possible conflicts between team leaders over how much each gets of each staff member's time, by keeping track of the planned workload of each individual. If necessary the director in charge of assignment may have to intervene if several team leaders are placing impossible demands on an individual.

Multiple clients

A further complicating factor is that in most professional firms people serve more than one client at a time. Thus in selecting assignments decision-makers have to balance the pattern and nature of existing client commitments as well as new ones.

It may be that the workload of some clients is always greatest at certain times of the week or month. It may be that certain clients require professionals to travel to particular places. All these considerations must be taken into account in trying to devise the right mix of clients for any one individual.

Professional firms also have to overcome problems of client conflict. In most firms team members will not be able to work simultaneously with clients who might be considered commercial competitors. In some firms professionals are marked for their whole careers as being associated with a particular client – and even during periods when no work is being done for that client those professionals would be designated as unable to work with any potential competitor of that client. Advertising agencies seem particularly sensitive to client conflict and it is very rare, in the UK or the USA, to find two competing brands being handled within the same agency.

Management consultants, accountants and law firms seem to have done a better job of convincing clients that teams of professionals within one firm will be able to keep client secrets and preserve client loyalties by the use of so-called Chinese walls to keep teams separate.

CLIENT LOYALTY

One of the large management consultancies numbers among its clients several large banks, brewers and consumer goods companies. Once an individual has worked on an assignment for one of the clients in any one category great pains are taken to ensure that he or she does not work for the potential competitors. Professional staff know which of their colleagues are associated with which clients and although it is not formally written down it is clearly understood that anyone who breached client confidentiality would probably have to leave the firm.

Length of assignment

Another consideration in the process of assigning people is the duration of the typical job and the relatively long-term nature of most client relationships. Clients like to keep the same people on their accounts as it reduces learning problems and gives a greater sense of security. However junior professionals often like to experience a variety of clients and to keep assignments short.

In management consultancy and the litigation departments of law firms assignments tend to be short and project-oriented even if the client relationships are long ones. In the audit departments of accounting firms and advertising agencies assignments and relationships tend to be much longer. In these cases the assignment tends to be to the client, often for the duration of the client relationship.

ASSIGNMENT MECHANICS

The mechanics of assignment will normally be carried out within the personnel function or by a secretary. The decision-making must be done by a senior person with sufficient experience and knowledge to balance conflicting needs.

Consultation and salesmanship

Because of the inevitable problems of keeping everyone happy, assignment must be seen to be taken seriously by the firm. The worst possible situation is when people feel it is all done by chance at the last minute. The pattern of past work and likely future prospects for an individual should be discussed at the time of the regular evaluation sessions. The firm needs to acknowledge the facts of past assignments so that some degree of objectivity can be applied when assessing, later, how well the assignment process did in meeting the individuals agreed career goals. Nothing is more frustrating than for people to be told, for example, that they need to get experience with international clients if the assignment process always, somehow, manages to assign them to domestic projects.

The assignment process must be consultative, with the individual given the opportunity to state preferences clearly and explain career needs. In the end, though, the needs of the client and the firm must be seen to take precedence over the individual although individuals can quite legitimately record the degree to which they feel they have lost out on each assignment to build a case for more consideration of their needs in the future.

The skill of the senior professional who oversees assignment is to sell each project to people to enthuse them and to convince them it is good for them. In many cases assignments have also to be sold to clients who would often prefer that their teams be unchanged. One of the by-products of good client relationships is that clients can be involved in the process and made to feel that their interests are also being considered.

Assignment success

A perfect assignment process would result in very high staff utilization. Clients would feel they had been served by the best people the firm had to offer. Professionals would feel they had been placed on the most interesting and rewarding assignments. Clearly such a perfect result is never achieved.

The most tangible indication of assignment failure will be low utilization as people are left on the beach or spend too long in training. There may also be complaints by clients about the quality of the teams working for them. A less tangible, though equally important, indicator of problems will be a widespread feeling among professionals that their careers are being held back because they are on the wrong projects. They may complain they have been unable to broaden their skills or even that they have been unable to work with a wide enough range of senior people.

When firms are concerned that something is going wrong with assignments they seek a solution by giving someone the assignment job as a full-time task, or by investing in sophisticated computer equipment to make it more automated. In fact a lasting solution is to involve managers of greater seniority in the assignment process which demonstrates the seriousness with which the firm takes the task. Senior people are more likely to be able to balance more accurately the needs of the various parties. At the very least the operation and relative success of the assignment process should be a regular item on the management committee or executive meeting agenda.

22

TRAINING

How can you use training to make the professional staff more valuable?

Our training is what makes the firm so successful. Our people are always known to be at the leading edge. People come to us and stay with us because we train them. We have a technical advantage but we also have a far greater common spirit and common philosophy than many others because our people understand what the firm is all about through training.

Manager, management consultancy

Training is regarded by many professional employees as an enjoyable benefit; it should be regarded by the firm as an investment in its intellectual capital and part of the product development process. It is one of the key ways for firms to communicate their culture and values to staff and it can be used as part of an incentive package. In short, training in professional service firms is a good thing.

TRAINING OPTIONS

Training broadly falls into three categories:

- General technical
- Company-specific
- Individual–specific programmes

General technical training

This involves the teaching of skills such as the use of computer spreadsheets, accountancy techniques and data analysis and language tuition. This sort of teaching can be done by subscribing to places on commercially available courses or organized by the company itself in-house. The general courses on technical skills make the individuals more useful on assignments and increase their marketability as employees which makes them keen to attend.

Company-specific training

This teaches things such as company information procedures, use of available company resources and use of proprietary company techniques. These have to be organized on the company's behalf. The company-specific courses play an important role in building and maintaining company culture and in achieving consistent quality standards. It would not be too strong to say that these courses can amount to indoctrination in the firm's culture. This is, in fact, a particularly important feature as it creates the sense of identity and commitment to professional values and quality standards that mark one firm out from another.

Individual-specific programmes

This area includes courses such as presentation skills, part-time MBAs, senior management development programmes and executive team building courses. These can be subscribed to or can be organized at the company's request. Individual programmes are particularly good for people who are at major turning points in their career – promotion to manager, election as partner – as they help them put their work and lives into context. Courses such as a residential senior managers' programme at a leading business school are also highly prestigious and are seen as a bonus or reward to the individual.

CULTURAL INDOCTRINATION

In professional firms the culture and values of the firm can be one of the key factors in assuring long-term success. New recruits and new clients will be heavily influenced by what sort of firm they are thinking of doing business with. Some of the cultural training is about what the firm stands for and some is to do with its underlying values – often those of the firm's original founders. There are numerous examples of the way firms seek to get their values understood and accepted.

SALOMONIZATION

In his book *Liar's Poker* Michael Lewis describes the Salomon Brothers training programme:

The training programme was without a doubt the finest start to a career on Wall Street. Upon completion a trainee could take his experience and cash it in for twice the salary on any other Wall Street trading floor. . . the [written] materials were the least significant aspect of our training. The relevant bits, the ones I would recall two years later, were the war stories, the passing on of the oral tradition of Salomon Brothers . . . . All the while there was a hidden agenda: to Salomonize the trainee.

LEONIZATION

Forbes Magazine (September 1990) in a profile of the very successful, privately-owned advertising agency Leo Burnett titled 'Lionising Leo' comments:

Photos, corny sayings and cartoons of the agency's founder – who's been dead for nearly 20 years – decorate the offices. Employees, who call themselves Burnetters say things like 'That's what Leo would have done' . . . . In short the Burnett agency has accomplished something that has eluded so many other businesses. It has managed to keep alive the spirit and drive of the founder.

ANDERSEN COLLEGE

Writing in the *Sloan Management Review* (Autumn 1985) Dr David Maister notes:

[Arthur Andersen, the accounting firm] is renowned for its training centre at St Charles, Illinois, to which young professionals are sent from all over the world. In the words of one Andersen partner: 'To this day, I have useful friendships, forged at St Charles, with people across the firm in different offices and different disciplines. If I need to get something done outside my own expertise I have people I can call on who will do me a favour.'

MCKINSEY INDUCTION

The international consulting firm McKinsey requires all new recruits to go on a two-week, residential training course called the Introductory Training Programme (ITP). This is often organized so that new American associates come to Europe and their European peers visit America.

Much of the two weeks is given over to sessions on how the firm works and even playing games as well as a team project to solve a business case. At the end of the two weeks participants are left in no doubt about how the firm works and where it stands on ethical and professional standards. In effect the course tries to prepare them to behave in a 'McKinsey fashion' in a very wide range of professional circumstances.

Commenting on the McKinsey programme, Dr David Maister (in the same *Sloan Management Review* article quoted above) says:

The programme is run by one or more of the firm's senior professionals who spend significant amounts of time inculcating the firm's values by telling Marvin Bower stories – Bower who ran the firm for many years is largely credited with making McKinsey what it is today.

The value of the cultural aspects of training are hard to quantify but there is no doubt that the major and well-respected professional firms all make a major commitment in this area.

TRAINING BUDGETS

The real cost of training tends to be in lost professional billing time rather than course fees. By definition individuals cannot be working on client assignments at the same time as attending a training course. The budget decision must, therefore, be based on a careful analysis of just how important training is. Leading management consultancies will expect staff to devote at least two full weeks every year to specific, often residential, training courses plus a large number of one-day and part-day sessions.

The belief that training people is a waste of money because they will simply leave and take their skills elsewhere is very short-sighted. The knowledge of a commitment to training will help recruitment and retention and may even produce benefits in winning new clients. If a firm is managing its people correctly the only ones who leave will be doing so with the firm's blessing.

Given that professional service firms, by definition, are attempting to do tasks for clients better than the clients can do them for themselves, a very high commitment to training in terms of cash budget and time seems correct. Although firms are loath to set exact financial targets there seems to be a consensus among the training leaders that, as a minimum at least five per cent of professional time, and more than five per cent of the overheads budget should be devoted to training.

ORGANIZING TRAINING

Training, like assignment, can be highly political. Going on most courses is seen as a perk. Attendance at some courses is seen as a clear indication of professional success. As with assignment there is a balance to be achieved between the individual's needs and the firm's current demands. What needs to be made clear is the level of the firm's commitment in terms of time and budget and the agreed programme for an individual over the next year. The potential disputes and arguments should come at the beginning of the year, when a programme is agreed in broad outline, rather than afterwards when it is too late and potential courses and opportunities have been missed.

The largest professional firms have in-house training departments but even the smallest company should ensure that a senior person is clearly assigned a training role and will fight for the training budget and champion the importance of training in the firm's future development.

One aspect of managing training is the systematic follow-up of courses. At its simplest all participants should be asked to fill in evaluations so the course can be updated or amended if required. Course tutors also should be evaluated in terms of ability and clarity, whether they are firm personnel or outsiders.

COUNSELLING

A crucial role for senior professionals is the on-the-job counselling of more junior staff. This goes far beyond the idea of training and is more a matter of learning by absorbtion. It was once the case that juniors were expected to turn up at meetings as 'bag-carriers' and just learn by being present. It is now important that formal attempts are made to explain why things were done in a certain fashion and what is happening in the overall project and client relationship.

TRAINING PRIORITIES

To be really successful in a professional firm training needs to be seen to be an investment in the future and needs to be championed by top management. If it is simply left to the training department or assigned to a junior director or partner it will not get the financial or emotional support it needs. Executives must look upon training as a perk rather than a chore.

To motivate senior people to participate in organizing training it needs to be made clear that acting as a tutor is regarded as one of the advancement criteria for professional staff. Likewise successful counselling should certainly be made part of the assessment criteria for the promotion and bonuses of senior professionals.

Clients must feel it is to their benefit when people who work on their business are sent to be trained.

23

SUPPORT STAFF

How do you manage the people who keep the firm running but are not part of the professional group?

I know it sounds patronizing – but that doesn't stop it being true – when I say that this business would collapse tomorrow if the main secretaries, receptionists and back office staff left. Many of them have been here longer than me. They really know how the place works.

Manager, PR consultancy

Every professional in a service firm will pay tribute to the crucial services of the support staff but, often, will do very little to help them. The blunt reality is that in many firms the support staff are simply not included in the firm's culture.

The real character of a business may come from its receptionists, security guards, messengers and caterers and secretaries – those who support the client service teams while not working directly for clients. There is a belief that support staff are replaceable and high turnover can be tolerated whereas professional staff are more difficult to find. In reality a secretary or receptionist who really knows how the firm works is an important part of the team.

SUPPORT STAFF REQUIREMENTS

Getting the support staff involved in the firm and helping them to work efficiently requires recognition that they have different needs from the professional staff and face different problems.

Lack of career path

A critical problem for many professional service firms is how to provide a satisfying career path and rewarding job for support staff who will find it very difficult to follow the same career track as a professional. In many professional areas such as the law or accountancy support staff would have to leave and obtain qualifications if they wanted to join the professional group.

In other businesses such as advertising and public relations, it is easier to move but it is usually best if a secretary is treated in exactly the same way as a graduate trainee. This can be difficult, trainees are often paid much less than senior secretaries, but it does ensure the transition from support staff to a professional role happens over a period of time.

This period of transition is necessary if only because clients will see professionals in a very different light from support staff and will have much higher expectations. It is quite unfair to expect anyone to make an immediate transition from one role to the other. Ideally secretaries given this sort of promotion should do their training in a different office as it can be very difficult for their colleagues to accept the changed status.

The development of professional executives like para-legals and financially literate but unqualified accounting staff will increase in future years as a shortage of professionals gets worse. The role of para-professionals is discussed in the next chapter but this offers another career option for support staff.

Different culture

The professional staff can look forward, ultimately, to an ownership position in the firm or the financial equivalent. Support staff tend to be paid for the job they do. Treatment of support staff in professional firms is often very bad as professionals tend to expect the same level of commitment and enthusiasm they feel themselves, overlooking the fact that they enjoy vastly better conditions of pay and prospects.

To build a feeling of loyalty to the business professional firms should provide support staff with the best equipment in terms of computers, fax machines and so on. They should make it quite clear to all professionals that it is unacceptable to be abusive or unreasonable in their behaviour towards support staff. Many firms make the proper use of support staff time and facilities part of the regular assessment of professional performance.

Different aspirations

Most support staff quite naturally want a good job with pleasant working conditions. They are often not so concerned with carving out a career and will be far less enthusiastic than professional or client service staff about working all weekend to meet a client's needs.

Support staff will look for security and reasonable working hours and working conditions. It is simply not reasonable to expect a 35-year old senior secretary with two children to stay at work until 8.00 pm because his or her 26-year old boss (who is hoping for promotion) wants to get a document out by the next morning.

SUPPORT STAFF MANAGEMENT

It is important that a senior member of the firm champions, and is seen to champion, the support staff cause. Without this backing they are unlikely to get the high quality of facilities they need. Without top management support it can be hard to justify investments in mundane things like computers, laser printers, copying machines and faxes. It is all too easy for a senior partner to fail to understand how much time is wasted in a fax queue – a problem that could be solved by buying one new machine – an expenditure equivalent to less than three hours of his or her billed out time.

Although a secretary will tend to regard his or her boss as line manager he or she, like all support staff, should actually report to an office manager to ensure consistency of treatment and equivalent job specification and perks. It is also often the case that the boss is not a good advocate of the secretary's cause as the boss may be too junior actually to get anything done.

THE ACCOUNTS DEPARTMENT

The accounts department in a professional firm is a special case. Many of the staff are professionals (accountants) in their own right, but they are different from the other professionals in the firm. Their careers will probably take them to similar work, but in more senior positions, in other firms. Often they are paid well but are usually not part of the same bonus schemes and so on, as the professional staff. One of the firm's professional partners or directors should be given responsibility for the accounts department so that they, like other support staff, can be seen to have a champion.

24

THE PEOPLE SHORTAGE

How should you plan for the future when there will be many fewer professional staff on the job market?

We find, even now, good graduates hard to find and there are many other professions after them. I've seen the projections for the next 20 years and its a terrifying prospect. Growing the firm will become very difficult indeed.

Partner, law firm

A major challenge to professional firms over the next few decades will be an acute shortage of people – particularly at the junior level. The number of potential young professionals in the main Western economies is set to decline dramatically in the near

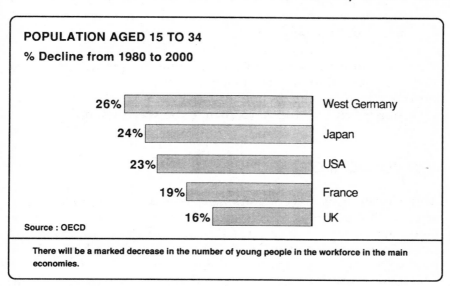

POPULATION AGED 15 TO 34
% Decline from 1980 to 2000

26%	West Germany
24%	Japan
23%	USA
19%	France
16%	UK

Source : OECD

There will be a marked decrease in the number of young people in the workforce in the main economies.

Figure 3.5

future. Even though many professional firms have laid off staff in the 1990s recession they will still have a recruitment problem in the future.

FEWER YOUNG PEOPLE

Figure 3.5 shows that the number of 15 to 34-year-olds in the UK will drop by 16 per cent between the years 1980 and 2000. In the US the decline is 23 per cent and in West Germany a full 26 per cent – more than one in four fewer young people than today.

These demographic effects are the results of the 1960s baby boom which pushed up the number of young people and changed the nature of society. Unfortunately other demographic trends are also going to put pressure on professional firms.

- The number of qualified women in the workforce is already quite high and unlikely to increase significantly

- The proportion of young people with the necessary qualifications is also quite high and again with education facilities being cut back in the face of the demographic decline in some countries it is unlikely to increase

- The convergence of the various professions means that young people will have a much wider choice of potential professional career all of which will carry the promise of status and financial reward

The net result is that competition for young people will be intense and firms will find salaries rising rapidly and growth severely constrained. The impending scarcity of people means that professional firms will have to change the way they do things.

NEW SOURCES OF LABOUR

Professional firms have traditionally looked to the most established and prestigious universities for their new recruits. Even senior appointments from other firms will have followed this route. In the future firms will have to look to other ways of finding staff who are capable of doing client work.

In some cases this will mean redefining what is required to be a professional, in others it will mean changing the way the firm works to allow people to contribute even when they are not prepared to work 60 hours a week or who do not want to follow the conventional professional career path.

Para-professionals

Para-professionals are those people who have learned and practised professional skills but have not gone through the same process of examination and qualification as a member of a professional body.

Although the term is most often applied in law firms (in America the idea of para-legals is very well established) the same basic concept is valid in many professions.

PARA-PROFESSIONALS

In an article in *The Times* (20 November 1990) Edward Fennell argues the case for more extensive use of legal executives (para-legals) who have many of the required skills but have not gone through all the same qualification stages as a solicitor:

Legal executives are a great under-utilised resource. Firms with scores of partners and hundreds of lawyers frequently have a dozen or fewer legal executives . . . They are under-used and under-appreciated because of one of the fundamental flaws in the modern solicitor's make up. Solicitors tend to be mediocre management delegators . . .

Professional firm managers will need to be clear about what type of work can and cannot be done by these skilled but unqualified executives.

DE-SKILLING AND UNBUNDLING

In another article in *The Times* (31 July 1990) Alan Grieve argues that the huge rise in legal costs is pushing the profession towards the use of para-legals:

One accepted way to hold down the costs revealed by a time sheet is to try to de-skill (or unbundle) the services being provided. For example, drafting a simple document or indexing documents in a heavy litigation case can be done by a para-legal.
The key to para-legal profitability is the ability of the

para-legal to take on work which lawyers would otherwise perform, at an effective hourly rate lower than the lawyer's top charging rate, and the ability, conversely, for the lawyer to convert these released hours into optimal charge-out rates.

Particular thought needs to be given to the career path of para-professionals. Can para-professionals become partners? Should some equivalent position to partner be created to give them a career path?

If firms do start to use para-professionals they will find they have created another group of employees in addition to professionals and support staff.

Part-time workers

Many qualified professionals find that they no longer want to work full-time. Examples are married women with children, professionals who are running their own business or want to be involved in other work or in teaching. At present most firms find it very difficult to accommodate such requirements but with some creative thought solutions can be found.

Part-time might mean three days a week or it could be four months a year. Some people may be able to schedule their various activities so that they could do one major project a year for a firm – in effect being freelance.

Married women

Some women with young children may be happy to return to full-time work. The issue this raises for firms is the provision of creche facilities or the financial incentive of paying for day-care or nursery-schooling for the children.

In addition managers will have to be prepared to make allowances for the inevitable emergencies which will require mothers (or indeed fathers) to put family before the firm.

Outworkers

Professional firms who have to be located in the centre of major cities face the twin problem of expensive office space and the pressures placed on many staff by commuting.

The recent development of technologies such as fax machines and modems mean that some executives can work very easily from home. Some firms (the best known example is Rank Xerox) took the radical step of providing executives with all the necessary technology and guaranteeing them a certain number of days' work per year. The executives were then encouraged to find other sources of income using their home office as a base.

Returners

These are qualified people who left full-time work but who now, after a gap of five, ten or even more years want to come back. Often they are women who married and brought up children, sometimes women or men who left professional work to go into industry, teaching or self-employment.

The challenge here is how to fit these people fit into the firm's structure. They may be much older than many junior partners and directors and will be expected to work alongside executives very much their juniors. Will this work? Will it destabilize the firm?

Radical thinking

All the above options are potential solutions to the people shortage. The challenge for firms is to be sufficiently flexible in their thinking and planning to make use of these various methods.

Those firms that stick to the old ways will find wage costs escalating and will lose business to competitors who are able to serve clients with first-rate people even though those people are not employed in the conventional way.

PART IV

RUNNING THE BUSINESS

How should managers control the day-to-day operations of a professional firm?

I think the biggest difficulty we face is that we don't really run our own company at all. I work more than 60 hours a week in the office. I take calls at home in the morning and at night but it is all fixing things for clients. I don't feel we really run the firm – it just exists.

Partner, law firm

The day-to-day running of a people business is about tactics rather than strategy. Previous parts of this book have outlined the concepts useful in understanding a professional firm, highlighted the key actions which can increase profits and described how to manage the people. This part considers the practical day-to-day operation of a professional firm.

Principally this involves making sure that your main assets, the people, are where they should be and doing what they should be, that they have the tools for the job and that clients are paying the right amount for the firm's efforts.

Almost without exception everyone in a professional service business will regard him or herself as an executive or as a manager. In many ways this is true as most professionals will be managing external resources on behalf of clients or doing work which clients would regard as executive tasks. The main distinction to make, though, is which of the staff are really involved in managing the business itself as opposed to doing client work only. The easiest test to use is which of the staff have responsibilities for the deployment of the resources of the firm.

Those people with responsibility for allocating resources of the firm can be regarded as managers. Those who mainly work by exercising their own professional skills are not managers of the business even though they manage resources on behalf of clients. Those who maintain the operation of the business without supplying professional skills to clients are support staff. Under this definition it is quite possible for someone to be a manager of the firm even though he or she may not be one of the professional staff.

The role of a manager includes both running the business itself and organizing the servicing of clients. The fact that it is a *role* and not a job is important as in most cases senior people will be both managers and professionals.

Running the firm itself includes the tasks of:

- Finding and managing premises
- Recruiting staff
- Personnel issues such as pay, promotion and training
- Invoicing and debt collection
- Managing profitability
- Strategic planning

Organizing client work includes:

- Assigning staff
- Constructing and motivating client service teams
- Personnel issues that relate to client work
- Client relations
- Seeking new business

Both the above sets of managerial tasks are in addition to the professional work carried out on behalf of clients. Actually doing the client work, which is the role of every professional, means applying the craft skills specific to the firm – legal work, architectural design, writing advertising copy and so on. As people become more senior the balance will tend to shift towards spending more time on managerial and less on professional work.

Unlike a factory or a department store the running of the business cannot be left to a few designated managers, simply leaving the majority of staff to get on with their own jobs. Running a professional firm involves all the staff in making good decisions about saving resources and improving client service. The role of top management is therefore, as with profitability, to create a culture which helps the firm to run well rather than simply issuing instructions about how things are to be done.

25

OWNERSHIP

Who should own the business?

---

*Don't forget we actually own the firm ourselves. We report to
ourselves. We set our own policy. We own the money machine. It
really feels different from being an employee. It makes a huge
difference.*

Director, advertising agency

An important issue for professional service businesses which needs
to be considered as a prelude to management structure and
leadership is ownership.

In broad terms the business may be owned in four ways:

- By shareholders and quoted on the stock exchange – a listed
  public company

- By a small number of shareholders, either external or senior
  managers – a private company

- By another corporation – a subsidiary

- By the senior members of the business – a partnership

Management behaviour will be affected by the form of
ownership. Senior managers will have a different psychological
contract with the business depending on their participation, or
possible participation in ownership. As a general rule the more
widely spread the ownership among the firm members the less
direct control will be required. Motivation to maximize income
and reduce costs will already have been built in by participation
in ownership.

Control versus profit-sharing

In considering the impact of ownership a clear distinction must be
made between control of the firm and participation in profits.

Profit-sharing schemes are part of a programme of employee incentives. The owners of the business (the shareholders) can decide to institute generous profit-sharing incentives if they believe it is in the firm's best interests, without giving up any control.

The actual ownership of shares is only important for those people who feel a need to be part of the control structure of the firm. Some people will be more motivated if they hold shares although, in practice, they would have no real voting power unless they had ten per cent or more of the equity. In partnerships control over the future of the firm is more a matter of being part of the partnership group than the legal holding of equity. Partners' shares are more a matter of calculating the division of profits than of control.

If managers and owners accept the premise that employees will be more concerned about the success of a business if they have a vested interest in its prosperity, then it follows that the firm will put in place some mechanism such as equity ownership or profit-sharing, to ensure that those employees who can effect the firms success are properly motivated.

Share options

Most share-option schemes are not intended to spread the *ownership* of the firm among the staff but are simply a way for employees to benefit from an increase in the value of the business. Most of the shares issued to staff following options (except in cases where capital gains tax is a big issue) tend to be sold immediately to provide the option holder with cash.

Change of control

The actual ownership becomes an issue when a professional firm gets taken over or merges with another and the managers of the smaller firm wish to retain some control over future policy. It can also be important when a firm goes public and sells shares to the investment community.

Going public

For most true professional service firms such as lawyers, small accountancy practices and management consultants there must be a real doubt as to whether it is viable to have the firm listed on the stock market. Senior professionals work in the firm because it provides them with a base from which to serve clients and enables them to share in the firm's profits.

If an earlier generation of partner/owners sold the firm to investors those investors will expect to share in the profits. The partners who sold will have enjoyed a one-off capital lump sum – in effect selling out their future rights to profits. Later generations of partners will, therefore, have a smaller pool of profits to distribute.

In a business where barriers to entry for any *new firm* (as opposed to any *individual*) are very low it is relatively easy for a group of senior people to set up on their own and make far more money than they would within a public firm. The barriers to entry to a profession for an individual can, of course, remain high with the hurdles of professional exams and apprenticeships to overcome.

The more a firm becomes dependent on a business system or international network, and the greater the degree to which it has *real* economies of scale, then the more likely it is to be able to prosper under public ownership. It is almost impossible for a small group of individuals to break away to set up an international network on their own.

Firms which wish to remain private will need to have some mechanism for transferring equity from retiring partners to new appointees but this is relatively easy to organize.

A professional firm which decides that it has to go public in order to raise funds for expansion (rather than finding those funds from internal resources) will almost certainly be at a long-term disadvantage to a private competitor in the crucial areas of recruitment and retention of staff.

The advantages of private control were discussed in the *Financial Times* (21 January 1991) in a profile of Young & Rubicam (Y&R) the largest privately owned US marketing group:

> *Alex Kroll, Chairman of Y&R sees private status as an asset for the company 'Back in the 1980s you might have gotten a few voices in Y&R saying there might be benefits in going public. Not any more,' he says. Private status has enabled Y&R to pursue a policy of slow, but steady, growth over the years. It has been able to make long-term investments that a publicly quoted company might have balked at.*

PARTNERSHIP – A SPECIAL CASE

The ideas of partnership as an ownership and management structure, and professional firms, are usually closely linked. Indeed in some countries certain professions *have* to be partnerships, as limited company status is not allowed. Because partnership has as much to do with culture and operations as it does with legal ownership it merits separate discussion. Even those professional firms which are, in legal terms, limited liability corporations, tend to exhibit many of the characteristics of partnerships.

Partnership has a mystique encompassing ideas about ownership, management, culture, philosophy, training and wealth creation.

Partnership characteristics

For most professionals election to the partnership (or the near equivalent of becoming a director) represents the major career goal. Although each firm will vary, in general partners (or directors) are a class apart from the rest of the firm. The partners are the aristocracy with their status reflected in a number of ways. The typical characteristics of partnership are:

- *Income* – partners are almost always better paid than more junior professionals

- *Security* – partners are much harder to fire

- *Profits* – partners almost always share the firm's profits (or losses) between them which can create a huge income differential with other firm members

- *Control* – partners usually enjoy far more autonomy over the assignment and conduct of their work. They are also directly involved in setting the policies for the firm itself

- *Status* – perhaps the most important partnership benefit is that both within the firm and outside it partners have a definite status and respect. Inside it is likely to manifest itself in larger offices and a better car. Outside it is a simple and easy concept to explain to friends and neighbours that one is a partner

It is the nature of partnerships that their finances are far less public than those of corporations but it is widely accepted that the top firms provide spectacular rewards. According to the *Wall Street Journal* (5 October 1990) in a highly revealing article about the leading investment bank Goldman Sachs:

A typical candidate [for partner] in his or her mid-30s already makes half a million or more a year [US $]. The first reward for *making partner is to take, maybe, a two thirds reduction in salary. But on paper new partners immediately become wealthy. They are entitled to a cut of Goldman's future profits which averaged $5 million a partner last year [1989] before taxes. A partner's cut typically starts at $1 million [annually], but within a few years can balloon to well over $10 million a year.*

Goldman Sachs (widely acknowledged as one of the best run professional firms in the world) provides many examples of the unique nature of partnership. *The Economist* (29 September 1990) in an analysis of Goldman observed:

> *Goldman's biggest challenge is it needs to find a way to integrate its new staff into its still very American hierarchy . . . . As a private firm, maintaining the corporate glue of Goldman's culture is vital. Problems have arisen from the intense recruitment of lots of potential bankers who all aspire to partnership.*

The Economist reports that Goldman is looking at early retirement for partners and at selling equity participation to non-partners as ways of keeping staff happy when partnerships are scarce. The article ends by observing:

> *Even so, internal critics insist, the panache of partnership has created fierce political competition and hurt Goldman's teamwork.*

The Wall Street Journal (5 October 1990) has its own perspective on the cultural aspects of partnership:

> *[In selecting partners] Goldman says it is simply looking for culture carriers, people willing to fit into a rich tradition . . . It says it is looking for team players. If you cannot sublimate your ego or work with others, you have a problem says Geoffrey Boisi, a top partner.*

Partnerships and wealth creation

The issue of partnerships going public is covered in a *Forbes Magazine* profile of the consulting firm McKinsey (October 1987):

> *Insiders say a recently elevated senior partner at McKinsey is likely to draw $600,000 or so. Compensation for veteran senior partners ranges up to $1 million. Nice money . . . but to be truly rich . . . it takes more than owning stock in a privately held consulting firm. Thus there must have been a temptation to take*

the firm public, cashing in on its golden reputation to make existing partners rich. Pure greed snorts Marvin Bower, principal architect of the firm. Does this philosophy sound pretentious? Maybe so, but McKinsey people behave as if they believe it and this contributes to the morale and the mystique. Would the Vatican go public? The First Marine Division?

Further insights into the nature of partnership comes from the excellent book on Salomon Brothers – *Liar's Poker* by Michael Lewis. Salomon is a private firm which went public in the early 1980s:

Salomon's loose management style had its down-side. It was the only major firm on Wall Street in the early 1980s with no system for allocating costs. When the firm was a partnership (1910–81) and managers had their own money in the till loose controls sufficed. Now, however, the money did not belong to them but to the shareholders. And what worked for a partnership proved disastrous in a publicly owned corporation.

Michael Lewis goes on to describe the effect that the switch from private partnership to public ownership had on top management:

John Gutfreund [Chairman of Salomon Brothers] openly criticised what he considered the overwhelming greed of the younger generation. It was easy for Gutfreund to say money did not matter . . . He had already made his fortune by taking $40 million out of the sale of the firm. His attitude – as well as those of the other old partners – towards the firm had changed since he cashed in his chips. He and others ceased to view Salomon Brothers as an instrument of wealth creation, and began to treat it as an instrument of power and glory, a vast playground in which they could be the bullies.

THE BEST SOLUTION

There is no single answer to the the ideal form of ownership. Partnership does have great merit but it can be very constraining to growth. Full public ownership only really works where the firm needs capital and is able to build a business with true economies of scale. Private limited companies have many of the merits of partnership – the only difference often being to do with commercial and tax legislation.

26

MANAGEMENT STRUCTURE

How should the firm be organized?

You know we don't even have an organization chart but everyone is pretty clear about who does what and the firm seems to prosper.

Director, management consultancy

In the conventional model of a manufacturing company or a bureaucracy there will usually be a clear organization chart showing exactly who reports to whom and who does what. Professional firms can very rarely draw such a chart and even when they do it is always out of date and always disputed, in terms of its implications, by those who appear on it.

Most professional service firms have a relatively flat management structure and some form of matrix reporting relationship – where people are members of specialist departments *and* separate client service teams – rather than a rigid hierarchy.

Any one individual will probably serve multiple clients, if not simultaneously, then over the period of a year. Each of those client teams will probably have a director or team leader to whom all the team members will report on client matters. At the same time individuals will probably report to a separate boss for employment matters such as salary reviews and conditions of work. In many firms that boss is the managing director or managing partner.

To show the business structure as a conventional, hierarchical organization chart is, therefore, potentially misleading. It is more useful to think of the business as layers of people of similar seniority and to describe the existence of a team structure where each team is a grouping (often temporary) of people from each of the layers of seniority.

STAFF PYRAMID

The idea of the staff pyramid was introduced in chapter 5 (see figure 1.9, p. 38). In running a professional firm managers have

155

STAFF PYRAMID

GRADE	% OF TOTAL STAFF NUMBERS		APPROXIMATE TENURE years	MAIN TASKS
	Flat	Steep		
DIRECTORS OR PARTNERS	10%	20%	6 →	Client relations New business
MANAGERS OR TEAM LEADERS	20%	30%	4 — 7	Project management Staff coaching
EXECUTIVES OR ASSOCIATES	60%	40%	2 — 5	Using professional skills
TRAINEES OR ANALYSTS	10%	10%	0 — 1	Learning professional skills

All firms have clear levels of hierarcy and must decide on the right balance of numbers at each level. The balance will depend on the type of work the firm does.

Figure 4.1

to find out what sort of pyramid is right for them and what sort of pyramid will enable them to deliver the services promised to clients in a profitable way.

Flat versus steep structure

Figure 4.1 describes the make–up of a typical professional firm in terms of layers of staff. It shows the relative weighting of the various layers of staff and how this differs between the flat and steep models. The trainee level is shown separately but for most purposes, certainly in considering the firm's economics, trainees should be considered as the same grade as executives.

The two firms in figure 4.2 show a flat and a steep pyramid model. In the flat, wide-base, model the excess of income over costs is £3,080,000 while in the steep, narrow-base model it is only £2,620,000. This results from the larger number of junior staff in the flat model. The really dramatic difference is in the profit *per director* which is calculated by subtracting the firms overhead costs (assumed to be £2 million) from the surplus income and dividing it between the directors. Splitting the larger amount (£1,080,000) among only five directors in the flat model produces a surplus per head of £216,000 compared to only £62,000 in the steep alternative.

STAFF PYRAMID – FLAT VS STEEP

FLAT PYRAMID :   Profit per director = £216,000

GRADE	NUMBER IN GRADE	BILLING RATE	UTILIZATION	INCOME* £'000s	SALARY COSTS £'000s	SURPLUS** INCOME £'000s
Directors	5	£130	50%	£650	£750	(£100)
Managers	10	£90	80%	£1,440	£600	£840
Executives	30	£60	90%	£3,240	£900	£2,340
TOTAL	45			£5,330	£2,250	£3,080

STEEP PYRAMID :   Profit per director = £62,000

GRADE	NUMBER IN GRADE	BILLING RATE	UTILIZATION	INCOME* £'000s	SALARY COSTS £'000s	SURPLUS** INCOME £'000s
Directors	10	£130	50%	£1,300	£1,500	(£200)
Managers	15	£90	80%	£2,160	£900	£1,260
Executives	20	£60	90%	£2,160	£600	£1,560
TOTAL	45			£5,620	£3,000	£2,620

* Assumes total of 2000 billable hours
** Surplus prior to meeting firm's overheads which are assumed to be £2m

The flat and steep pyramids produce very different economics. The total surplus income (= profit) of the flat pyramid is £460,000 greater than the steep. The surplus per director is therefore much greater in the flat example.

Figure 4.2

The flat pyramid

At first sight the flat structure may appear to be the one to aim for but it will only be possible to operate this wide-base model when the client work requires this sort of servicing. It would be a mistake simply to assume that a flat model is better.

The flat pyramid tends to be a bit more of a sweatshop with juniors working hard on tasks defined by others. There tends to be a higher (and therefore more costly) staff turnover. Client projects tend to be less predictable as senior members of the firm have less time to develop close, counselling relationships with clients. The relative number of senior people out in the market-place is smaller so there will be less time for marketing. This model might suit a few stars of their industry who want to create the maximum income for themselves. They will be very good at winning new business because of who they are, and simply need a large team of arms and legs to carry out their bidding and do the work.

The flat, wide base, model will do well when there is a great deal of work around and there are client projects which need a team in a hurry. However it is less resilient in recessionary times because if the overall workload of the firm drops off the high staff overheads can make it quickly unprofitable. Making a large number of the junior staff redundant will, of course, create a steeper, narrow-base structure.

The steep pyramid

The steep, narrow-base model will suit a number of professional practitioners who group together to share common costs and assist in mutual marketing. A group of family doctors or a general legal practice are examples.

The steep pyramid tends to produce a more collegiate and friendly atmosphere as there is less delegation and more time spent on client issues by senior people. Client relationships tend to be longer-term and the utilization of staff is better, over long periods, as the proportion of senior people is much higher and therefore client workloads are more predictable. In times when there is a relative scarcity of work the steep structure firms have an advantage as they can field far more senior people to do marketing and to undertake client work. The directors of flat structure firms are trying to sell the work of their teams. The directors of steep structure firms are trying to sell themselves.

COUNSELLING FROM A STEEP STRUCTURE

A PR firm specializing in high level client counselling will be heavily weighted towards managers and directors as clients will usually require the time of senior people to help them with politically sensitive and complex issues and to do hands-on work. This sort of business will be forced to adopt a steep, narrow-base, pyramid but will be able to achieve high profitability by increasing the utilization of senior people as they will spend more time on client work and less on managing the firm.

ANALYSIS FROM A FLAT STRUCTURE

A management consulting firm specializing in analytical support for acquisitions will tend to have a flat pyramid with a large number of executives and analysts working to a small number of senior directors. Here the billing utilization of the directors may be low but the firm is very profitable as they leverage themselves by managing a larger number of juniors.

The best ratio and pyramid structure is clearly that which maximizes *long-term* profits. Assuming that clients are rational and pay for what they get (in many cases a false assumption) then the best structure and ratio is that which delivers maximum client value (and therefore fee income) at the minimum internal cost to the firm.

SELECTING THE BEST STRUCTURE

There is no simple answer to the best shape of pyramid but in moving towards a solution for any specific firm the following issues should be considered:

- Workload
- Promotion
- Client needs
- Partner's aspirations

Workload

The first issue is how many clients a director can take on simultaneously. If just one the director might as well go and work, full-time, for the client. More than about six and the clients will start to feel unloved.

The number of clients per director (or senior partner) will tend to dictate the ratio of managers to directors. As a general rule a manager will find it hard to service more than two or three clients at any one time as each client will require regular access to the manager. When a director has, say, six clients he or she will usually have two or three managers reporting to him or her. To have less than two managers per director is very top-heavy; to have more than five would either mean that each manager only had a very few clients or that a director had too many accounts to handle.

If firms make relatively junior people managers then they, as individuals, will each have a smaller number of accounts creating, in effect a flatter pyramid with a wider base. If, on the other hand, managers are very experienced they will usually have several accounts and be acting almost like directors: this produces a steeper pyramid with managers acting more like directors.

Promotion

If it is stated policy that all junior staff have the possibility of promotion then the business must be growing fast enough to allow the pyramid to expand at such a rate that people can move up through the levels. If, for example, there were five executives to every manager then in order to maintain this ratio five new executives would need to be appointed for every one promoted to the manager grade. In reality no firm is like that as gaps are created when people leave but the principle holds good if the shape of the pyramid is to be maintained.

The flatter the pyramid the more difficult is the problem of recruiting fast enough to maintain the shape. If a very flat structure required ten associates to support one director then each directorial appointment has major recruitment implications. Also if staff feel that because the pyramid is so flat promotion is most unlikely, they will become demotivated.

To maintain a flat pyramid a firm will have to grow very rapidly so that a large number of new junior staff can be employed to keep the ratios intact when people are promoted. Alongside this the firm will need a strict up-or-out policy under which senior people will be asked to leave if they are not able to justify promotion by bringing in and serving new clients.

Client needs

If clients require a service which is based upon experience and expertise with a large amount of counselling by senior professionals, the firm will be forced towards a steep structure (with relatively high average billing rates). If clients want a mainly execution based service with the prospect of getting a large amount of basic work done quickly under supervision then the firm could have a flatter pyramid (with relatively low average billing rates).

Partner aspirations

If the partners/owners want to build a firm with a long-term future which is not dependent on them as individuals, a steep structure would be preferable. If they want to maximize their income during their own working time with the firm a flat pyramid would be more appropriate.

People who enjoy close client contact and like the idea of being practitioners will favour a steep structure while those who are more entrepreneurial and see themselves as leaders and architects of a business will prefer the flat structure.

STEEPENING THE STRUCTURE

The main warning about ratios for managers is that there is a tendency for professional firms to become top-heavy over time, as a flat pyramid gives way to a steep one. This is inevitable because of the high growth rate required to sustain a flat structure.

If a firm with four partners decides to grow at the rate of adding one partner a year then after five years it would have nine partners. The flat model firm with a ratio of five professionals to one partner would have to find, and find work for, an additional 30 professional staff to keep its ratios. The steep model firm with three professionals to a partner would only need 20 new posts.

The gradual change to a steeper structure can only succeed if the firm simultaneously changes its work to the type where clients will require more senior staff to service their needs. Doing this will justify a steeper pyramid and will create a new, and viable, set of economics for the firm.

One solution to becoming top heavy is to encourage a senior team to set up a new organization with a different work orientation. This will enable the remaining people to keep the original orientation and structure.

GROWTH AND CHANGE

A successful public relations consultancy developed a good name and made good profits for itself doing straightforward consumer work. Over time the senior team started to outnumber the rest of the professionals as the growth of the business was not great enough to justify the employment of enough junior staff to maintain the structure.

Members of the senior team set up a new division which was a sub-brand of the original firm and offered clients high level crisis counselling concerning consumer issues such as food contamination which required much more of the senior people's time. Clients were happy with the two brands because they were getting what they wanted and paying accordingly (high daily rates for the counsellors, low daily rates for the consumer work). The firm prospered as the two divisions had their own separate economics.

A particular lesson for those seeking to acquire professional service firms is to be very cautious of high past profits which have been generated by firms with a flat staff pyramid. Over time the pyramid will get steeper, the base will narrow and profitability will reduce. Also when the two or three top key managers of a flat structure are demotivated, by wealth or loss of control after selling out, then the profitability of the firm can reduce dramatically as the firm is so dependent upon them.

The best firms to buy are those with a steep structure with a good brand name and solid reputation in the market. They may appear less profitable because of the need to share surpluses with a large number of partners but that profit will be more sustainable and the firm is less at risk from a few individuals. These sort of firms do not have a built-in time bomb of poor future profitability as a result of structure.

CLIENT SERVICE TEAMS

Professionals almost always work in teams, partly so that junior people can work under the supervision of their seniors (allowing the seniors to leverage their expertise) and partly to bring together the mix of skills required by the client.

There are various ways for professional firms to organize their teams to serve clients. The way chosen will depend on the type of business the firm is in, the way competitors organize themselves and the beliefs of the firm's founders about what is best.

There are broadly two types of team:

- Flexible teams of professional staff made up for the duration of a client project
- Fixed teams which can serve a number of clients

These teams can either be drawn from a common pool of professionals or drawn from specialist departments. In businesses where there is one main professional skill (e.g. strategy consulting) the choice is between fixed or flexible teams from a common pool as most individuals in the pool have the same skills. In businesses where a number of different professional skills are employed (e.g. advertising) fixed or flexible account groups are usually drawn from fixed specialist departments.

CONSULTING – A FLEXIBLE TEAM

A typical engagement team on a consultancy project might be a partner, a manager, three associates and a business analyst. Every one of them might have a degree in economics and an MBA from an American business school.

162

All might have the same degree of experience of the client's industry. All have come from a common pool of staff and will work together for the client in question but might not do any other mutual work. Although they have similar skills they have different levels of experience and will break up the work between them to reflect their different roles in the team. If required, however, each could, probably, do the other's work.

ADVERTISING – A FIXED TEAM

An account team in an advertising agency might be made up of an account director (team leader), an account executive (administration and client contact), a copywriter (the words), an art director (the pictures), an account planner (market research/consumer behaviour) and a media planner (audience research/media costs). Each of the individuals will have a different background and different skills. Each is necessary to serve the client. The same team may have several, separate, client projects.

The decision between fixed and flexible teams in any professional firm is often driven by the need to maximize staff utilization. In most cases fixed teams are easier to administer but can produce far lower utilization rates as there is less room for manoeuvre. As a very general observation those firms which rely on some form of hourly or daily rate tend to use the flexible system. Those firms which are remunerated on a commission-or success-fee basis often have fixed teams.

The use of flexible teams puts more emphasis on the role of the partner or director in building client relationships and then picking a team from the firm's resources to serve that client. The client tends to see the director and appoint him or her and only then become involved with the team.

With fixed teams the client usually knows from the start who the members of the team will be and what they have achieved, in the past, as a team.

Some firms make a virtue of their team structure in marketing their services. Some public relations consultancies and firms will argue that a client will work with a tried and tested team who have a proven track record. Others will say that the client will be served by a hand-picked team drawn from throughout the firm to suit the client's special needs. In either case it is much more likely that the work will go to whichever people have the most spare capacity.

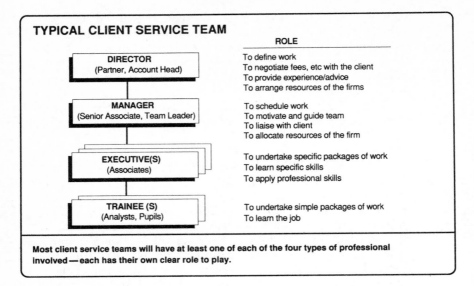

TYPICAL CLIENT SERVICE TEAM

ROLE

DIRECTOR
(Partner, Account Head)

To define work
To negotiate fees, etc with the client
To provide experience/advice
To arrange resources of the firms

MANAGER
(Senior Associate, Team Leader)

To schedule work
To motivate and guide team
To liaise with client
To allocate resources of the firm

EXECUTIVE(S)
(Associates)

To undertake specific packages of work
To learn specific skills
To apply professional skills

TRAINEE (S)
(Analysts, Pupils)

To undertake simple packages of work
To learn the job

Most client service teams will have at least one of each of the four types of professional involved — each has their own clear role to play.

Figure 4.3

Team structure

Figure 4.3 describes a typical client service team. While the titles may change greatly according to the type of business the basic structure will remain the same. The number of managers, executives and trainees on any one team will depend on the size of the client project. In terms of the three levels of the staff pyramid trainees are, in effect, the same as executives.

The four basic elements of the team shown in figure 4.4 can be organized on a flexible or fixed basis.

Flexible teams

On a flexible basis any one individual can be a member of several teams. While the individuals will be responsible to the team's leader or project director for the specific project or client they will probably have similar relationships with other team leaders and, quite separately, will report to a boss for personnel matters. That ultimate boss will often be the managing director but it could be any of the directors acting in a *firm* management rather than *team* management role.

In the example in figure 4.4 there are five project teams serving five clients and two of the directors are running two projects each. The junior membership of teams A and B are likely to be quite different even though they are both run by the same director.

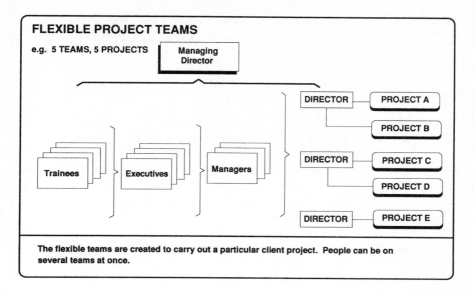

Figure 4.4

Fixed teams

In some firms the client teams are permanent and thus the client team head is also the individual's line manager (e.g. a team of designers who always work together). This is shown in figure 4.5

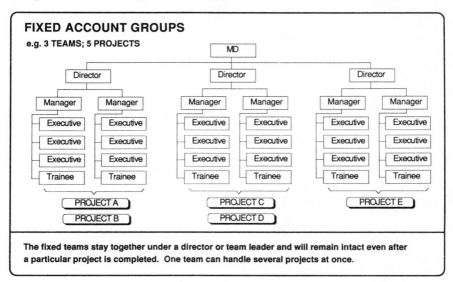

Figure 4.5

which again shows five projects but this time with only three teams. In this case the teams on project A and project B will be drawn from the same fixed group.

The fixed team approach simplifies management in that client organization and business organization is combined under one person, but can be restrictive in that it creates a number of firms within a firm and can deny individuals the opportunity of working for a range of directors and a range of clients. Clearly individuals could change from team to team over time to provide more variety but this can be difficult to achieve except when people leave the firm. Fixed teams also increase the risk of a group breaking away from the firm and setting up on their own having got used to working together.

Matrix structure

In those firms where there are clear functions of specialized skills such as an advertising agency the specialists can be grouped together for management purposes, for example, creative department, media department and so on, but can be organized into flexible or fixed client teams for client service.

Figure 4.6 shows the classic matrix structure where individuals report to their functional director for employment matters and to their team leader for client service issues. Within the matrix of line

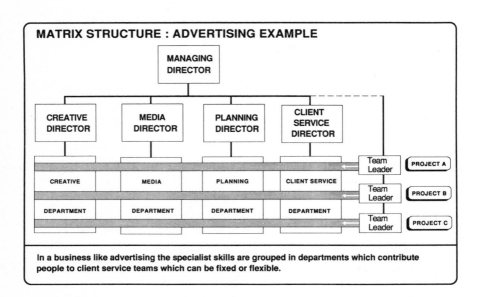

Figure 4.6

166

management and client teams the client service teams themselves can be fixed or flexible but any team changes will need to be negotiated with the individual's line manager (the department in which he or she works) as well as the client team leader (the person who controls the client work).

DECISION-MAKING STRUCTURE

As well as organizing themselves to serve clients professional firms must have a mechanism for running their own business.

The staff pyramid is an expression of the relative numbers of each grade of professional staff within the firm which is important in an understanding of the firm's economics. The client service team structure is an expression of the way the firm organizes itself to serve clients. The committee structure is an expression of the way the firm controls its own affairs – its own management and decision-making structure. Figure 4.7 shows a typical committee structure for a professional firm.

The board

A board or partners' committee will exist to ratify major policy decisions. The exact status of this group will depend on the legal

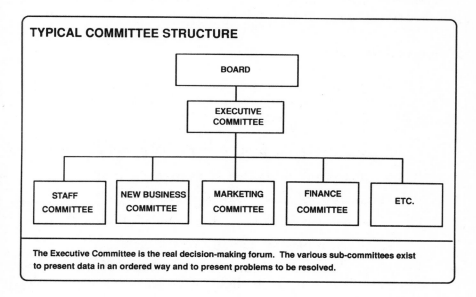

Figure 4.7

structure of the firm – a listed company, a public company, a subsidiary, a partnership, and so on will all have a slightly different legal status and required procedure.

The executive committee

Day-to-day management of the firm will be in the hands of an executive committee which will meet at least once a month and will, in reality, take all the key decisions which will be later approved by the board. This committee tends to base its decisions on practical reality, whereas the board may be more political in its operation. In some firms the executive committee is, in practice, just one person – usually the chief executive or managing partner.

Sub-committees

Reporting to this executive will be a series of sub-committees (sometimes, again, a sub-committee of just one person) each of which cover specific tasks such as premises, recruitment, staff and so on. The decisions as to what tasks or titles to give to these sub-groups will depend on the overall problems and opportunities facing a business. Thus a firm planning to move will almost certainly have a premises committee. At other times in its development the firm may leave everything to do with the building to the office manager.

Management tasks

There can be no hard and fast rules about the overall structure for running the firm but some framework must exist to carry out certain key tasks. These tasks are:

- Regular analysis of the profitability of all accounts or clients
- Regular analysis of utilization of professional staff
- Regular analysis of new business in prospect
- Decisions about promotion and remuneration of staff
- Decisions about planned rate of growth of firm
- Decisions about any changes in the nature of the service offered by the firm in the light of projected changes in the market, that is, strategy

Too much democracy?

Professional firms exist to provide services to clients rather than to make crucial decisions about the allocation of resources the way a manufacturing company or financial holding company might. Professional firms are not required to make rapid decisions about their own operations and, indeed, most have a reputation for being indecisive and dithering.

One of the key decision–making challenges in professional firms is to try to keep all the staff happy and involved. This can present a major problem as the inherent level of democracy and the need to syndicate all major decisions can make a firm very political and slow-moving. A manufacturing business with a clear distinction between workers and management can take decisions about investment, new products and new client opportunities with a very low level of consultation (although there are many who argue more consultation would be a good idea). It is inherent in professional firms that any change of direction will need the support of the vast majority of staff or it will not happen.

This complexity of decision-making is one of the reasons that most professional firms (including strategy consultants) are so bad at devising and implementing strategy. The very act of forward planning often forces a firm to confront issues about who will be doing what in the future which it normally prefers to leave undiscussed.

A similar problem is trying to obtain a clear positioning for a professional firm as part of its marketing efforts. When confronted with the need to decide what we stand for and what we are many partnership groups will discover they are deeply divided on the answer.

A cast of thousands

A special structural problem in some professional firms, particularly advertising agencies and public relations consultancies, is the almost insane desire of all the staff to get on the board. Top management frequently make someone a board Director to motivate him or her and avoid giving a large pay rise. Writing in the *Sunday Times* (20 May 1990) Ivan Fallon observed, after some directors resigned from the advertising agency Saatchi & Saatchi:

> *When Charles Saatchi heard of the latest defections from his Charlotte Street agency last week he exclaimed. But who are they? I've never heard of them. Although technically the five who left were directors in an advertising agency everybody is a director . . .*

At Charlotte Street there are – or were – 95 directors in a London agency which is a subsidiary of a worldwide one which in turn is a subsidiary of a holding company.

In addition to enhancing personal status the creation of a multitude of directors is also thought to help with clients who prefer to feel they are dealing with a director.

Executive responsibility

The problem of a multitude of directors is that boards become far too large to be of any use in management terms thus making the executive committee even more crucial. If you really want to know someone's standing in a professional firm ask if they are on the executive. From the client's point of view being served by an executive member might not be a good thing as the individual concerned will have many calls on his or her time in respect of managing the firm as well as being part of the client's team. Clients often get more attention from someone less involved in the firm's management.

The active management of a professional firm is important to keep it profitable but it will almost always be done on the side by professionals who are, primarily, concerned with client work. The management structure must recognize this and must seek to provide a mechanism within which firm members are informed of and consulted about key decisions.

27

LEADERSHIP

How should the firm be run from the top?

I think my job is to be consistent and clear about what this firm stands for and what the future holds. It's not about checking the budgets, finding clients or signing expenses. It's about setting the tone and knowing where the firm is going.

Managing Partner, consultancy

Leadership in professional firms is not just about management but goes further and involves developing and maintaining the firm's attitudes and standards.

Leadership could be described as management style but only in that it is the style of the most senior people. The choice of chief executive, senior partner, managing partner or whatever the title might be, is a key leadership question and that individual will be seen as embodying the values of the firm.

Vast amounts have been written about leadership styles with many academic theories about what is best. From practical observation of many people businesses most styles can be seen both to succeed and fail. The secret, although it is blindingly obvious, is to have the right style at the right time – different leadership approaches seem better suited to certain stages of a firm's development and certain types of market conditions. Rapidly growing firms need to exude energy and a sense that everything is possible; a more established, and larger, company must ensure that its quality standards are maintained.

In thinking about leadership of their firms professionals should ask themselves what sort of style seems most appropriate and then question if that style is, in fact, being implemented. The most rapid and effective way to adopt a new leadership style is to appoint or elect a senior partner or chief executive who exhibits the sort of qualities which are required.

LEADERSHIP ROLES

Leading a people business has three key elements:

- Maintaining the quality of output
- Providing craft skill guidance
- Resolving political and resource conflicts

Quality of output

Achieving a consistent high quality of work will be greatly assisted if the firm's leaders are seen to set and pursue clear, high standards. This is important in a business where much of the output is intangible and where the final quality of the product depends on the conduct of individual members of the firm's professional staff. By action, by anecdote and by instruction the leaders must be seen to refuse to compromise on quality.

Craft skills

Professional firms ultimately succeed or fail according to the level of their professional skills.

Leaders of the firm must provide craft skills guidance by demonstrating, in the way they go about their work, very high levels of professional competence and by being known to support the development of skills through training and coaching of junior professionals by their seniors.

Political conflict

Leaders must resolve the political conflicts between the firm's senior managers over issues of policy and allocation of resources. This is an important leadership role as the formal decision making processes in professional firms tend to be slow and unwieldy. Whether leaders resolve these issues by seeking a political consensus or simply by taking a decision themselves is a matter of their style.

LEADERSHIP CREDENTIALS

It is virtually impossible to be accepted as the leader of a professional service firm – by staff and clients alike – without being seen to be an outstanding practitioner of whatever the firm's professional skills are.

Marvin Bower of McKinsey in consulting, Frank Lowe of The Lowe Group and David Ogilvy of Ogilvy & Mather in advertising, Felix Rohatyn of Lazards and Henry Kravis at KKR in investment banking are examples of individuals who are accepted as successful leaders through their demonstration of outstanding craft skills in their chosen profession.

CRAFT SKILLS

An example of the importance of craft credentials in professional form leadership was cited in *Forbes* (18 February 1991) in a profile of the consulting group Bain.

Bain brought in Peter Dawkins, the former Heisman Trophy winner and Army brigadier general, as a rainmaker and soon made him head of the firm's North American operations. Though Dawkins had impressive contacts, his lack of consulting experience upset many younger and old 'Bainies' who were fighting for more control. Some of the company's best people jumped ship.

A clear distinction needs to be made between leading a professional service firm and running a financial holding company which happens to include professional firms in its portfolio. Martin Sorrell of WPP was described by David Ogilvy of Ogilvy & Mather, an advertising agency Sorrell was then in the process of buying, as an 'odious little jerk' who had never written an ad in his life.

This expression of lack of confidence in professional craft skills might, quite rightly, have put paid to any hope Martin Sorrell had of actually running the advertising agency Ogilvy & Mather. However it was, of course, no barrier to him being an investor and having financial control of the firm as for that he needed the approval of the financial community.

Writing in the *Financial Times* (19 June 1990) about the Ogilvy acquisition correspondent Alice Rawsthorn observed:

Mr Sorrell also had to raise morale, which had been badly damaged by the takeover. The Sorrell management style is limited to finance. Advertising agencies, he says, are best run by advertising executives and should be left to their own devices.

It is noteworthy that the Sorrell approach, essentially *management* rather than *leadership*, was effective when he took over the agency group J. Walter Thompson which had lax financial controls and poor margins, but had far less to offer when he acquired Ogilvy & Mather which was a better-run business and needed leadership to pull it through a time of recession in advertising.

Despite all the traumas both suffered it is arguable that the agency group Saatchi & Saatchi is better placed for the future than its rival WPP simply because Charles and Maurice Saatchi are still seen by many of their staff as having a valuable contribution to make in terms of craft skills.

LEADERSHIP STYLES

While it is not possible or even useful to attempt to describe the correct leadership style for people businesses it is possible to point out the implications of the way certain broad types of behaviour can affect the firm and other managers.

Most key leadership decisions in professional firms are about the allocation of resources and the resolution of conflict. There are different ways of approaching the same problem.

In broad terms very senior managers tend to be either democratic or autocratic when it comes to taking decisions. The autocrats simply take a decision and force it through. The democrats seek a consensus. It would be a grave mistake to assume that the right way to run people businesses is always to be democratic as often the inability to achieve consensus will leave the firms lacking direction.

When it comes to finding solutions to business problems and identifying courses of action again there are two broad alternatives – the analytical and the political. The analysts tend to be very fact-based and data-driven. The politicians try to assess what will actually work rather than the theoretically best solution.

Four types of leader

Figure 4.8 shows how the problem-solving style and decision-making style generates four broad types of leader. Each leadership type has its own characteristics and produces its own culture within the organization. Success of the different styles will depend on the internal characteristics of the firm (the type of staff, the rate of growth, the size) and external factors (the structure and state of development of the industry, the types of client). It is most unlikely that any firm will be led in a way that exactly corresponds to any of the four types but they are given as extreme examples for purposes of developing a framework within which to describe the differences between various firms. The four types of leader can be summed up as follows:

Professors will be most successful in firms with a flat hierarchy and a high percentage of professionally qualified and potentially mobile staff, who stay together because of mutual convenience. People will be promoted on the basis of a scientific analysis of their contribution to the firm. Clients will be looking for relationships with one or two key people they respect. Typical of strategy consultancies and smaller law firms.

Presidents do best where the client is king and where senior client service managers create their own empires by building close client links with them personally. The main leadership task is to hold together a federation of strong groups. Although the decision making is political – balancing the interests of various conflicting groups of people – the process of reaching the decision is by consultation with the various barons. People will be promoted on the basis of peer group approval. Clients will be looking for the reassurance of consistent quality of work and will require access to well managed teams. Typical of large accounting firms.

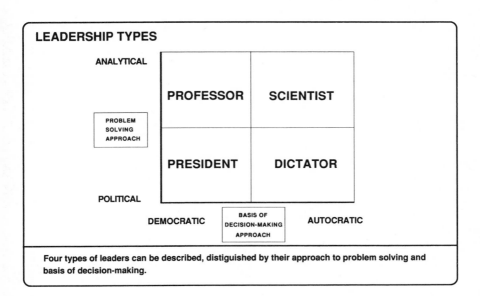

Figure 4.8

Dictators do best where the success of the firm depends on one or two key clients or projects and decisions must be made rapidly. Those key clients or projects need to be favoured above all others. This works best in firms where there are a number of different professional skills and a certain level of gut feeling is accepted by the staff in decision-making. People will be promoted with an eye to how this will affect the attitudes and motivation of others in the firm. Clients will be looking for outstanding work and a quick response to their requests. Typical of advertising agencies.

Scientists will help their firms thrive when very fast decisions based on hard facts rather than human behaviour or political considerations count. In the end a course of action will be followed because it is accepted as the right thing to do rather than being the most popular. People will be promoted on performance not professional contacts. Clients will talk of such a firm as being hard-headed. Typical of architects.

The above framework is useful in describing how leadership works and for identifying what sort of style a firm has and to what sort it might consider changing.

Firms which are simply *managed* and not *led* will always be second rate as they will lack the personality and sense of differentiation that attracts the best recruits and the best clients and which helps all members of the firm develop their own commitment to quality and client service.

28

MANAGEMENT INFORMATION

What do managers need to know to run the firm effectively?

If we just left everyone to their own devices they would make a perfectly good living but they would make far less money and miss many opportunities. In order to run this business, or at least to run it well, we have to know exactly what is going on in terms of costs and income. We collect a lot of information – that way the business runs as a business.

Partner, accountants

'If you can't measure it you can't manage it,' is a common rallying cry for management consultants who often fail to follow the advice in their own firms. Chemical engineers want every scrap of data on how the production plant is operating so they can work out 'exactly what is going on in there.' Managers of professional service firms looking out at an office full of people busy on the telephone or working on documents should ask themselves the same question.

The main components of a professional service firm's management information system are shown in figure 4.9. Procedures must be put in place to collect the information from each of the three main data inputs: the staff, client service costs and business overheads. The firm also needs a process for developing budgets and plans. On a regular basis (usually monthly) the main outputs of the management information system should be analysed by the finance department, or its equivalent, and a report made to the executive committee on client profitability, product profitability, staff utilization, performance against budget and how much is owed by the various debtors and for how long it has been owed.

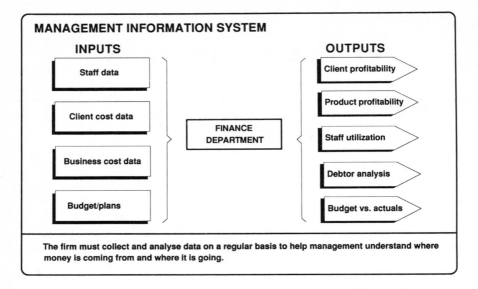

MANAGEMENT INFORMATION SYSTEM

INPUTS

- Staff data
- Client cost data
- Business cost data
- Budget/plans

FINANCE DEPARTMENT

OUTPUTS

- Client profitability
- Product profitability
- Staff utilization
- Debtor analysis
- Budget vs. actuals

The firm must collect and analyse data on a regular basis to help management understand where money is coming from and where it is going.

Figure 4.9

STAFF DATA

As a starting point a firm needs to know who works for it, what their skills are and what they cost to employ. It's important to know more than just the basics of name, address and salary. Special skills and interests should be recorded. A wine expert, albeit an enthusiastic amateur, may prove a valuable resource for a management consultant seeking a drink account. A half-forgotten geology degree might be useful to a law firm in the early stages of mineral rights litigation. Ex wolf-cubs might be a starting point for a PR company pitching for the Scouts account.

STAFF INFORMATION

There is a story (probably apocryphal) that the London advertising agency J. Walter Thompson used to record the hobbies of all staff. An advertising campaign required a picture of a rare butterfly sitting on a product with colours that complemented those of the pack design. Through an oversight a very quick solution was required and the normal sources of external professional advice moved too slowly. Using the staff database the account team discovered that one of the catering ladies was a keen butterfly collector and, when asked, she was able to name and supply a suitable insect within the day.

This sort of personal information is best collected via a self-completed form which is given to each staff member who is asked to update it when things change. The data should then be computerized for easy access. As a minimum firms must know things like home telephone numbers in case people are needed in a hurry at weekends.

In respect of the professional staff, full information is also needed on how much they cost the business in terms of salary, perks and bonuses. Each professional should be regarded by the accounting system as a cost centre and all the costs associated with him or her collected and analysed. This cost information is important in calculating the true cost of that individual servicing clients and doing other firm work.

CLIENT COST DATA

To understand client profitability – which is one of the main levers of profit described in part II – the major question to be answered is: what does it cost us to serve each client?

Use time-sheets

The fundamental information required is how people spend their time. This is obtained by getting everyone to complete a time-sheet such as the one in figure 4.10. The time-sheet is the single most important management information input in a professional firm. It helps managers to calculate the cost of almost all the activities the firm undertakes, as the time of the professional staff will be, by far, the largest single element of cost.

In some cases this time-sheet data will also be used as the basis of charging clients, but this should not be confused with its main purpose which is the identification of costs.

Some people are very resistant to completing time-sheets as they feel spied on. They feel the firm is trying to monitor the *total* number of hours that they work. The truth should not be that the firm is trying to run a sweatshop by watching people's hours but it should be trying to allocate costs between clients and other activities. It should be made very clear to staff that the total number of hours worked will not be used as a basis for compensation or promotion. The total is far less important than the split between various activities.

TYPICAL TIME-SHEET					MONTH :			**X**	
ACTIVITY	**Mon**	**Tues**	**Wed**	**Thur**	**Fri**	**Sat**	**Sun**	**TOTAL**
Client work								
Client A								
Client B								
Client C								
Firm work								
Interviewing								
Training								
Administration								
Other time								
Vacation								
TOTAL								

The time-sheet is the single most important management information tool of professional services firms. It allows managers to calculate the cost of most activities.

Figure 4.10

Analysing time-sheet information

The most useful way of using the time–sheet data is to calculate a cost per hour for each professional and use this to assess the cost of servicing each client. To do this the accounts department must work out the total employment costs of each person (salary + national insurance + car + any other perks) and divide that by the total number of hours worked. This gives an average cost per hour.

For two members of staff with identical total costs the one who puts in very long hours will have a lower hourly cost to the firm but is not, necessarily, more valuable.

Assessing the relative merits of staff on the basis of total hours worked is an error and should not even be done informally. The correct assessment should be of the value that each individual generates. A person who can meet a client's needs as a result of 50 hours worked (and billed to the client) is as valuable to the firm as another who works 100 hours to achieve the same level of client satisfaction.

Other, non-time costs

Other aspects of costs associated with each client should also be captured. Directly attributable overheads such as photocopying, telephones and postage and external services such as printing and deliveries should be recorded for each client using some form of client number or job number system.

If an identifiable overhead is incurred on behalf of a client it should be an active decision *not* to charge it on to the client but for the firm to absorb it as part of the firm's own overheads. Items such as client entertainment or the print costs of a job which went wrong are typical examples of costs the firm may choose to pay itself – reducing the profit on the client in the interest of good relations.

Client profitability report

This information about staff costs from the time-sheets and other costs from the recording system is combined with details of the income from the client (both from fees and from the mark-up on services and goods purchased) to create a client profitability report like that shown in figure 4.11

The reason for collecting the client cost information and producing client profitability reports is that this enables managers to identify poor performing accounts and take steps to improve them as described in chapter 9 on client profitability.

The most important column in figure 4.11, in management action terms, is contribution, which is the contribution made by

TYPICAL CLIENT PROFITABILITY ANALYSIS		MONTH :			**X**
£000	Income	Direct staff costs*	Direct overheads	Contribution	Contribution as % income
CLIENT					
A	30	20	4	6	20%
B	50	40	5	5	10%
C	15	10	1	4	26%
D	20	16	2	2	10%
E	40	38	3	-1	-2%
F	10	10	3	-3	-30%
AVERAGE	27.5	22.3	3.0	2.2	10%

* derived from time-sheets

The monthly analysis shows which clients are producing the profits and highlights those clients where changes must be made.

Figure 4.11

each client account to firm overheads. This is the total income less staff costs and direct overheads which leaves the contribution made by each client. This is the surplus income which goes towards paying the overheads of running the business as a whole. The figure shows clients E and F to be loss makers with client C the most profitable in percentage terms and client A the largest contributor to the firm's overheads and profits in cash terms. The general overheads to be covered include things like the annual audit fee for the firm and the heat, light and power.

Devising an information system to allocate the firm's general overheads can be the source of much fruitless argument in professional service firms, particularly when directors are rewarded with financial incentives linked to their own clients' profitability or contribution.

Cost elements such as support staff, heat, light, rent and so on can be treated as general overheads or can be allocated to clients on the basis of hours worked by professional staff for the client as a proportion of total hours worked for all clients. On balance it is probably useful to allocate these headcount related costs as it gives a better idea of individual client profitability by highlighting the real cost of servicing big and/or time consuming clients. It must be remembered though that this is purely an accounting exercise. It will still be the number of hours worked for each client that really drives the costs.

The main problem with *allocating* costs is that some people will always feel (with some justification) that the basis of allocation is unfair to them.

COST ALLOCATION

A small British consulting firm rewards its partners with bonuses related to the profit contribution of their own clients. The firm chooses to allocate all its office costs against client income by dividing the costs in direct proportion to the number of professional hours worked for each client. Among those office costs are the receptionist, the post room and the catering. One partner had three clients all of which were abroad and he, and his entire team, spent the best part of a year away from the office. He spent a good proportion of management committee time arguing that the general office costs should *not* be allocated to his clients when calculating profitability as he and his team made no use of the services. The argument lasted for a year and he came close to resigning over the issue.

To be really 'honest' long-term client profitability should include all the costs of pitching for an account and the interest charges incurred if the account is a slow payer and produces large outstanding debts which the firm has to fund out of its own working capital. Pitch costs (perhaps written off over two years) and interest charges can be included in the information system as part of the client overhead.

As well as the regular monthly monitoring client profitability needs to be assessed on a to-date basis as this will smooth out the inevitable fluctuations which occur when there are mismatches between the costs of staff working on the account (driven by the volume of work required) and the agreed payments by the client (a product of the initial client agreement).

In those businesses where the time-sheets are used as the basis of charging (as in many law firms) the client profitability will obviously not fluctuate as much as when the time related costs rise so does the income.

Product profitability report

A product profitability report is very similar to that for a client, the main difference being that all the costs and income are collected by product rather than by client. Thus a legal practice which has as a conveyancing of domestic homes product would capture its data accordingly and discover how profitable this activity is.

Analysis will probably show that certain products are far more profitable to the firm than others. This will either be because the firm's own economics make a product cheap or expensive to make or because clients seem prepared to pay a significant premium for a product above its cost of manufacture. For example a large law firm in a capital city is unlikely to be able to prepare wills or defend minor motoring offences as cost-effectively as a firm in a small provincial town. The will product will be more attractive to the smaller firm because of its costs structure.

PRODUCT COSTS

A public relations firm has two products – a brand audit which assesses consumer attitudes towards a brand and a corporate audit which assesses public attitudes towards a corporation. Both products have the same manufacturing costs in that they both require the same amount of staff time, external research and analytical work.

In selling to clients, however, the corporate product commands a higher price (and therefore yields more profit) than the brand product because the customer for the brand product is a price-sensitive brand manager and the client for the more expensive corporate audit is the company chairman.

For as long as it can command premium prices it makes sense for the PR firm to concentrate on corporate audit work.

BUSINESS COST DATA

In addition to client specific information, managers also need to understand how much it is costing them, in total, to run the firm itself. These running costs are items such as total staff costs, business overheads (telephone etc.) and premises costs. This is nothing more than an aggregate of all the individual client information plus the general overheads but it is the measure of the success of the whole business.

The client information is analysed to help in sorting out poor performers in the client list. The total business information is analysed to identify trends and variances against budgets and to highlight those costs which look as if they may be getting out of control.

The accounts department should capture this data virtually every day and it should be part of the monthly information pack reviewed by the executive or management committee. The budget information comes from the annual budgeting process. The actual spending information comes from the accounts department who should monitor the firm's outgoings and report how money is being spent under the various cost headings.

The actual cost headings used will vary from firm to firm but when designing the accounting and reporting system managers must focus on those cost elements which are most controllable in running their particular type of firm. Thus, for example, in an advertising agency it might make sense to analyse entertainment costs separately from the general business overhead.

Figure 4.12 shows a typical monthly report for review by the executive committee. Much greater detail supporting each of the main line items must be available if required. The key management actions will be to understand why variances from budgets have occurred.

£000's	MONTH 4			YEAR TO DATE		
	ACTUAL	BUDGET	VARIANCE %	ACTUAL	BUDGET	VARIANCE %
INCOME						
Fees	50	70	-40%	200	250	-25%
Handling	10	10	0	40	40	0
Total Income	60	80	-33%	240	290	-21%
COSTS						
Professional staff	40	40	0	160	160	0
Support staff	10	10	0	40	40	0
Business overhead	4	5	-25%	18	20	-11%
Building overhead	5	5	0	20	20	0
TOTAL COSTS						
OPERATING PROFIT	1	10	-900%	2	40	-190%

TYPICAL MONTHLY PROFIT REPORT

Managers need to monitor performance against budget to identify where problems and opportunities are located.

Figure 4.12

The handling line of income is the *net* income to the firm from the mark-up or commission it charges on goods and services it buys in for clients. In the firm's published accounts the full value of the goods or services handled would appear as turnover but for the purpose of management analysis it is usually best just to look at the actual net income to the firm from this source.

The picture of the business provided by this format of report highlights different issues from those of client profitability. Managers should watch for overheads getting out of control and for shifts in the balance of income between fees and mark-up. Figure 4.12 shows a somewhat extreme example of a very significant decline in fee income compared to budget which has not yet been matched by a reduction in staff costs although a small saving against budget appears in the business overheads. If managers were convinced that the fee income was going to remain low they would have to cut staff costs to return to acceptable levels of profit.

STAFF UTILIZATION

The data collected from time-sheets tells management how the professional staff actually spent their time. Equally important for managing future profitability is to know how the business expects its professional staff to be used. This gives insights into likely utilization rates which are a major element of profitability.

All account directors/partners must forecast how they expect to use staff over a future period (often six months but it depends on the nature of the business). Each director must estimate how much time each professional on each of his or her client teams will spend on that client. This is usually the amount of time that the client has agreed to pay for. The individual directors will be aware of new clients coming on-stream and of particularly busy or slack periods on any one account. Each director gives an individual forecast to the accounts department and these forecasts are then collected together to provide an aggregate picture of the firm's staff utilization like the example shown in figure 4.13.

This sort of analysis shown in the figure is particularly important for firms operating a flexible team system where any one member of the professional staff might work for several different account directors. No individual director will have a complete picture of probable staff utilization.

For example in figure 4.13 staff member C is scheduled to work at 120 per cent of his or her time in May and June – presumably because two or more account directors are expecting to use that person on their client teams but are unaware of each other's plans. Staff member D looks under-utilized at only 40 per cent and could be used on any accounts which are starting up after March. In

---

PREDICTED STAFF UTILIZATION (% of hours billed to clients)

NAME OF PERSON	Jan	Feb	March	April	May	June	AVERAGE % USE
A	80	80	80	80	80	80	80
B	80	60	40	40	40	40	50
C	80	60	80	80	120	120	90
D	80	60	40	40	40	40	50
E	80	80	80	50	50	50	100
TOTAL	80	72	64	58	66	66	74

Forecasts of the likely utilization of professional staff will give early warning of people who will be under (or over) worked and also if new business or new staff must be found.

Figure 4.13

aggregate the firm is expecting to achieve utilization of 74 per cent over the period, which is quite good.

Figure 4.13 is an oversimplifation as an example because it only shows the percentage of billable hours allocated to clients. It does not reflect the billing rates of the individuals concerned. An under-utilized director (who could command a billing rate of £1,200 a day) is a far more costly wasted asset than an under-utilized executive (who might only bring in £300 a day). Thus the firm's aggregate utilization should always be analysed at the individual level to see where the real problems might be.

This type of analysis (which should be regularly updated and available for review by the executive committee) will provide early warning of certain individuals who will have a low utilization and also if the whole firm is going to drop below acceptable levels (which will make it unprofitable). Equally the analysis will highlight the need to recruit new staff and will show at which grades the greatest shortfall/surplus of staff time will occur.

WORKING CAPITAL

Unlike manufacturing businesses, professional firms should not have large amounts of money tied up in work-in-progress. Professional firms do not make things and do not build up stocks for later sale. They might need some working capital to pay their own staff if clients pay the firm after the professional staff have been paid for the work done. However this working capital can be kept down which will reduce the interest charges paid by the firm – assuming it has to borrow to provide the funds.

In managing working capital there are three main areas for which it is important to collect data about and to understand:

- Debtor days for the firm as a whole and for each account
- Creditor days, again for the whole firm and for each supplier or creditor
- Daily cash balances

Monitor debts

The firm's finance or accounts department should set up systems to monitor the payment of invoices and record the average amount outstanding on each account. It is important to inform account directors if their clients are poor payers as this may be

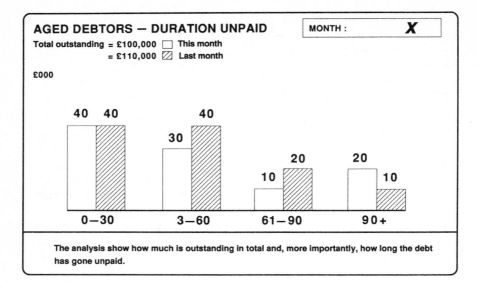

AGED DEBTORS — DURATION UNPAID   MONTH :   *X*

Total outstanding = £100,000 ☐ This month
= £110,000 ▨ Last month

£000

The analysis show how much is outstanding in total and, more importantly, how long the debt has gone unpaid.

Figure 4.14

an indication of some discontent with the service or may even be an early warning of a client in financial difficulties which could end up as a bad debt.

At the aggregate level the firm should analyse all the debts that it is owed to identify not just the total amount outstanding but how long it has been outstanding for.

Figure 4.14 shows a typical aged debtors report. The total amount outstanding has decreased from £110,000 to £100,000 since last month implying that more debts have been paid than have been incurred. However it must worry management that £20,000 of the total has now gone unpaid for more than 90 days (up from £10,000 last month), which apart from running up interest charges may indicate a possible bad debt.

Monitor creditors

In respect of creditors it is important to know who the major creditors are — again so that those managers who are responsible for the sums owing can manage the relationship well. If their accounts go unpaid suppliers like mobile telephone companies might cut the firm off. Some suppliers could be getting paid *too quickly* and the firm might be able to enjoy extra credit by slowing down the processing of certain invoices.

The accounts department should analyse the total sums

outstanding to major suppliers as this can also reveal the amount of business being done with particular suppliers which can offer the firm an opportunity to negotiate better terms.

SUPPLIER MANAGEMENT

A US-based PR firm left each of its account directors to organize the provision of visual aids (35 mm slides, flip charts etc.) for the various client presentations. An analysis of creditors showed that more than half the account directors were using the same external contractor to make their slides. A further analysis showed that the PR firm accounted for more than 30 per cent of the slide-makers total turnover. Each account had been operating as an independent customer. Following negotiations with the slide contractor prices were reduced by 20 per cent to reflect the volume of trade.

Monitor cash

Cash balances should be monitored so that the firm can ensure it makes the best use of any spare funds. Bank systems can be set up to inform the firm of how much is in its various accounts each day.

In businesses like advertising agencies which make very substantial purchases on behalf of clients it may be possible to have *negative* working capital – that is other people's money on free loan to the firm if it is possible to collect payment from the clients before paying the suppliers. However that money is only useful if the firm knows it has it and uses it to generate interest.

29

QUALITY CONTROL

How can you ensure consistent quality of work when the firm's output is services which are intangible?

We can always be very good on any one job (particularly one of my own!). It's being very good all the time that is so difficult.

Director, design consultancy

Quality control in a car plant or a fast food restaurant is relatively easy to monitor. The product is there to be seen and to be tested. Managers can try it for themselves. Consumers can respond to something tangible when asked for their reactions. The nature of a professional service firm's output was described in part I with the four challenges of intangibility, perishability, localness and consistency being described. The task for management is to ensure consistency as the firm's reputation will always be at risk on every project it undertakes.

In professional firms like advertising or up-market hairdressing aspects of the client service work are highly visible and feedback from clients and the outside world is available. For most professional firms, however, some process must be created to establish criteria for quality and ways of regularly assessing the firm's work against those criteria.

PROVIDE A TOTAL SERVICE

Quality is not just the work itself but also how the client is dealt with, accuracy of invoicing, speed of response, efficiency of meetings and so on. Quality from the clients point of view is the effectiveness and value for money of the overall relationship.

Writing in *The American Lawyer* (April 1984) the consultant Dr David Maister observes the following about quality:

Consider the following scenario: You have had your car repaired at a new local garage. A week or two later your neighbour, curious about whether she should also use this new garage asks 'Did they fix the car?' 'I think so' you reply, 'it seems to be running smoothly so I guess they did a good job.'

Then your neighbour asks an interesting second question: 'Did you get good service?' What does this second question mean? Surely fixing the car is the service, isn't it? Well yes and no. Fixing the car is part of it and an important part it is, but by itself it doesn't constitute good service.

Dr Maister goes on to describe his own concept that 'Goods are consumed, services are *experienced.*'

The difficulty, as the above anecdote illustrates, is that the primary reason for a client to use a lawyer, accountant, advertising agent, doctor and so on will not be the only thing upon which the success of the professional relationship is judged. Firms must recognize that they are in the business of providing a total service, *not* just the professional skill of their staff. From the perspective of the client quality will include the speed with which telephones are answered, the punctuality of the firm's staff for meetings and the clarity of the invoicing for the firm's bills.

CREATE STANDARDS

One approach for many professional firms is to invent criteria of performance which are tangible and which can give clients a sense of quality service and performance. The other, possibly the main, benefit of having these measurable performance standards is that they help reinforce the idea of quality service among the staff. Examples of performance standards include:

- Telephones will not go unanswered for more than 20 seconds.

- Clients' telephone enquiries will be answered within four hours

- All client letters will have a reply within two working days

- All client invoices will be accompanied by a personal letter of explanation from the account director

- Written notes of all client meetings will be sent to the client within 24 hours

These devices might not actually improve the core professional service but they will help the client's belief in it. As a client you can never really know if your lawyer or PR consultant is giving you their very best but you can tell if the notes of the last meeting were accurate and prompt. You can tell if your professional adviser gets back quickly with answers to any questions you have.

QUALITY STANDARDS

Attempts by professional firms to introduce objective standards were covered in *The Independent* (21 February 1991) under the headline 'Solicitors win badge of Quality':

A firm of Manchester Solicitors (Pannone Blackburn) has become the first law practice entitled to display the British Standards Institute 'kitemark' guarantee of quality of service. The accreditation cannot guarantee quality of advice and representation but the firm's clients will benefit from systems aimed at ensuring the quickest possible service.

The physical outputs of the firm such as letters and reports are one of the few ways of judging its commitment to quality. New secretaries and associates are often driven to distraction by senior managers' apparent obsession with things like spelling, grammar and lay-out but experience has shown that, albeit illogically, it is these things upon which the firm will be judged.

LISTEN TO COMPLAINTS

Ideally the managing director or senior partner of the firm should have a line of contact with all clients to provide a safety-valve for the communication of dissatisfaction. Where sheer numbers make this impossible a system of client service roles for other directors should be introduced so the client has someone senior to complain to about (or to praise) his or her client service team.

By providing a mechanism for listening to clients their critical observations, even if made in jest, can give an insight into where the firm is falling down.

EXTERNAL REVIEWS

A firm can assess its quality standards by asking clients what they think of it. (Figure 1.16, p. 49 shows a typical client feedback report. A far more detailed survey is shown in figure 4.15, p. 199, and discussed in the next chapter.) The information collected in this way should be analysed *and taken seriously* by the firm's top management. If any problems are identified the client service director or managing director (senior partner) should contact the client directly.

More informal feedback can be obtained by senior members of the firm (*not* the client's own account director) meeting regularly with the client for a general chat about how the relationship is working. These meetings can be embarrassing and difficult if things have been going badly. Top managers must avoid the urge either to defend their people without question or, worse still and far more common, to agree with the client that a certain account manager or associate is clearly not up to the job and to promise his or her replacement without investigating all the facts.

CLIENT FEEDBACK

A PR company with consumer and corporate divisions worked with a major blue-chip company on several of its food brands and had tried for some years to gain an introduction to the client's finance director to see if it might work on investor relations issues. It was told that the client was satisfied with the financial service of a competitor.

After two years of trying the client suddenly appointed a new financial firm without asking the PR firm's corporate division to pitch for the business. The firm's managing director raised this issue in his once-a-year lunch meeting with the client's marketing director and was told that while the client was very happy with the consumer work it had been reluctant to suggest that their financial colleagues might use the PR firm as the firm's executives were always late for meetings. Although this did not trouble the marketing department, it was felt by the client to be potentially very irritating to its financial colleagues. The PR firm thus discovered the true nature of the obstacle they had to overcome.

These informal meetings should *never* be decision making forums but should simply allow senior people to get information for use in decisions later after having involved the account team concerned.

Professional firms can even employ external researchers to conduct surveys among clients (and potential clients) to assess the firm's reputation, strengths and weaknesses, and can focus questions on quality of work. The most formal sort of external review is a client audit which takes the idea of the regular feedback questionnaire further by involving the client in discussions of the firm's performance. The client relationship audit is considered in detail in the next chapter.

INTERNAL REVIEWS

Firms should make their professionals' own work subject to the scrutiny of their peers as well as the firm's top management. Architectural designs, advertising campaigns, consultancy projects, legal cases, even audit projects can be presented to other members of the firm as examples of best practice and models for quality standards. Professionals crave the approval of their peers and will often be even more diligent on a project if they know that, at some time, their fellow professionals will be assessing the quality of the work.

Regular reviews of work done on behalf of clients (advertisements, press coverage generated, contracts negotiated etc.) should be conducted by senior members of the firm who are not involved in the client's account. If objective quality measures such as the speed of telephone answering listed above are in place the firm's performance against the criteria should be regularly measured and *the results communicated* inside the firm.

If quality standards are considered too low a number of questions will help identify the source of the problem which may stem from:

- Lack of any quality standards – or standards too low

- Lack of knowledge of the right way to do things

- Lack of motivation to achieve quality

- Inadequate resources – computers, telephones and so on

Senior management should identify the cause and then work on the solution.

QUALITY TRAINING

Training in the context of quality control could almost be called indoctrination. The object is to get all members of the firm to appreciate and *agree with* the drive for quality. People must *really feel* that they will be letting themselves and their colleagues down if they allow work of less than a certain standard to get through.

In training sessions and even in social conversation the senior members of the firm should recall anecdotes of the benefits of high quality work and the obsessive adherence to quality of the firm's leaders. *All* companies have these sort of war stories – some, like McKinsey, go so far as to write them down to help build the commitment to excellence. A commitment which, by and large, clients will seek out and pay for.

Quality in professional firms cannot be enforced by management with regular checks and instructions. It must be a desired end–product for all staff, so the job of management is to win their approval rather than to invent systems to identify lapses.

30

CLIENT RELATIONSHIPS

What is really meant by a client relationship and how should these relationships be managed?

---

*The most valuable asset we have is the good will of our clients.
Every day I look at our client list and wonder – do these people still
like us? Do they like us enough to keep paying the bills?*

Partner, executive search firm

Managers in professional firms who worry about recruitment or
keeping overheads down often do not give much thought to the
formal management of the most important aspect of the firm –
its relations with its paymasters, the clients. Without clients there
would be no professional firms, but more than just being the
people who pay the bills clients can be the best source of
information about the market-place and can provide crucial help
in developing the firm's services to best suit the customers. The
relationship with the client is one of the critical management
issues for professional firms but it is frequently not actively
managed but is left to chance.

Clients are wooed and seduced when they are at the stage of
being prospects but are often ignored once the conquest is made.
Providing an annual trip to the opera and a Christmas card is *not*
managing client relations. Equally just having a client on the
books or doing work for a client is not having a relationship. A
client *relationship* implies that the firm will be consulted about
various aspects of the client's business and that there will be a
regular dialogue between the firm and the client. The existence of
a relationship implies a degree of mutual trust and dependence
and brings significant benefits to the firm in terms of the
profitability and duration of the client relationship and the degree
of flexibility with which the firm can serve the client.

RELATIONSHIP MANAGER

The management of the relationship with the client, as opposed to the management of the professional tasks on behalf of the client, is best done by someone other than the individual in charge of the client's projects. The professionals will tend to be too bound up in the task in hand and too focused on achieving immediate professional goals to think about the overall development of the business relationship.

Clearly all the team involved in the project have a role to play in making the two organizations work well together but it is difficult for them to assess accurately how things are going and what changes may be required. What is needed is a senior person from the professional firm who can monitor the *relationship* itself and not just professional progress.

In small firms this role of relationship manager for all clients is often taken on by the firm's managing director or senior partner. In larger firms, directors or senior partners can be given the formal task of managing relationships for the clients of other senior people. Typically a senior person might be an engagement director to certain clients (responsible for the execution of the work) but will be a client service director (responsible for the relationship) to others.

Having a clearly designated relationship manager gives the client someone to turn to. It can also help the firm if senior executives (who make up the client team) break away and seek to take the client with them. No matter how much the client respects their professional skills his or her key relationship will be with another person in the firm.

The issues to be discussed between the relationship manager and the client will include:

- Staffing on the account. What does the client feel about the skills and personalities of the team members?

- Invoicing and terms of payment. Are bills clear? Might the client be prepared to pay more quickly in return for a discount?

- Client satisfaction. Is the client getting value for money?

- Long-term plans. Are there future projects the firm might be able to help with?

As with other aspects of managing professional firms it must be stressed that the relationship task is a *role* not a job or position.

When performing in this role senior firm managers must resist the temptation simply to act as an alternative professional trying to solve the client's problems but must concentrate on managing the client relationship. A relationship role provides a safety valve and it is not unknown for a client to request the removal of the engagement director while expressing satisfaction with the rest of the team.

CLIENT FEEDBACK

In addition to appointing a relationship manager professional firms should actively seek to get feedback from their clients in other ways. One of the most successful is some form of questionnaire which clients are asked to complete at the end of specific projects or two or three times each year.

Figure 4.15 is a typical client questionnaire developed for a PR firm but which is broadly applicable to a wide range of professional firms. The main objective is to identify areas of potential discontent which can then be explored further with client executives.

CLIENT RELATIONSHIP AUDIT

It is worth involving long-standing clients in the process of formally auditing the nature of the relationship to seek ways of helping the firm and the client to work more successfully together.

The best professional firms foster the idea that a business partnership exists between themselves and their clients and an audit of that partnership done once every couple of years can make it more mutually rewarding.

The full audit process is much more than just an assessment of satisfaction with the quality of the work. It seeks to understand, and improve, the basis of the client relationship and to cement the partnership between the firm and the client. In conducting the audit (which must be done with the full approval of the client) the firm should look for guidance in many areas in addition to feedback on the professional work. These include:

- The existence of shared professional values – do the two organizations think the same way about ethical issues?

- The nature of the chemistry between the firm's staff and the client's staff – are there any clashes of personality?

Figure 4.15 XYZ Public Relations: Confidential

Dear Client Executive

As you know we run a programme to monitor the quality of our work on your behalf. The attached brief questionnaire provides you with the opportunity to let me have confidential feedback on our professional services. I would be most grateful if you would complete it by indicating the degree to which you agree or disagree with the statements about our work and our firm.

Should you wish to discuss any aspect of our work in more detail please do not hesitate to contact me and we can arrange a meeting.

(signed)

Managing Director
XYZ Public Relations

Please indicate your reaction to each of the statements below by writing the appropriate number against each. (1) strongly disagree, (2) disagree, (3) neutral, (4) agree, (5) strongly agree. Each statement refers to our firm and to our staff.

PROFESSIONAL WORK

Your people understand my business
Your people understand my market
Your people understand the PR profession
Your people understand the media
Your people understand marketing
You keep us in touch with new ideas
You are creative
You give us the right balance of senior and junior staff

ATTITUDES

Your people keep us fully informed
Your people communicate well
Your people are easy to get hold of
Your people quickly respond to calls and letters
My people like your people
Your people are helpful

ADMINISTRATION

We understand the basis of your charges
You administer the account well
You do not waste our money
Overall you provide value for money

- The existence of mutually beneficial business plans – do both the client and the firm want to open an overseas office?

- The likely development of future budgets for professional services – will the volume of work for the firm be likely to increase or decrease?

- The degree of overlap between the firm and the client's other professional advisers – is the firm at risk of being replaced or could it replace others?

When conducting the audit the firm's senior people should use face-to-face interviews and desk research as well as reviewing the results of the regular questionnaires. They should talk to people from the client as well as the firm's own staff. It can even be useful to commission an external research firm to interview client executives and firm professionals and to report back on how the relationship is working.

CLIENT CONTACT

In addition to the relationship manager, questionnaires and the formal client audit there are other ways for the firm to keep aware of a client's state of mind. These include:

- Social contact with client executives

- Inviting clients to professional seminars and discussion lunches and dinners

- Client workshops. Arranging meetings of the engagement team and client executives to ask the question: 'How is the work going?' and to consider changes to working practices.

As a general rule all executives should be encouraged to report on the state of the client relationship in an attempt to sense problems before they become unmanageable.

A sense that the relationship is as important as the work should permeate the successful professional firm. Again it shows the value of having a relationship manager as junior professionals may feel more comfortable talking to him or her about client problems than they would raising them with the designated team leader.

CLIENT SERVICE ATTITUDE

The cliché that the customer is always right prevails in retailing. In all too many professional firms the idea that the client is an idiot is common.

Liking clients

Professional firms group together highly skilled, highly motivated people who have a common base of professional expertise. The vast majority of their clients will not have the expertise and can seem to the professionals less gifted than their own work colleagues. Arrogant is all too frequently the word applied by clients to their professional firms. The most successful firms go a long way to overcoming the idea that the client is a turkey and virtually make a crime out of denigrating the client and client personnel.

Clients will nearly always be more risk averse than their advisers and will take longer to reach decisions. This is hardly surprising because they usually have more to lose and they are paying for it. Given this, it is important for top management to provide clear leadership and to show that good client relations are desirable and to foster a general attitude among the firm's professionals and support staff that the maintenance of client relationships is an important part of their work.

Formally making successful relationship management one of the criteria to be looked at when considering promotion and remuneration of professional staff is certainly a good start but some rallying cry like the professional version of the customer is always right needs to be found. The retailing maxim is *not* applicable in a professional firm, as frequently the client is not right and it is crucial that a good professional should be objective enough to explain that. What is true, though, is that the client is a human being too and the client is always smarter than you think.

Sensitivity to feelings

Professionals need to be constantly reminded that clients are frequently using them under very difficult circumstances (a financial or legal crisis, an architectural problem or a health difficulty). Even very junior professionals can sometimes be seen by client executives as very threatening and even dangerous. The development of a good bedside manner is of particular importance in projects which involve working with a large number of client people. Stray remarks about the client's business prospects or the ability of members of the client's management team can be taken out of all proportion because of the role of the professional who has said them.

Don't promise too much

A critical part of having a good relationship is to ensure that the client's expectations do not fall out of line with reality. It will always create bad feelings if the client feels let down. This is particularly important at the start of the relationship. In defining the service to be given at the beginning of a project, the firm's management must be confident that it can deliver.

OVER-PROMISING

The managing director of a medium–sized London PR firm used to insist on being at the final new business pitch for all potential major clients. He was so keen to win the account that he was prone to make offers of numerous extra services without any attempt to renegotiate the fee. He tended to be very successful in winning business but caused despair in his staff who knew that the client relationship was doomed from the start as they would never be able to match delivery to promise. When the account is subsequently lost this tends to be seen as the fault of the account team rather than as a flaw in the initial negotiations.

The elements of achieving a good client relationship are summarized in figure 4.16

PROFESSIONAL INDEMNITY

A particularly important issue in recent years is what happens when the relationship goes wrong. At best the firm will have to eat humble pie and perhaps agree not to be paid for any poorly executed work and change the members of the client service team. In some cases the firm will lose the account but, increasingly, firms are finding themselves being sued for millions of pounds for alleged neglect. The most dramatic cases are the accounting firms where the creditors of failed companies will sue the accountants on the basis that they did not make a good job of doing audits.

Business Week (24 December 1990) commented on the problem faced by accountants citing the example of Ernst & Young being

Figure 4.16 Achieving successful client relationships

Use the idea of a client service director (or relationship manager) to create a safety valve mechanism and provide feedback.

Seek client feedback through a formal process such as a questionnaire.

Provide the client with written notes on all meetings.

Always write confirming any action points agreed with the client. This provides a checklist for them to monitor the firm's activities.

Discuss the performance of team members and the quality of the work with the client on a regular basis. At least every 6 months.

Ensure the senior client and his/her accounts staff understand the basis of your firms charges.

Never send an invoice without a covering letter. Wherever possible invoice regularly and do not flood client with numerous small invoices.

Seek to make the firm part of the client's problem solving mechanism.

Constantly manage client expectations about what will be achieved by when. Aim never to disappoint.

Make the successful management of the client relationship a key element of the assessment of the firm's staff and one of the criteria for promotion and remuneration.

sued for US$560 million by the US Federal Deposit Insurance Corp over some past audit work.

MALPRACTICE

Above all, the industry (accountancy) suffers from the ravages of a five-year epidemic of malpractice suits. Creditors and investors in failed companies like to sue auditors because those firms are often the only participants left with any cash. This, plus the use of anti-racketeering laws against professionals, has inflicted huge litigation expenses, even when firms eventually win the cases.

The difficulties of the accountants are rapidly spreading to other professions. Architects and lawyers are becoming very cautious about negligence suits and even advertising agencies and

PR consultants are reporting legal actions against them by consumers alleging misleading claims about products or by clients alleging poor workmanship. In partnerships with unlimited financial liability the threat of a legal action is particularly concerning as the partners could face personal as well as professional ruin.

The cost of providing various forms of professional indemnity insurance is rising rapidly and many smaller professional firms now feel they are getting to the stage of being like doctors in the USA where certain types of client are just too risky to accept. In addition to insurance premiums going up many insurers are now limiting the maximum pay-out leaving the firm liable for potentially huge amounts.

Managers should ensure that all staff in the firm are aware of the potential penalties of negligence and stress to all professionals the importance of demonstrating the highest levels of diligence on client issues. Many firms are investigating contracts with clients which protect the firm from many potential liability claims, but this is a complex legal area and in many cases legal precedents have not been established. It is likely that professional indemnity will become one of the most important issues for firms in the 1990s and, at the minimum, managers should factor sizable insurance costs into their business plans.

31

GETTING PAID

How should you charge for the firm's services?

---

*We always knew that fixed commissions let us make out like
bandits – a lot of people got very rich back then.*
Stockbroker

The actual mechanics of collecting payment were covered in part
II and the importance of a good client relationship to achieving
prompt payment was mentioned in the previous chapter. This
chapter is about how to be paid – what mechanism to use for
judging the value created by the firm on a client's behalf and what
mechanics to use to charge for that value. The mechanisms by
which a professional service firm chooses to collect payment for
its work can have a profound impact on its profitability and on
the way its services are perceived by its customers. To take an
extreme example a hairdresser could charge using the following
alternatives:

- By the weight or volume of the hair cut off irrespective of
  the amount of staff time or level of skill involved

- By the actual time taken by the staff with the cost per hour
  set by the skills and experience of the staff

- By a scale of pre-agreed charges reflecting the estimated
  complexity of the job to be done

- By agreement with the customer based on a mutual
  assessment of the quality of the work after the job was done

In reality almost all hairdressers offer a fixed set of charges and
happy clients can leave a tip; but the four alternatives illustrate
the issues affecting service firms. The weight of hair example is
analogous to charging on the basis of completing an agreed task
irrespective of what this actually cost the firm to do it and without
regard to how well the task was done.

The use of some form of performance-related bonus (the corporate equivalent of the tip) is particularly attractive in service businesses where it can be very difficult to assess the degree of success of a project at the beginning of the relationship

There are three basic methods of getting paid as a professional firm:

- Time-based fees – hourly or daily fees for each person involved which usually reflect the differing seniority of the people concerned. This is typical of law firms. This is a low risk, cost-plus approach

- Fixed or project-based fees – for the job which are agreed at the outset but which are usually calculated by the firm based on an estimate of professional staff time involved. This is typical of management consultants and auditors. It requires an estimate of the amount of professional time needed to achieve a product acceptable to the client

- A commission – based on the size of the transaction completed or the value of the goods/ services purchased on behalf of the client. This is typical of estate agents or advertising agents. This can be risky to both client and firm as the actual cost of the job may be much greater or much less than the commission

Each of these methods has its pros and cons. As a general rule the more closely the fees charged reflect the value received by the client the more satisfactory the basis of charging will be in the long run.

TIME-BASED FEES

The time-based fee is the safest for the firm and the simplest to administer. It is safe in that there is very little chance of the client being overserviced by staff working on projects that have not been paid for. It is simple as staff fill in time sheets and clients are billed for their hours. The billing rate is calculated to cover the individual's salary costs and all overheads and to provide a profit.

The problem with the time-based fee is that clients may feel the clock is running and may, therefore, feel under pressure to minimize the use of the firm. In addition time-based fees are, by definition, almost completely transparent so that clients can easily compare one firm's with those of a competitor. For less highly skilled professional work this can be a problem as it tends to reduce the firm's offering to a price-based commodity service rather than a special professional relationship.

The fact that the more hours that are billed the greater the cost of the job to the client can also be an irritant if clients do not trust the firm to work as efficiently as possible and are concerned that they may spin out the work to keep themselves busy. For jobs which have a long, but uncertain, duration there is also the problem for the firm that while it can be sure it is not operating at a loss it can be hard to plan its future staff requirements if the client keeps asking for a few more weeks of people's time.

On balance the time-based system is best used for open ended projects without clearly identifiable end-products such as in situations where the main benefit to the client is simply having the professionals available rather than expecting them to complete some mutually agreed project. Although a company's lawyers can work on an annual retainer many firms and their clients find it easier simply to charge on the basis of hours worked letting the client and external factors (like law suits) govern how much time will be needed.

FIXED OR PROJECT-BASED FEES

From the perspective of clients the great attraction of this method is knowing what they are committed to and being able to budget accordingly. It is best used where a clearly defined end-product can be identified, such as an audit or a will.

To succeed on a fixed-fee basis the firm needs to be skilled at assessing the complexity of a job at the start of the process. Fixed-fee contracts have the particular danger that the client will be overserviced – that is more work will be done on the client's behalf than has been paid for.

An extension of the fixed-fee contract is the idea of the annual retainer. The firm is paid to provide an agreed package of services. A typical example might be a public relations consultancy which would provide a service of responding to press enquiries and would guarantee the client a certain minimum level of service. The major advantage for the professional firm is capacity planning.

The fixed fee is more opaque to the client who is less certain of how many of whose hours went into a project. This makes comparisons with other firms far more difficult and the client simply has to assess if the professional charges were less than the benefits of having the work done.

COMMISSION CHARGES

The payment of a commission almost always requires that the firm complete some task for the client and that the client pays a fee related to the size or value of the task. A certain percentage of the value which is generally accepted throughout the particular profession is the basis of charging. A major problem with commission systems is that the cost (to the firm) of doing the work may bear no relation at all to the amount charged to the client and may also bear no relation to the value received by the client.

In a domestic context many people have had the experience of feeling aggrieved that an estate agent was able to sell their house within days of getting the job and yet will charge the same fee as on another occasion when they took four months and spent heavily on advertising.

Employing firms on commission has a high element of gambling from the clients' point of view. From the firm's point of view there is the hope that the huge profits made on some jobs will even out the losses made on others.

Contingency fees

The no foal, no fee idea taken from the analogy of stud farming is used by investment bankers and some lawyers involved in deals and, in effect, is the way many estate agents sell houses. A refinement of it is that a small percentage commission is paid if the project fails and a much larger one if it succeeds.

Where there is a genuine risk/reward trade-off clients tend to accept contingency fees as being reasonable. The investment banker on the takeover bid or the American lawyer on the damages claim will do far better, financially, if the client is successful but will suffer if the client loses. The bank's (or the lawyer's) high profits on successful jobs will compensate them for fruitless efforts on other occasions. Where clients have a cause for annoyance is where a fixed commission is charged but the professional firm runs no risk if the project fails.

The end of commissions?

The commission system is under attack in almost every profession. Stock markets across the world have been abolishing fixed brokerage fees. Solicitors' fixed charges for house conveyancing are much criticized. Advertising agencies are finding clients increasingly refusing to pay the previously accepted 15 per cent commission. Clients are seeking to match the fees paid to the work done. In his book, *Liar's Poker*, Michael Lewis comments:

> The stock market had once been Wall Street's greatest source of revenues. Commissions were fat, fixed and non-negotiable. Each time a share changed hands, some broker somewhere took out a handsome fee for himself, without necessarily doing much work. A broker was paid twice as much for executing a two hundred share order as a one hundred share order even though the amount of work in either case was the same. The end of fixed stock brokerage commissions had come on May 1st 1975 after which, predictably, commissions collapsed. Investors used the broker who charged them the least. As a result, in 1976, revenues across Wall Street fell by some 600 million dollars.

The *Sunday Times Business World Magazine* (November 1990) said of the approach to charging taken by one of the newer British advertising agencies, Howell Henry Chaldecott Lury:

> Because it treats advertising as a profession Howell Henry does not use the old-fashioned and slightly iniquitous commission system under which agencies take 15 per cent of whatever a client spends on advertising (this system is breaking down and many different types of deals are being struck). 'We're not estate agents' says Rupert Howell 'We are professional business advisers just like accountants and lawyers.' Howell Henry operates on a mixture of fixed monthly retainers and hourly fee systems – £120 per person per hour – and is trying to move all accounts onto the latter basis. Interestingly Howell calculated they made more this way than they would have done on a 15 per cent commission.

THE BEST SOLUTION?

Potentially the most effective way for a professional firm to charge is to use all the methods depending on the nature of the client and the work. A basic system of annual retainers may be supplemented by fixed-fee projects and time-based work. Certain work may be taken on a contingency or commission basis. In theory the firm will be able to ensure basic, profitable, operation on the basis of the annual retainer and fixed fee work. Spare resources can be offered to clients on a time sheet basis and bonus profits can be achieved from commission work. The key management decision becomes which basis of charging to use.

The difference between the basis of charging becomes very clear when looking at the advisers on a typical contested take-over bid.

The investment bank will usually charge a commission – often calculated as a percentage of the value of the bid; the lawyers will charge on an hourly rate basis, the management consultants on a fixed project fee and the public relations people on a monthly retainer. In the event of success all firms may receive bonus fees but the bankers are almost certain to receive the largest bonus.

Professional firms, quite reasonably, want to be paid as much as they can get for doing their work. The trade-off is that they must keep their clients happy. If the feedback from clients is, consistently, that they are unhappy with the *basis* of charging (which may simply be that they feel they are paying too much and do not know why) then firms should heed the warning and come up with a new way of charging which meets the needs of both parties *even if the new basis is not widely accepted in their profession*. The client *not* professional practice should have the last word.

RECHARGABLES

Most professional firms charge some element of overheads to their clients. Telephones, postage, photocopying can be very expensive. Some firms simply pass these expenses on at cost; others absorb them. In some cases virtually everything is charged to the client. Some firms will charge the client for hospitality costs incurred entertaining client personnel. As witnessed by the City diary column of *The Independent* (9 June 1990) this can be taken to extremes:

> *Clients of Mercer Fraser, the employee benefit consultants, are used to paying stiff fees. The firm acts as consultant to most major companies and charges accordingly. What has not been widely appreciated until now is the full impact of a lunch with a Mercer Fraser executive.*
>
> *Not only does the company charge the client for the lunch, but it also costs out the time of the executive entertaining the client at anything between £100 and £140 an hour. It pays to be a fast eater and leave before the brandy.*

Many professional firms charge relatively low fees and ensure that all costs incurred on behalf of clients are charged including a mark-up in the belief that the client will feel it is getting good value from the low fees. What these firms fail to understand is that from the perspective of the client the equation is a simple one of what is the total cost of employing this firm compared to the value of their services. Excessive charges for photocopying, for example, which is rife among legal firms, can be a source of great irritation to clients. Not only do they feel that the amount of copying is beyond their control but they recognize that they are being forced to pay for the lawyers' high overheads and staff salaries.

Some firms, particularly consultants, are trying the policy of charging the client a large fee and absorbing all overheads as a demonstration of the incentive to keep these overheads down. Other firms have a policy of passing on expenses strictly at cost.

MARK-UPS

A British PR firm had an aggressive policy of charging a 17.65 per cent mark-up on all costs incurred on behalf of clients and charging 20 pence per sheet for photocopying to cover staff time, the argument being that fees only related to professional staff. The level of these charges often caused resentment. Before a major press conference one of the firm's clients, which was also a professional firm, sent two of its own executives round to the PR company's office to help with preparation of documents which subsequently appeared on the invoice as copy charges. The following month the client's managing director sent an invoice for the time his people had spent photocopying, asking for it to be removed from his bill.

A TOTAL COST APPROACH

In assessing the overall cost of a relationship with a professional firm clients are increasingly taking into account the overall amount they pay (fees, commissions, mark-ups, expenses etc.) and asking themselves 'Are we getting value for money?'

No matter how professional firms care to dress up the basis of charging they cannot escape from the fact that the client's accounts department should be able to work out what the total costs of the relationship have been.

Firms which have unwittingly benefited from unsophisticated clients who pay too much will, in the end, suffer and they may find their own cost base and management control are unable to deal with a new situation where clients are more concerned about the cost of using professionals. Clients always have the opportunity of using alternative professionals or, if total charges become too exorbitant, they will simply do without the service or do it for themselves.

32

PREMISES

How should you house a group of professionals?

I remember we moved a small business to some low-cost offices about five miles from where they had been. I think we lost every single secretary and three of the eight main designers within six months. I don't know what we saved on the office move but I dread to think what it cost us in lost business and recruitment fees.

Director, marketing services group

For a professional firm its offices are its factory, administration block, sale room, research laboratory and, often, staff canteen. Even in those businesses where the staff spend most of their time on client premises the office is an important statement of what the firm is all about.

As set out in part I, professional firms need to invest in substantial offices to give confidence to clients who are buying intangible services. The look and feel of the office affects the firm on a number of fronts:

- Recruitment and retention of staff
- Motivation of staff
- Operating efficiency
- Winning clients
- Keeping clients

In terms of the *type* of accommodation firms must consider the trade-offs they need to make:

- Open-plan *versus* closed offices
- Single floor *versus* multiple floors
- Shared building *versus* own building

At one extreme an open-plan office on one floor of a very large building will allow even quite big professional firms to get maximum efficiency in terms of use of space and ease of internal communication. At the other extreme a converted Victorian house will provide a number of comfortable individual offices but will result in a lot of wasted space and will make the location of secretaries, support staff and computer systems difficult.

Decisions about options such as lease, buy or rent are best made with the help of property professionals and are dependent on the specific nature of the firm, the desired location and the state of the market. But the issues such as private offices or open plan, single floor and single building have to be considered in the light of how the firm actually functions and what it is trying to say about itself, what the firm does for clients and how the firm's staff interact. consider in choosing the type of accommodation is what the firm does for clients. A legal firm where senior partners assist clients in solving complex legal problems – mainly by their own efforts – simply does not need the big open-plan format as the individual offices provide all that is required with the additional benefit of privacy and reassuring prestige. An advertising agency which functions on teamwork and a high level of staff interaction will benefit from a far more open-plan arrangement.

A RABBIT WARREN

The current affairs department of the BBC, although not strictly a professional service firm, provides an interesting example of the impact of a building on operation. For many years it was located in an ancient building in London's Lime Grove with a complex warren of offices located over many floors. Staff regularly got lost moving from one place to another. People who worked both there and at more modern ITV equivalents were convinced that the cost of programme making and the rate of staff turn-over was significantly increased simply because of the lay-out of the place.

In respect of *where* the office is to be managers must ask:

- Does our location affect our chances of winning client business?

- Does our location affect the costs of serving clients?

The main trade-off in terms of location is city centre versus out of town. City centre will, usually have higher rents but will be closer to many client head offices and will reduce travelling costs. As a very general rule professionals will prefer city centre locations but support staff will often prefer somewhere out of town nearer to where they live.

A key premises issue for professional firms is flexibility. Unlike a factory which can work more shifts to meet increased orders a professional firm almost always has to add more staff which means finding more office space. Firms which start off very small in a self-contained house sometimes expand into similar houses next door. Firms which start on one floor of a modern building can expand onto other floors.

The most successful premises policy is to plan on a three or even five year basis and to calculate accommodation costs as an average through the period.

PLANNED GROWTH

A firm of 30 staff might decide that, on average, they needed 100 square feet per person and therefore would need 3,000 square feet. If at the end of three years the firm expected to grow to 50 people they would then need 5,000 square feet.

If they rented a property of 5,000 square feet at an annual cost of £40 per square foot their total costs would be £200,000 a year or £6,666 per head in year one and £4000 per head by year three. In planning terms it makes most sense to consider the business as having accommodation costs of £5,000 per head (the average) over the three-year period and to make all profit calculations accordingly.

The figures above also focus attention on one of the main management tasks – keeping down the head-count of support staff. It is easy to justify £5,000 a year (a typical figure) against a professional's total client income which will be well into six figures but it adds greatly to the employment costs of extra secretaries and so on. The above figures also illustrate why professional firms will make an error if they spend too much time trying to cut accommodation costs, as the penalties which result from having professional staff demotivated by bad offices will almost always outweigh the relatively tiny savings.

It is most unlikely that building-related overheads will be more than ten per cent of a firm's running costs and thus even a 25 per cent cut will have a far less dramatic impact on the bottom line than say, a five per cent cut in professional salaries or a five per cent increase in utilization rates. Because of the nature of professional firms, watching the pennies in respect of the building does not yield dividends.

33

TECHNOLOGY

What sort of hardware and software do professional firms need?

There's no doubt clients are impressed when they see the amount of kit we have in our offices – I do wonder though if we are making anything like the use of it we could. I only have the vaguest idea of what our computer network can do.

Partner, management consultants

The application of technology is of great importance to professional firms and should quite rightly represent a significant investment. People are expensive and scarce resources; the use of technology helps them to make the most of their efforts. The availability of the right, state-of-the-art, equipment brings benefits in several ways:

- In terms of recruitment and retention of staff it sends a clear message that the firm aspires to industry leadership. People will be much happier at work if they feel they have the best possible technological support

- In terms of client service and new business clients will draw reassurance from the fact that their professional firm appears up to date. The very intangibility of professional services means that the output in terms of documents, presentations and even the way the telephone is answered are critical in providing reassurance

- In terms of profitability the use of technology, particularly computers, will significantly increase the value of the work done in a given time by individuals and can cut down on the number of support staff required

The principal technologies available to firms are computers and telecommunications but without thorough training much of the value of the investment will be wasted.

COMPUTERS

All professional firms must use computers if only for basic word processing and doing the accounts. The main decisions required are:

- Whether to use a system of linked terminals, networked personal computers or stand-alone personal computers

- Which software packages to use for the main applications of word processing, spreadsheets, databases, accounting, computer-aided design and so on

- Whether to have special software application written for things like accounting and to support any products the firm creates

- Whether to have one fully integrated system encompassing accounting, word processing, databases and so on, or whether to keep the various systems separate

Which system?

The type of system will be dictated by how much information the business needs to process and share. A stockbroker's dealing room has such a high need for rapid processing and shared information that some form of mainframe or mini-computer which supports workstation terminals is the only viable option. Architects who require computer-assisted design will probably need a central computer and workstations simply to give them the processing power needed to support complex graphics applications (but as PCs develop more and more capacity they are becoming an alternative).

The vast bulk of professional businesses, however, have a much simpler choice between a network of personal computers and a series of stand-alone machines. Increasingly some form of network is the best solution as it offers the following advantages:

- Users can share files and information. Even though the business may not immediately see the need for this, once the facility is offered it will usually find applications. Common databases of names, addresses and telephone numbers can, for example, be created and updated every day

- Users can share peripheral devices such as printers. This can significantly reduce costs as, for example, four secretaries can share one expensive printer

- The computers can be used as communication devices. This is not to suggest that people will accept the paperless office; the reality is that people like having hard copies of documents and memos, but there are some other possibilities. A very simple example is that telephone messages can be taken and sent to the recipient's computer

- Cost savings can be achieved as relatively cheap individual PCs with low memory capabilities can have access to almost unlimited memory via the network

- Professionals who would normally use their machines just for word processing or spreadsheets can be encouraged to enter time sheets and other profitability data directly into the systems rather than filling in forms and can be given access to certain profit related performance information which helps to generate an attitude of profit consciousness

Desk-top publishing/presentations

The application of desk-top publishing (DTP) is a natural extension of having computers in the office. The DTP system can take text typed in normal document form and represent it in a compelling manner to improve the look of the documents and the effectiveness of communication. Professional firms need to look good to prospective clients and when reporting to existing clients. The use of DTP and associated techniques is now widely available and those firms which do not embrace the techniques will simply look shabby against the more enlightened competition.

The principal benefit is the marriage of text and graphics to create an attractive document, but many firms now discover they can produce in-house the sort of presentation that used to be sent out to designers' studios. On-screen computer presentation techniques like VideoShow or IBM Storyboard can be very impressive.

In selecting a DTP system (both hardware and software) firms should ensure that it is fully compatible with their existing word-processing systems as this will allow easy interchange of text between the secretaries, professionals and DTP operators. A decision also has to be made about how widely to spread the DTP skills. At one extreme all secretaries and professionals can have the software available on their machines and can be trained to use it. At the other a single operator (or a small group) will carry out all the DTP tasks for the firm.

The best results are usually obtained by centralizing the resource but allowing any secretaries or professionals who have a special need or special talent to have access to the necessary software and hardware. Firms with a DTP set-up must guard against the temptation to use it for all documents for although this will enhance the documents' appearance it may be a waste of resources.

TELECOMMUNICATIONS

Communication within the firm itself and with the world outside can now be carried out with a very wide range of technologies which all, ultimately use a telephone line.

Telephones

All professional firms should have a policy about how long it is acceptable to have a telephone ringing unanswered. The technology exists to ensure that, for example, no more than five rings are made before the phone is answered either by the executive being called, a secretary, the switchboard or a sophisticated answering machine such as a voice-mail system. As with documents the degree to which a telephone system is impressive and efficient will help win clients' trust.

Facsimile

The ubiquitous fax is another technology which professional firms must master. Ideally fax machines should be liberally spread around the building and people wanting to send information in should be given the appropriate number nearest to the recipient. Those individuals who have a heavy outgoing load of faxable documents can be given fax boards in their computers which will send documents without the need to create hard copies.

Modem links

The use of modems to send data along telephone lines and the associated technology of electronic mail can be very useful to firms which have to send information to their own offices or to clients which will be processed once received. Raw data on spreadsheets can be sent from a remote computer to an electronic mail-box and can then be processed without having to be retyped into another spreadsheet. The computer images used to make 35mm slides for presentations can be created in one office and sent via modem to another which has a slide making machine.

Whereas once a presentation in France might have to be prepared in England and transported across the Channel, the presentation can now be created in London, the electronic images sent to Paris and the slides made up in Paris to await the arrival of the presenter. Last minute changes can be telephoned to London, the image altered and the new image sent immediately to Paris for a new slide to be created.

Video-conferencing

Professional firms with multiple office sites may find that video-conferencing facilities will prove cost-effective by allowing executives to have conferences without the cost and time loss of travel.

TECHNOLOGY TRAINING

It is, sadly, a common experience to telephone an executive in a professional firm and at the end of the conversation to ask to be transferred to someone else only to be told 'Er, hang on I'm not sure I know how to do that. Why don't you just ring in again.' No amount of investment in computers and telephones will work unless there is a real commitment to training both professional and support staff.

Particularly in the area of computers, professionals can be trained to produce many of their own documents and notes by direct entry. This cuts out the process of dictating notes or handwriting documents for secretaries to retype. Increasingly professionals draft documents on computers themselves, leaving secretaries to clean up the spelling, grammar and layout.

Support staff can be taught the full power of word processing and data management packages which will allow them to work much more efficiently. Mailing lists and contact notes can be very effectively handled by the right software.

Senior people who fear some loss of status if they are seen behind a keyboard need to be shown the benefits of computers. It may, literally, be worth installing computer games on executives' machines so that they will have the incentive to turn them on and play – which increases familiarity. Many senior executives are much happier using a mouse to control their machines by pointing to icons than they are tapping away at a keyboard.

Much of the technology now available will work without detailed training but is much more effective if the trouble is taken to explain it to staff. Most fax machines can be programmed to improve efficiency but in every office people are to be found laboriously dialling the same numbers time and time again. Advanced word processing packages have numerous features such as automatic columns or macros which allow the user to automate frequently-repeated operations but which go unused and wasted through lack of training.

A technology champion

To make the most of the investment in technology senior management must accept that the investment in staff training may be as great as the original investment in the hardware and software. In addition to providing *enthusiastic* leadership, top management needs to identify a champion of the use of technology (probably a junior manager or senior member of the support staff) who will enjoy looking for new applications of technology within the firm and who will encourage others to learn to make the best use of what has been provided.

OUTWORKERS

The combination of computers with fax machines and modems provides the opportunity for the firm to allow people to work from home or from remote offices. With the predicted shortage of professional staff described in chapter 24, the use of technology offers a way to provide the facilities for married women who wish to stay at home or part-timers who do not want to commute, to do valuable work and to be as in-touch as if they were physically in the office. A firm can also set up some of its back-office functions in low-cost locations which suit the staff and link these to the prestige, high-cost offices to create one single organization by using technology.

A professional firm will nearly always benefit from the use of technology to improve efficiency and to make use of lower-cost labour. The main obstacle is not the willingness of staff to make use of the new equipment but the reluctance of senior professionals to embrace the idea that technology has a place in their sort of business.

PART V

BUILDING THE BUSINESS

How do you grow a professional service firm and remain profitable?

The most difficult thing for us has not been doing good work – it's been growing our own business.

Chairman, market research firm

Running a one-man or one-woman consulting business is easy. The quality of work is assured, there are no problems in managing issues of capacity or personnel conflicts. Unfortunately the income of the firm is limited by the number of hours the individual can work and the firm will close when the individual retires.

Clients of professional firms are increasingly looking for services to be carried out across national borders, they are looking for teams from professional firms to supplement their own staff in times of corporate change, and for relationships which are long-lasting with firms of high reputation. Professional staff seek promotion, increased personal wealth and the prestige associated with being part of a well-known and successful firm. Technological developments such as the use of computers, telecommunications networks, faxes and so on are creating potential economies of scale for professional firms.

All these pressures are driving firms to grow and to take on more professionals. There is a need to build the business but the nature of professional firms means that growth is one of the hardest things to manage. The downfall of many professional service firms has been overambitious growth.

FAILURE THROUGH GROWTH

In August 1990 the world's second largest design firm Michael Peters Group (MPG) went into receivership. Writing in *The Sunday Times* (26 August 1990) Rufus Olins commented:

223

> *MPG, the most flamboyant design company in the UK, fell into the hands of Arthur Andersen [as receivers] when Security Pacific [the bank] withdrew its support. Its banking debts are estimated to be around £7m. Murdoch McKillop, a partner at Arthur Andersen, said: 'It is a top-notch quality business with a superb client list. But it made mistakes in its expansion plans which cost it dearly.'*
>
> *After becoming one of the first companies to join the USM in 1983 Peters opened up businesses in Europe, Australia, America and Japan and diversified into consultancy and financial public relations. From then on things went wrong.*

The problems of Saatchi & Saatchi and WPP Group in advertising and marketing services, the collapse of VPI in public relations and Michael Peters in design and the bankruptcy of one of America's largest accounting firms, Laventhol & Horwath, have all been traced back to badly managed expansion.

At its simplest, growth is achieved by seeking out more clients, by selling more services to existing clients or by acquiring other businesses or teams of people which bring with them clients as well as resources. The key issue for managers is how to match the expansion of resources to any extra work identified, how to keep the profitable balance of the firm. Do you increase the level of resources and hope the work will follow, risking unused facilities and idle staff? Or do you win new work and then scramble to find people and facilities, risking a loss of quality and reputation? There is no simple answer.

Decisions by managers about how to grow will depend on special conditions in their industry. Issues such as availability of trained staff, availability of premises and delivery times of specialized equipment will all be constraints on growth.

Growth in professional service firms is usually defined as growth in total income or turnover which is, of course, closely linked with growth in head-count. If total income is growing much faster than total head-count it probably implies the firm is moving into a different type of business where the daily fees paid to each individual are higher – reflecting the greater value of the work being done.

If the senior people in the firm wish to increase their wealth they must either increase the number of people in the business and thus increase the profits in which they share or they must seek to increase the fee-earning capacity of the firm by helping all the professionals to do higher value-added work.

Increasing the per capita fee income is what an individual does as he or she gets more experienced and thus charges more for his or her services. For most firms this is very difficult to achieve as clients will resist paying more for what they regard as the same service and it will take some time for a large firm to reposition itself in the client's eyes as a firm which provides additional value for money. Increasing the size of the business places particular stresses on the economics of professional firms and presents problems of maintaining the balance between the three levels of the staff pyramid (directors, managers and executives) and of keeping staff utilization rates high.

Although most firms will seek to grow by simply recruiting more people and finding more work – this is the organic growth described in chapter 34 – firms can also grow by joining with or acquiring other firms as described in chapters 35 and 36. Growth for professional firms is desirable and necessary if junior people are to realize their ambitions of promotion. The challenge is how to manage that growth profitably.

34

ORGANIC GROWTH

How do you grow bigger while keeping a balance between the firm's resources and workload?

We've grown solidly for ten years now but we always either seem to have too many client assignments for our team to handle or we have people on the staff without enough to do. You can never seem to get it just right but at least we didn't go crazy buying up all our competitors.

Chief Executive, market research firm

Organic growth is the natural way of building the firm by taking on more work and finding more people to do it. This approach has many benefits in respect of building on already proven and understood business systems and in terms of maintaining a strong culture manifested in professional and ethical standards. It is the way most professional firms grow.

Organic growth can only come from two sources:

- New work from existing clients
- Work from new clients

Additional work from existing clients tends to be more profitable and easier to win than new business.

The American trade magazine *Advertising Age* noted (20 August 1990) that Saatchi & Saatchi appeared to have got this message:

> *Saatchi & Saatchi Advertising Worldwide, an aggressive pursuer of new accounts, is shifting its focus to current clients. Andrew Fraser, Saatchi's Director of Business Development, said 'Real revenue growth at a worldwide company such as ours comes from incremental business. Most long-established agency networks have generated new assignments from their major clients but Saatchi, a relatively new network, hasn't focused on that area until now.'*

The main constraints of this approach are for firms anxious to increase their size rapidly or to build an overseas network in a hurry. They would not be able to find the additional staff or client work on an incremental basis. The only options for them will be joint ventures or mergers which are discussed later.

Organic growth, then, is an expansion of the business achieved by taking on more people within the existing structure and by finding additional work from existing or new clients. This growth can be achieved under a variety of different management approaches but there are three broad options:

- Forecast staff numbers

- Revenue reinvestment

- Zero-based budgeting

The first option requires decisions about increasing the firm's resources *before* new work has come in on the assumption that a certain growth rate will be achieved. The second and third options dictate that new resources cannot be committed until *after* new sources of revenue have been signed up. The revenue reinvestment approach allows for new resources to be added automatically, the zero-based budget approach requires that resources are only increased if management can prove they are required.

FORECAST STAFF NUMBERS

Growing by adding additional people in anticipation of new work raises one of the key issues of profitable growth which is capacity planning. Under this approach managers set targets for recruitment and promotion and make assumptions about resignations. The advantages of this approach are in building a well-trained and well-motivated staff as it gives people a relatively high degree of certainty about their immediate futures. It also helps greatly with recruitment especially for those firms who take on the bulk of their new staff from universities or business schools and are, therefore, linked to the pattern of the academic year. The main drawback is that having a fixed staff size and therefore planned future 'capacity' can be very unprofitable if the hoped for extra work fails to come through.

To adopt a forecast or planned staff-numbers approach firms must be very confident about the future growth prospects for their market and about their ability to retain or gain share within that market. Having set the professional staff targets, other budgets such as premises, equipment and support staff are increased to reflect the increased size of the firm. It is important that these other budgets are carefully monitored to ensure they do not go up faster than the size of the professional staff warrants.

Forecast growth in numbers is very appropriate to firms who require scarce skills and have to invest significant training in their staff. If a firm gives the top priority to successful recruitment and really believes that its future success requires it to recruit the best ten per cent of that year's Harvard Business School class then it must achieve the recruitment target almost irrespective of the certainty of having work for them to do. This approach is probably most applicable in single professional discipline firms like lawyers and strategy consultants where the supply of good professional staff is the main key to success and the recruitment benefits of being able to plan ahead outweigh all other considerations.

Clearly there is the opportunity within the forecast growth approach to grab the chance of a huge new client account which doubles the size of the firm in a three-month period and requires a sudden additional influx of staff. The main problem with this is that many aspects of staff and work quality control will be lost and the firm may find that it creates short-term dramatic revenue growth at the expense of long-term profits. There can be times when the bravest decision is to *refuse* new work on the grounds that, at the moment, the firm cannot manage it!

REVENUE REINVESTMENT

This is a variant on the planned staff approach. Rather than fixing a recruitment target for staff the firm simply decides to reinvest a fixed percentage of its budgeted new revenues (often 30 per cent) in growth (usually in extra staff numbers). In other words *all* budgets grow in direct proportion to new revenue. Managers of all departments know they can grow staff numbers and expenditure (*not* simply increase the salaries!) but the exact implementation of that growth is left up to them.

This approach does not require that a targeted amount of new business is won (unlike the forecast numbers approach) but it does imply that new business must be serviced at a particular level of operating margin if profit margins are to be maintained.

A particular difficulty of this approach is that the decision to invest in new resources must be made at the time that new revenue is expected (i.e. contracts signed etc.) but ahead of the new revenue actually coming in. This leaves the firm at some risk if the new projects do not materialize. Another problem is that all the spending will go up by the selected percentage but that income will not rise resulting in reduced profits. Top management must watch the development of new business very carefully and be prepared to cut back on budgets if new work is not being found that is as profitable as past work.

This approach is suited to mature businesses in stable markets – particularly large departmentalized, firms where it would be very difficult to set straightforward head–count targets.

ZERO-BASED BUDGET

The zero-based budget approach says that no new resources i.e. recruits, equipment and so on can be taken on until after new business is won and even then management must make a case that additional costs are necessary to service the new work. This has the great advantage of keeping utilization high but risks overworking staff and reducing the quality of client servicing as incremental business will have to be handled by existing staff until successful recruitment is approved and can be achieved.

The approach is appropriate if analysis shows that the firm has very poor profit margins as a result of overmanning and that far more work could be handled by the firm from higher productivity.

If managed well the zero-based budget will keep short-term profitability high but can be bad for long-term development as it will result in less of a drive for new business and a more haphazard approach to recruitment.

The approach will be most successful when a firm is in a market where either staff skills are low (something like a direct mail fulfilment house) or where the necessary skills are widely available in the jobs market (like a basic auditing accounting firm). Suitable staff can then be quickly located if the workload increases. It is probably most useful when applied to recently acquired, low-productivity subsidiaries by a holding company such as some of the international marketing services groups which are driving their own growth by acquisition and are mainly concerned with improving the short-term profits of subsidiaries.

KEEPING THE BALANCE

In earlier chapters it has been suggested that the economics of professional service firms are very simple. By contrast planning profitable growth is probably the most complex management issue. The most difficult aspect of growth is keeping the firm balanced.

The decisions are essentially driven by the type of work a firm does and the type of clients it serves. However the type of firm and the shape of the staff pyramid also has a profound effect on growth rates. In his article 'Balancing the Professional Service Firm' which appeared in the *Sloan Management Review* (Autumn 1982), Dr Maister describes the problems of managing the balance of the staff pyramid as the firm develops. Part IV of this book includes a discussion of the pros and cons of high-ratio or low-ratio firms.

One of the main incentives for the professional in a professional firm is the prospect of promotion and, eventually, election to the partnership or management group or the equivalent and a determining factor for any individual will be the average length of time he or she might expect to stay within any one level in the firm. A typical length of tenure in any one grade might be five years.

How fast can you grow?

If a firm has 26 executives, ten managers and four directors then without any growth and any resignations only one in three of the

---

GROWTH RATES UNDER FLAT AND STEEP MODELS

	Start	YEAR 1	YEAR 2	YEAR 3	YEAR 5
STAYING FLAT (High Ratio)		This model maintains the staff ratios			
Directors	4	5	6	7	8
Managers	10	12	15	18	21
Executives	26	33	39	45	52
Total	40	50	60	70	81
Ratio directors/total	10	10	10	10	10
Annual growth		25%	20%	17%	16%
BECOMING STEEP (Low Ratio)		This model allows the ratios to reduce			
Directors	4	5	6	7	8
Managers	10	11	12	13	14
Executives	26	29	32	35	39
Total	40	45	50	55	61
Ratio directors/total	10	9	8.3	7.9	7.6
Annual growth		13%	11%	10%	11%

To maintain a flat structure calls for very high growth; moving to a less leveraged structure is easier to achieve but will change the economics of the firm.

Figure 5.1

executives can expect promotion to manager and only one in six will make director. That might be regarded by the executives as an unacceptably low probability. If they believe, however, that the firm will grow over five years to have eight directors and 21 managers then the odds look much better for nearly all of them to become a manager. However, as figure 5.1 shows, in a flat pyramid, wide-base, high-ratio structure this calls for a doubling in size of the firm from 40 staff to 81 over a four year period if the firm is to retain its ratios and keep the pyramid the same. This rate of growth is very hard to sustain.

The second model in figure 5.1 shows how the pyramid is allowed to get steeper (in effect to become shaped more like a column) and the directors are happy to let the ratios of directors to managers and executives reduce with time. The rates of growth required to create an eight director firm are much lower with total staff numbers only going up by just over 50 per cent. Unfortunately this will almost certainly make the firm less profitable.

The mathematics of growing professional firms is described in more detail in Dr Maister's book *Professional Service Firm Management*.

UNSUCCESSFUL GROWTH

A US based PR consultancy was set up with three directors who specialized in basic consumer public relations work associated with supporting advertising and sales promotion campaigns. After two years they had an excellent business with 15 executives to help them. The partners had a counselling relationship with clients and the executives did the basic 'leg-work'. To keep senior staff happy a number were appointed to the board until there were nine directors. However the simple constraints of growth meant there were only 30 executives so the pyramid had to get steeper.

The problem was that the basic type of work remained consumer PR and that clients were not prepared to pay extra for having a larger number of more senior staff on their account. The firm had to use directors to do executive work. Inevitably this resulted in significantly reduced profits which de-motivated senior staff. After five years three of the directors broke away to form their own firm.

Manage staff expectations

The ability to grow fast enough to meet the aspirations of the staff is the main dilemma of professional firms. There is no one single solution but success is a mixture of the following policies:

1 Make it clear that only a certain percentage of recruits will succeed in being promoted. Reasonable targets are 60 per cent to 80 per cent. This means making it easy for people to leave by cultivating relationships with executive recruiters, by building the reputation of the firm's staff as top quality professionals and by removing any stigma from departing from the firm.

2 Make it clear that the length of stay in any one grade is limited. If people do not achieve promotion they will be expected to leave the firm. This is the so-called 'up or out' policy adopted by many consultancy firms.

3 Allow the pyramid structure and ratios to change over time. Let people get promoted but avoid impossible growth rates by allowing the pyramid to become steeper. This only works if the firm actively plans for it and seeks the sort of client work that can be profitably served with a steeper pyramid. This means increasing individual billing rates or, in effect, putting up the firm's prices which can only be justified if the firm is doing higher value work.

4 Be *very* rigorous in the criteria and decisions to make people partners or directors. Only those individuals who are really capable of bringing in new clients and thus expanding the work base of the firm should be considered.

SUCCESSFUL GROWTH

A London-based strategy consultancy was set up with three partners and 12 executives specifically to support hostile takeover bids and bid defence. In the mid 1980s the firm prospered. It had a flat staff pyramid with a high degree of leverage. The founding partners provided leadership and the executives, mostly, did number crunching. As the business grew the founders had to offer partnerships to several of the executives to keep them from leaving. However at the same time the partners sought to develop long-term consulting relationships with their bid clients and as the original executives stayed with the firm they actively built their general consulting skills and started to run general client projects themselves. After seven years the firm had seven partners and 15 executives. The pyramid had changed radically but so had the type of work and the firm was still profitable.

To confront the growth problem a firm must have a very clear idea of the sort of services it plans to offer and the structure and staff skills that are right to provide these services. Clear targets must be set for the number of people in each grade over each of the next three to five years. Individual professionals must be told what they can expect in terms of promotion and rate of advancement.

So the main point about *planned* growth is that the firm takes decisions about its future level of resources (people, equipment, premises) based on assumptions about future revenues and therefore profits. It does not just grow as fast as new business wins allow and then start to worry about the effect this has on its economics. The need to grow is mostly dictated by the desires of the junior professionals as well as the wish of the firm's owners to see an increase in their wealth. The problem is that if the balance is lost owners can very quickly find themselves controlling a larger but *less* profitable business.

THE PROBLEM OF BALANCE

The problem of balance was clearly illustrated in a feature in *Business* (June 1991) on the firm PA Consultancy. Quoting the chairman and chief executive John Foden:

We had geared up for 20 per cent growth. When that target was set – in 1989 – it was not unreasonable; PA had been growing by 20 per cent a year throughout the 1980s. Planning for that kind of growth meant hiring extra staff and taking on more office space. The need for those staff never materialized; revenues were flat, meaning, in real terms, that demand had fallen by about 10 per cent. But the staff and office space still had to be paid for. Result: a steep drop in profitability.

35

JOINT VENTURES/STRATEGIC ALLIANCES

How can you work with another firm to win and manage profitable business?

Informal alliances among small service companies are one way to grow without putting dollars on the line. It doesn't cost us anything and it adds revenues without adding overhead.

William Morton, chief executive Jack Moreton Productions. (Wall St Journal 24 October 1990)

Professional firms that wish to develop an international network quickly or want the advantages of economies of scale without raising the funds to buy other firms are increasingly turning to some form of joint venture or alliance. The joint venture is a particularly appropriate growth mechanism for people businesses as it allows individual firms to retain their identity and culture while giving them both benefits. A classic example of the value of a joint venture is where a firm needs to service a client in a remote location and needs a partner. Rather than set up a new office or acquire a local firm it can find some basis for sharing the work with an established local business getting the benefit of local knowledge very quickly.

International expansion can be achieved by the organic means described in the previous chapter but that has problems. The alternatives are summed up in the Canadian official history of the accounting firm Touche Ross:

INTERNATIONAL EXPANSION

When the founding firms [of Touche Ross] set about building a structure for global business they had to choose between two procedures.

They could set up their own branches abroad, with direct control over their personnel and be in a position to set and enforce standards and methods. But they would face inescap-

able problems in trying to do business as foreigners in strange places.

The other choice was to make contact with existing accountancy firms in other countries. The advantages would be great. The founding firms would have their international work carried out by indigenous foreign firms, in each case by people who spoke the language of the country, who were of its race and culture, familiar with local conditions and had a basis of local work.

As professional services converge with lawyers doing consultancy, management consultants getting involved in mergers and acquisitions, accountants moving into management consultancy, and so on, there are increasing opportunities for joint ventures between firms from different professional areas as well as between similar, potentially competing, firms.

The main mechanisms for structuring joint ventures are:

- Negotiating a contract for cross referral and fee-sharing

- Buying a small, mutual, equity stake in each other

- Setting up a joint venture company

- Franchising or cloning a brand and business system

CONTRACTUAL AGREEMENTS

Linking two or more firms by using a contract defines certain basic elements of how their relationship will work.

- What is the minimum input expected from each party?

- To what degree can any party commit the joint resources of the others?

- How will costs and profits be shared?

The development of loose networks among law firms has been very rapid, particularly as they try to find ways of benefiting from the reduction of cross-border barriers in Europe. Writing in the *Financial Times* (24 October 1990) Rachel Davies comments:

The objectives of the individual groupings vary. Some concentrate on a referral system similar to a dating agency, matching up UK-clients' needs with appropriate foreign law firms or vice versa. Others concentrate on the sharing of expenses or expertise. Others offer a one-stop service for local clients who intend to operate abroad.

The attraction of the contractual agreement mechanism is that it is quick to put into effect and simple to end it and the individual firms retain their independence. The main problem is, usually, in defining how the spoils are to be divided.

Rewards for finding new business

Most contractual tie-ups are mainly aimed at generating new business for the partners by giving them access to each other's clients. This always raises the issue of compensating one partner for finding work for another. Should a cross-referral payment be a one-off finder's fee at the start of the new business relationship (which resulted from the contractual tie-up) or should it continue over the life of the account thus keeping the two firms tied together? Should fees shared between two firms who work jointly on an account be split on the basis of the costs incurred by each firm in winning a particular account or by some pre-agreed formula which will apply to all accounts irrespective of what each account cost to win and service?

A PAPER NETWORK

One European PR 'network' which, in reality, is a co-operative of independent firms pays each other ten per cent of the value of the first year's fees of any cross-referred business as a one-off reward. Another US-based group pays between three per cent and seven per cent of the annual fees and other income from the account for as long as the cross referred account is operated. The actual percentage depends on the size of the account with three per cent for the largest billing clients.

The one-off, up-front, finder's fee type arrangements only really work when the client does not require joint serving but simply needs a local contractor. It can be most appropriate when the professional service required by the client is actually different with, for example, a law firm recommending PR consultants or designers suggesting an advertising agency.

If the client needs a co-ordinated service something different is required. If the original firm is going to be involved in passing on guidance and information to the newly appointed firm or if they are going to work together on the same client issues, some basis to maintain the incentive has to be found. The long-term joint fee will be required when both firms are required to put in work. For example a British advertising agency might seek partners in Europe to buy the media time and space to place the advertisements it had made on behalf of clients. The British agency would continue to create the advertising and the foreign partners would have to constantly update their media plans to meet the client's needs. Some form of long-term fee sharing will have to be negotiated to motivate all parties.

Gross income or profit

Another issue is whether to base the shared incentive on gross income or profit. Assessing the real 'profitability' of any one client account is very difficult as the amount of profit is often a function of the allocation of the firm's overheads. Because of this problem the ongoing incentive paid from one firm to another is almost always based on total income from the client irrespective of how the two firms choose to service the business. The logic is that it is up to each firm to organize itself to achieve the maximum profit from any revenues. In effect the firm who received business from a cross-referral should look upon the client as cheap to service, as the original marketing costs and many of the ongoing costs of the client relationship (entertainment, top management time etc.) are borne by the original firm. In this light it is not unreasonable for the receiving firm to give up, say, seven per cent of the gross income from the client on the grounds that over the life of the account this represents the amount it would have had to spend itself to bring in *and keep* the client.

'Gentleman's Agreement'

In its very loosest form the joint venture may have no formal revenue sharing mechanisms but will simply be an arrangement that the firms' principals will 'always keep each other in mind' and may pass over a case of champagne by way of thanks for the referral of a particularly lucrative account. This can be a surprisingly successful formula as both firms can benefit greatly even though no hard cash changes hands. For both firms the marketing costs of finding new clients are reduced and as the respective teams get used to each other the costs of servicing clients are reduced as information transfer becomes more efficient. Without the need to negotiate a division of the spoils the relationship between the two firms can remain very good while both benefit from increased work.

A lawyer's dream?

As can been seen from some of the above the biggest problem with contracts is the need to define, unambiguously, how a relationship will work and to anticipate a wide variety of situations.

The need constantly to police the arrangement can mean that more time and resources are consumed on trying to make the tie-up operate fairly than are spent on winning new business. Unfortunately many contractual arrangements end up being disputed in court. This leads many professional firms to look for arrangements which place less emphasis on the *mechanisms* of sharing profits but simply involve a declaration that two or more firms will work together in their mutual best interest.

The ways of making networks work better are discussed in chapter 37 – the success is as much related to culture as to systems.

EQUITY STAKES

Two firms wishing to co-operate could sign a joint venture contract simply saying they would work together and help each other 'whenever possible' and would, at the end of each year give each other ten per cent of their profits. If, as a result of the co-operation, one firm did much better than the other they would both benefit because of the profit swap. In effect this sort of profit swap is what happens when firms buy equity stakes in each other.

The mutual minority equity stake is a system under which two firms provide an incentive for both to cross-refer business to each other and to try to assist each other's profitability. Long term co-operative client programmes can work under this arrangement. It also provides a useful first step towards one of the partners taking full control of the other. It can provide a 'getting to know you' period as firms begin to understand each other's accounting systems, recruitment policies, market-place and so on.

Equity advantages

The equity stake brings a number of benefits:

- In terms of control both firms are able to have a say in the setting of policy and the general direction of each firm

- The equity stake makes sharing the mutual benefits simple. There is no need to have complex negotiations. The two partners simply receive profits from each other by way of dividends

- Information about the two firms will flow naturally and easily particularly if both are represented on each other's boards

- Clients will find the arrangement easy to understand and there is less concern about finder's fees which can make clients suspicious of professional firms recommended by others.

Equity drawbacks

The main problems with equity stakes are:

- They can be a very inefficient way of transferring funds between the two firms (dividends will be taxed)

- The stake needs to be quite large if the firms are growing to justify including the equity related profits in their own pre-tax profit statement

- If the firms decide to end the arrangement agreeing a value for the equity can be difficult unless the firms are quoted companies

- Mutual equity stakes are also, clearly, a problem for two partnerships where the legal structure does not create straightforward equity. If two partnerships wish to get more closely involved than having a contract or a joint venture some form of merger is really their only solution.

JOINT VENTURE COMPANIES

A joint venture structure is used where two or more firms want to start a new business and both are willing to share in the costs and want to benefit from the profits. The joint venture company is potentially the most flexible arrangement under certain circumstances. The venture may be an actual physical office set up by the partners jointly funded and staffed by them to focus on specific client work, or it could simply be a paper based accounting mechanism.

For example, a London based consulting firm may have a client who wants a two-year efficiency study undertaken in a large factory it has just purchased in North America. For practical reasons the consulting team has to be based in Atlanta, Georgia and in London. The London firm identifies a Georgia-based consulting company with the necessary resources. The two firms have various joint-venture options. They could set up a joint project office which may seek to serve other Anglo–American clients as well as the original one. Cost and later profits would be shared on an agreed basis. Alternatively they could simply use their existing separate accounting systems to charge all the project costs to a paper company which later can remit its profits to the two firms again on an agreed basis.

Joint venture advantages

What makes the joint venture particularly attractive is ease of operation. Partners take out profits in the same proportion that they put in investment and resources. The success of the venture is in the best interests of both. Joint ventures can trade under the name of one or both of the partners or can develop identities of their own.

Joint venture disadvantages

The main difficulties with the joint venture is who manages it. Is it an entity in its own right or is it an off-shoot of one of the partners? In terms of systems, approach, culture and philosophy, which of the parents does it resemble? In joint ventures between firms from different countries what language will be used? These questions are often resolved by physical proximity as the closer of the two partners will become dominant. In many cases one of the partners may support the joint venture with administration such as payroll or even by providing accommodation and office services. If the partners are contributing in kind (office space, use of expertize etc.) problems can arise in defining the financial value of this contribution which is similar to the difficulties experienced in contractual tie-ups.

FRANCHISING?

The idea of franchising immediately conjures images of McDonalds or Holiday Inns where a well-tried and tested business system with a strong brand is made available to a local management team who operate it faithfully and reward the franchise-holder with a share of the profits. In some cases a similar idea can be successfully used as a growth mechanism for a professional firm.

The key differences between a professional franchise and that of say a fast food chain is that in the McDonalds example the franchisee benefits from a very strong consumer brand which is promoted and protected by the franchisers and also is subject to a fairly high degree of central management and quality control. The professional franchise gives a methodology but it is likely that the brand name will be far weaker.

At the heart of most large and successful professional firms is a business system, a way of doing things and a set of corporate values. These things can be codified and written down and can be transferred to a new group of people. It could be argued that professional firms which encourage partners to set up offices in new territories are operating a sort of franchise. Baker & McKenzie, often described as the world's largest law firm, has expanded very rapidly from a base in Chicago. Writing in *Canadian Lawyer* (March 1988) Deborah Watson notes:

BAKER & McKENZIE

The way Bert Stitt [founder of Toronto based Stitt Baker & McKenzie] got started typifies how the firm has managed to expand so rapidly. Instead of sending US lawyers to a new country the firm hires local lawyers and trains them for up to three years in other offices and then sends them home to establish a practice . . . When Stitt visited Baker in Chicago he found a mini-United Nations of lawyers. He spent the next few years working at various offices before he returned to Toronto.

Baker & McKenzie reject the idea of being a franchise and with some justification To be a pure example of franchising a firm needs to sell its franchise on some geographical or other basis to a group of people who can then operate in that market. If a firm chooses to expand by allowing one or two of its partners to set up an office in a remote market and then to operate under the firm's name using all the firm's methods and approaches this is more like cloning than franchising. In the context of using joint ventures to grow the business the encouragement to people to set up new offices is, in effect, a joint-venture agreement between the firm and the new team.

If a professional firm was able to develop a very strong proprietary methodology or technology it might, then, be able to franchise in a more classic sense. Firm managers wishing to expand should certainly ask themselves if they have a brand that could be exploited.

36

ACQUISITION/MERGER

How do you buy another firm and what do you do to merge the two together afterwards?

The best and worse times of my professional life were to do with the merger. Best because it was exciting to be twice the size. The worst because of the endless pettiness in bringing two organizations together.

Partner, law firm

This book is about the management of individual professional service firms rather than the activities of financial holding companies. A very clear distinction must be made between merger as a mechanism for two or more firms to combine and grow and an acquisition programme under which a financial holding company seeks to build an empire. The well publicized problems of Saatchi & Saatchi, WPP, Laventhol & Horwath, VPI, Michael Peters and others illustrate the difficulty of building groups in the professional sector by financial holding companies.

Acquisition or merger is examined, in most of this chapter, as a mechanism for growth between firms. It can also help the growth of parts of firms where a small firm is acquired and merged into an existing division.

PRE-MERGER CONSIDERATIONS

The key points to consider when thinking about whether to merge or not include:

- Is the target firm more or less profitable than the would-be acquirer?

- If less profitable, can the acquiring firm add value by bringing to bear skills and systems which will improve the profitability of the target?

- Are there client conflicts which could cause clients to leave resulting in surplus staff resources?

- Are there staff conflicts ? Do both firms have specialists who would clash?

- Are there operating systems and policy conflicts? Do both firms use the same computers? Are the terms of employment the same?

- Are there cost saving synergies to be captured? (Typically these are found in administration and accounts departments.)

MUTUAL BENEFITS

Leaving aside the financial engineering considerations which drive the acquisition programmes of some publicly quoted companies, the real motive for a professional service firm to buy another should be the belief that once acquired the target firm will perform better and that the economics of the two combined will be better than either alone.

There will be examples of two firms perfectly suited to merge. A young, aggressive firm with strong management can bring real benefits to a long-established firm with good clients but lacking top-level direction. The young firm will get the scale and growth to satisfy its people. The old firm will be able to keep its clients in the face of aggressive competitors

A good example of a merger of two firms based on mutual benefit was the one that created the Saatchi & Saatchi advertising empire in 1975 when the relatively new and aggressive Saatchi & Saatchi London advertising agency merged with (in effect staged a reverse takeover of) the very long-established and rather sleepy Garland-Compton agency. In his book on the Saatchis, *The Brothers*, Ivan Fallon comments:

> *[Ken Gill, Chairman of Compton] outlined the problem that faced him. The London end [Garland-Compton] was a good, solid, day-to-day agency but he could not see anyone among the younger people who could provide the new burst of energy needed; he had no obvious successor. He had seen these two young men [the Saatchis] producing some of the best advertising he had ever seen; they were financially bright as well as creative. He was thinking of taking over their business and getting them to set the direction of the agency . . . . His operation was full of good administrators. What he did not have were bright young creative people.*

The perception among clients was that the world divided into bright creative people of which Saatchi & Saatchi was a good example; or bigger, more conservative operations which were strong on marketing. Garland-Compton was very much in the latter camp, while Saatchi & Saatchi on its own, no matter how fast it grew, could never get there.

It is generally accepted that the resulting merger (which was a merger of two professional service firms and not the takeover of a firm by a financial holding company) was a great success as it brought together two organizations which needed each other.

VALUATION

One basic issue which has to be addressed when acquiring or merging firms is how much should one pay for the other? How much is a professional firm *worth*? There are a number of different techniques for putting a value on a professional business.

P/E ratios

The most conventional way of valuing a business is to use a price/earnings (p/e) ratio where the price of one share in the business is expressed as a multiple of the earnings of the business (the operating profits less taxes) attributable to each share. In other words the total value of the business is regarded as a multiple of its total post-tax earnings. For example if a firm made profits of £100,000 pre-tax then with a tax rate of 40 per cent it would have post tax profits of £60,000. If the *right* p/e ratio was nine times then the value of the firm would be £540,000 (i.e. 9 x £60,000).

This approach has two main problems.

1 The *right* p/e ratio is hard to determine. The whole stock market has an aggregate p/e ratio, currently about 13. Each sector of companies has its own ratio.
2 A p/e ratio is based on historic profit performance and does not involve a close analysis of the company's prospects although in theory a company with bright prospects will have a high p/e.

The p/e ratio is, in effect, saying: this is what I am prepared to pay for the privilege of owning the organization that makes this amount of profit. Or in buying a stream of earnings the p/e ratio gives the immediate cash value of that earnings stream. A high p/e ratio is the market's way of saying that it expects profits to grow, that is, you will be buying a stream of income that will grow as the years go past. A low p/e ratio implies that the market thinks the amount of earnings may fall or not grow as fast as the market in general.

Net present value

An alternative approach is some variant on discounted cash flows or net present value. An estimate is made of the cash flows or profits the firm will make in each of the next five or ten years. An estimate of what the firm would be worth at the end of the five or ten year period is also made. These future values are then restated at today's value, that is, next year's profits (which arrive in twelve months time) are restated as what they are worth today. This is done by taking into account the time value of money.

For example if a firm is expected to make £100,000 of profit in 12 months time what is that worth today, that is, how much money would you give today for the guarantee of receiving £100,000 in 12 months time? In very simple terms the answer depends on interest rates. If interest rates are 15 per cent then £100,000 of next year's money is worth £100,000/1.15 or £86,950 in today's money. If you invested £86,950 for 12 months at 15 per cent annual interest you would have £100,000 in 12 months time

The great advantage of attempting to value a firm on the basis of future cash flows is that it forces managers to look hard at what is likely to happen in the future and to assess the firms real strengths and weaknesses. It can be a very useful forcing mechanism for discussion of strategy and an assessment of the firm's potential.

Asset values

Assessing the value (or potential purchase price) of a professional firm based on the assets it owns is virtually meaningless. The real value of a professional firm is its ability to generate income and to produce surplus income or profits. In almost all cases this is related to its *human assets*, which will not appear on any balance sheet, rather than its buildings and equipment. If a firm does own substantial assets such as a building then this must enter into the value calculation as must the ownership of any large cash reserves held by the firm in the bank. But these hard assets must always be viewed as value *additional* to the ability of the firm to make profits.

Artificial ratios

Valuing department stores, for example, can be done using a multiple of turnover – the assumption being that good management will be able to extract a certain level of profit (established historically) assuming the trade is there.

Cable television companies are valued by the number of homes signed up for their services or by the number of potential customers whose homes might be accessed by their cable service. The assumption is that good management will be able to turn these opportunities into a certain level of profits.

Radio and television stations and newspapers can be valued on the basis of the size of their *potential* audience (rather than past revenues and profits) on the assumption that good management can achieve a certain market share and profit level.

Professional firms could be valued by ratios based on things such as total professional head–count or current size of client income, the assumption again being that good management can achieve certain profit norms. The problem with such ratios is that they fail to force managers to look at likely trends in the industry or special features of the firm in question.

The best valuation

In the end the best way of deciding how much to pay must be based to create a model of what the *merged* firms will look like when combined and calculating how much more surplus income (i.e. profit) the merged firm will make than was made by the two components. This takes into account the inherent value of the acquired firm as well as any benefits from the synergy and cost cutting of bringing the two together. It will force all assumptions about the future to be overt.

MERGER NEGOTIATIONS

The majority of professional firms are partnerships or limited companies with a very small number of shareholders. Plans to merge two such organizations or to have one taken over by the other inevitably become far more about politics than economics. In some cases it is easily possible that as much negotiating time will be devoted to selecting the name of the new entity as is spent on discussing the purchase price of the shares. When the decision is taken to merge there is great merit in involving a third party, such as a lawyer or investment banker, to conduct negotiations and to draft the terms of the merger.

A critical fact of merging people businesses is that the principal assets – the senior people – will have to work with each other after the event. A bruising succession of late-night merger negotiations can badly damage the potential working relationship. Certain contentious issues have to be confronted and clarified *before* the merger occurs because if avoided they will come back to haunt the businesses later. These include:

- Basis of director's/partner's remuneration. It will commonly be different in the merged firm

- An *exact* and clear statement of the merged firm's positioning in the market. The two parties will often have different views

- A commonly agreed mission statement which may not be made public but the writing of which will force both firms to confront exactly what they stand for

POST-MERGER INTEGRATION

As part of the acquisition or merger planning considerable emphasis must be placed on the post-deal integration programme. Endless political issues will arise.

Post merger problems

Acquisition can create significant difficulties during the post merger period:

- Redundant resources – who needs two computer systems?

- Incompatible systems – accounting procedures, staff bonus calculations and so on, may well be different

- Culture – working hours, attitudes towards competitors

- client conflicts – two brewers might not like having the same advertising agency or lawyer

If the two firms are in the same city there will be great pressure to merge central functions to save resources. Firms will frequently face the problem of what to do with two finance directors, two marketing directors or even two managing directors. Key appointment decisions must be made very early – preferably before the merger occurs as they will affect nearly all staff who will view their own career prospects in terms of who is seen to win out in the post-merger fight.

It is often the case that the cultural differences between two firms will create as many problems as structural and legal ones. Writing in *Canadian Lawyer* (June 1988) Bruce McDougall describes the following:

CULTURE CLASH

The Canadian law firms of MacDermid & Co and Lamarsh & Co merged because they were able to make better use of staff, better use of the computer system and capture economies of scale (one library instead of two) however the partners found small details can spoil a merger.

Lamarsh allowed its staff an hour for lunch, MacDermid gave an hour and a half. Lamarsh paid overtime after seven and a half hours, MacDermid after seven. One firm had a no smoking policy, the other did not. 'It may sound insignificant', said a partner, 'but the small things gave us more trouble than the big ones.'

MERGER PROBLEMS

Two London legal firms merged because one had become top heavy with partners while the other had embarked on a vigorous and successful recruitment drive but was not finding success in winning new clients. From a professional point of view the merger was a great success but it threw up substantial cultural problems. Partners of the top-heavy firm had a relatively modest lifestyle having no company cars and low expenses. The other firm had far more generous perks packages. Failure to agree on the appropriate partnership perks nearly prevented the merger.

This sort of cultural problem needs careful handling as staff can become quickly demoralized. Mergers also create external problems. Writing in *Canadian Lawyer* (November 1989) Patrick McKenna and Gerald Riskin comment:

THE CLIENT'S PERSPECTIVE

Your merger will create new uncertainties for even the most sophisticated of your clients. For example, some may have a concern about losing the long-term relationship they had with certain lawyers or even the status they enjoyed within the firm. Others may worry that your increased size will create a bureaucratic system, with their once informal contacts becoming rigid. Nearly all your clients may suspect that your increased size will mean increased fees. After all, who is going to pay for the physical move and the more lavishly decorated offices that usually follow a merger?

Integration management

To assume that things will go smoothly once the main directors or partners are agreed and the documents are signed is naive in the extreme. The first step is to recognize that the integration itself is a major management challenge. A senior individual must be identified whose task it is to push the integration through. Specific integration tasks must be identified and task forces composed of people from both the merged firms must be created. Typical task forces will include:

* Development of common computer systems
* Harmonization of personnel policies
* Common financial reporting formats and systems

A clear and agreed timetable must be set with deadlines accepted by both firms by which phases of the integration must be completed.

In most business projects it is argued that an agreed strategy must precede discussions about structure. In the post-merger integration of people businesses, structure must come first as people must be given a very clear picture of who is in charge to prevent endless and destructive politics. Professional service firms are, by their nature, highly political and people must understand very early on in a newly-merged business who is in charge and from whom they are expected to take their cultural and professional lead.

QUICK AND CLEAR STRUCTURE

When the accounting firms Ernst & Whinney and Arthur Young were merged in 1989 to form the world's largest accounting firm the merger committee took the brave decision (later proved correct) to announce immediately the identity of the holders of all senior posts to prevent the inevitable political jockeying for position which would have occurred had they left the question open during the post-merger phase.

Making the merger work is sufficiently important to be made the specific responsibility of several senior people *from each firm* and for a budget to be created which is devoted to post-merger integration. In firms with more than a few dozen employees there is probably benefit in employing external consultants to manage the merger process. They will be able to identify and confront political problems which could prove intractable for an internal manager who is expecting to stay on after the merger is over.

A very clear post-merger timetable is required with well-publicized target dates for events such as:

- Inform all clients in person
- New chief executive to meet all staff
- Adopt new corporate identity
- Move into new offices
- First management conference of merged firm

The most attractive of mergers, on paper, will fail if the whole process is not given top priority.

EMPIRE BUILDING

In general the use of acquisition as a mechanism for creating an empire of professional service firms is not successful. *The Economist* (November 1990) commented:

WPP GROUP

Is there anyone left to speak up for the acquisitive service-conglomerates of the 1980s? The Saatchi brothers are now in semi-retirement; accountancy firms' attempts to become global know-how firms have backfired; and Mr Martin Sorrell, one of the most eloquent and skilful of the empire-builders has fallen flat on his face . . . . The market value of Mr Sorrell's WPP Group plummeted by 70% in two days . . . . following a warning about expected profits.

And in a separate article in the same edition, *The Economist* described the bankruptcy of one of America's largest accountancy firms, Laventhol & Horwath:

LAVENTHOL BANKRUPTCY

At the root of Laventhol's problems was its ambitious drive for growth in the 1980s. Though revenue increased fivefold, it was at the cost of taking on a lot of debt and being less choosy than it should have been about new clients.

The concern of the investment community – the City – was highlighted in the *Financial Times* (7 September 1990) by Alice Rawsthorn, commenting on the commercially successful Shandwick which has built the worlds largest single PR group:

SHANDWICK'S SHARE PRICE

Life is rarely fair . . . . Shandwick, like almost every other marketing services company, has watched its share price slide steadily . . . it had sapped the City's sympathy by staging a stream of acquisitions which left it with many of the characteristics – heavy debts and hefty earn-out commitments – that the City associates with accident-prone marketing companies.

The heart of the problem with many of the acquisitions motivated by financial engineering is that all they really amount to is a change of ownership without any real integration or cross-referral benefits to firms. Indeed the change of ownership often demotivates the firms' key staff.

Firms like Shandwick are probably unfairly treated by the City. Because they have a very single-minded focus and by only having public relations companies in their group they will be able to see some benefits of mutual learning and mutual client servicing. In some ways they are following the same path as major international law or accountancy firms, but by using the mechanism of public ownership and acquisition rather than mergers agreed between equity-owning partners. Peter Gummer, the founder and Chairman of Shandwick, says his approach is 'always to buy market leaders' and 'to provide quality assurance to clients.'

One-stop shopping

The concept of building a professional services firm to meet clients' needs across a wide range of professional services has been the subject of hot debate, particularly in the marketing services area with the example of Saatchi & Saatchi which ranged across advertising, marketing consultancy, management consultancy, public relations, design and other activities. At one point there was even talk of buying a bank.

The professional one-stop shop or services supermarket is built on two, flawed, assumptions:

1   That clients need someone, external, to co-ordinate their professional advisers. In most cases they do not.
2   That clients will be assured that the various professional firms within the supermarket are all of equal quality. Usually they are not.

Professional services depend on a close working relationship. Long-term success requires a close fit with their client in terms of philosophy, approach, operating methods and culture. The very term supermarket shows one of the main problems. A good supermarket will nearly always carry the two or three leading brands of any item. The consumer can choose between the market leaders. In a professional supermarket this is not the case as there will usually be only one firm on offer in any one area of skill and there will be no guarantee that the firm in question will be a leader in its profession. It would be very cynical to say the main reason that a particular firm was taken into the ownership of a professional supermarket was that it was for sale but often this is the case.

If the firms within the supermarket would not normally be within the client's top three choices of advisers within that profession the client is most unlikely to be happy with the arrangements and will feel it has been forced to accept second best. If a client wants to do business with an outstanding team at an advertising agency but is told everything will work better if you also use our associated PR consultancy (which the client loathes!) then the original relationship will find itself under strain.

Another problem of the supermarket approach is that there is no guarantee that the various firms within it will respect each other or work with each other. Indeed there is a real tendency to denigrate firms within the group as the feeling sometimes builds that others are mere passengers riding on the success and profits of one's own business.

CROSS-SELL FAILURE

Evidence of the problems of the cross selling concept comes from *The Wall Street Journal* (7 January 1991) in an article by Joanne Lipman:

WPP Group's Martin Sorrell, the advertising industry's chief proponent of cross-selling is now sharply curtailing his ambitious plans to sell clients one-stop advertising, public relations, and marketing services . . . . Although Mr Sorrell has spoken often about cross-selling, the theory hasn't succeeded much in practice . . . . Most clients simply aren't interested: just because a client uses a WPP ad agency in New York doesn't mean it wants a WPP unit in London to design its packaging, or a WPP company in Washington to handle its lobbying.

CONGLOMERATE FAILURE

The Economist (22 December 1990) also has harsh words about professional service empires in an article headed 'Blowing the whistle on accountancy':

Accountants deserve most of the stick they are getting. Like advertising agencies and investment bankers, they fell for the 1980s fad of the service conglomerate. The big eight firms became the big six as they merged and remerged, struggling to push under one roof a whole range of business services, like tax advice, management consultancy, corporate finance and, yes insolvency. This left them woefully dependent on non-recurring fee businesses like consulting; it also encouraged them to cut auditing charges to win other business. When auditing becomes a loss-leader it is scarcely surprising that it gets done badly or misleadingly.

37

MANAGING GROWTH

What mechanisms are available to manage the growing firm? How can you accommodate new people and new clients?

In the early years managing the firm itself seemed difficult but, as we now know, it was a breeze compared to managing the process of getting bigger.

Managing Director, advertising agency

Growth within a single firm is mainly a problem of keeping the balance as described in chapter 34. When a firm grows beyond one office a whole new set of challenges must be met irrespective of whether the extra offices came by organic growth, joint ventures or acquisition. Previous chapters in this section have been about the mechanisms of achieving growth. This chapter is about how to manage it and how to achieve it profitably.

Consistent quality

Having more than one office creates particular problems of quality and administration. One of the main selling points of the multi-office firm is that it can deliver consistent and high-quality work from all of its locations. However clients will quickly become very dissatisfied if they experience shoddy service from other offices. They will feel they have been forced to accept inferior service on the back of a satisfactory original relationship. If some or all of the additional offices were acquired the problem of quality control is even greater.

In practice many of the major international firms have put their businesses together by acquisition and professional firms, unlike manufacturing businesses, are not run by a top-down hierarchy. Much of the firm's culture and philosophy come *up* from individual offices – this, in itself, creates problems of managing a network. The creation of a management structure and systems is relatively easy. Creating a shared culture is far more difficult.

MULTIPLE OFFICES

New office locations may be required simply to accommodate an increased number of staff when the firm outgrows the original site. There may be a desire to achieve greater geographic reach to improve the ability to service clients. Most professional service businesses benefit from being relatively close to their customers in order to reduce travel time and to keep the professionals in touch with local market conditions. If the firm has a strong, distinct service philosophy and a strong brand additional offices can quickly win business. The firm will already be well-known and well-understood. Local clients who desire the firm's help but did not find it practical to do business with a far distant office will probably seek the new office out. These factors can lead to new office openings simply to exploit market opportunities.

Another motive for opening distant offices is when specific clients require it to service their needs. Lawyers may need to help a London client involved in litigation in New York. An advertising agency may need a network in Europe for a Paris-based client who requires a pan-European campaign. Meeting clients' needs may be served by opening offices or by acquiring or creating joint ventures with local firms.

Separate profit centres?

Having to run multiple offices whether they came by acquisition or organic growth raises its own special problems. A decision is required as to whether each office will be a profit centre in its own right or will be seen as part of the overall firm.

For those firms where the individual offices are virtually self-contained with no shared clients and the only thing in common is their name (such as for example a chain of accountants) then the individual office as profit centre works best. However if each office is a separate profit centre there will be endless disputes about the allocation of central overheads and rewards for cross-referral of work as each office will be in it for themselves.

For those firms where joint servicing of clients is crucial such as an international management consultancy or a major commercial law firm the single, firm-wide, cost-base concept is preferable where costs and profits of all offices are regarded as one pool of resources. However if the offices are regarded as part of one business there is the risk that individual office costs will be slackly managed. Everyone will feel that housekeeping economies are someone else's problem.

A common culture

Organizational issues such as culture and shared values become significant considerations with multiple offices but a common approach and shared values can be very important in recruiting, training and producing quality work.

SHANDWICK'S OFFICES

The Shandwick public relations group has a particularly informal approach to running a large network of offices. By mutual agreement there are no cross-referral fees paid unless specifically requested and chairman Peter Gummer feels in the end the flow of new business between offices will all even out to mutual benefit.

To keep a family feel to the group, which has a very small central management, Gummer claims he spends more time worrying about culture than management structure and says he travels the world to shake the hand of every one of the 2,600 employees at least twice a year and does not object to being described by his managers as 'a mother hen.'

CENTRAL OR FIRM OFFICE

If a firm is large enough it may justify having a central or firm office which exists to service the whole network. For the smaller firms the central functions will be carried out by the largest (usually the original) office.

The biggest danger of the firm office is that it tends to be pure overhead as it does no client work and simply exists to provide internal services such as pensions, public relations and conference organization. As overhead it will often be very unpopular with the fee-earning local office partners. The analogy with a national defence or road-building budget is not too far fetched. Most tax payers understand these shared national services have some value but they would prefer not to have to pay for them personally.

The central office can have the role of simply acting as a postbox for client referrals, it can assist individual offices in seeking and winning international clients or it can take on international clients for itself, using local offices as a delivery mechanism.

TRANSFER PRICING

Offices within a network and the central office itself will often do work for each other. Each office in a network has resources (its professional staff time etc.) which it can devote either to its own clients or to meet the requests of other offices. The key issue is the basis upon which these resources should be charged out to other offices.

Accounting for work for a shared client is easy. One office is regarded as having the client relationship and will issue the invoices. The professionals from other offices involved simply bill the lead office at their normal, full, billing rates. The client will pay the bills and each office will benefit from the profit element of its professionals' time. The only difference is that the professional was sold through another office rather than his or her own. There is no question of charging other offices at cost and allowing them to enjoy the profit element.

However when people become involved in other work, for the firm itself, such as training, product development, new business pitches and so on it becomes more complex. To work for other offices for nothing would be foolish as all offices would start to try to get value from others by getting them involved in work without regard to the real cost of doing it. Charging non-client work at the full billing rate of professional staff seems unfair because the office providing the people will be making a profit at the expense of the others. This might also tend to discourage inter-office projects and co-operation which will damage the firm and reduce the benefit of having multiple offices. Another approach is simply to charge the professionals at their cost – that is their salary and share of overheads expressed as an hourly rate.

The ideal basis for charging would be to reflect the lost opportunity cost of professionals' time – that is to say the potential income they are passing up by working on inter-office projects.

One international group has experimented with an inter-office points system under which each hour of professional time is worth a certain number of points (related to the individual's billing rate and thus reflecting seniority). At the end of the year those offices who are net *users* of other peoples staff and those who are net *contributors* are identified. No money changes hands but the system acts as a control mechanism to prevent abuse of potentially free labour.

COST SHARING/ALLOCATION

A firm with multiple offices will have some shared resources. Typical ones include a central information library, a desk-top publishing/visual aids unit, specialist professionals, public relations and so on. The management task is to decide how to share these costs among the offices.

The best principle is to say that those services which are *consumed* as and when required, such as the desk-top publishing unit, should be charged out on a time or unit of work basis with the charges calculated to recover all the unit's costs assuming that it is used for, say, 80 per cent of available time. To charge at below cost is to provide a subsidized service which would be abused. To charge at full commercial rates (which would be equal to those outside) will remove the motivation for using the unit and thus deny the firm the cost saving associated with doing it yourself. Services which are not consumed by all on demand, but which are deemed by the firm as a whole to be necessary, such as public relations, must be charged out to all the offices on a mutually accepted basis.

There are two models for operating the central office which dictate the way the allocatable costs are dealt with. The choice of model is really a function of the way the firm is owned and therefore the mechanism by which profits are distributed:

- In one model the central office is the recipient of the operating profits of all the member offices. The central office acts as a holding company. It simply deducts its own costs (which include all the shared services) and then distributes the resulting profits back to partners or shareholders depending on the company's structure

- In the other model the central costs (including those for shared services) are allocated to each office on some basis (usually in direct proportion to headcount) and each office then declares its own operating surplus for distribution

The basis of the cost allocation can vary but is usually done on professional head-count or gross income. The central costs are simply spread, pro rata, across all the firm.

The main problem with any form of allocation is that managers will always quibble over the way it is done. An ideal solution is to have only one cost and profit centre, that is, a one firm concept (which will be discussed on page 263).

MAKING NETWORKS WORK

The firm must invest significant sums in helping its various offices communicate with each other. Any firm with a multi-office structure can do things to make the network function better.

As a basic principle firms should try to bring their offices as close together as possible by removing or reducing barriers to communication both technological and cultural. Networks of offices can create electronic communications to improve the flow of information. All offices should use the same computer equipment and software. Electronic mail boxes and modem links should be installed to allow transfer of data and documents. Firms which can justify the cost should install video-conferencing facilities to enable senior people to have easy, face-to-face contacts.

The real problem, however, with getting networks to function is not with practical aspects like computer compatibility but with the political dimension. In most professional firms the local office is the main business unit and the main source of business will be local clients. While every office might welcome the income from multi-office clients most will resent paying the costs to win and service it.

Network benefits

Networks bring benefits to clients:

- Clients requiring multinational or just multi-location services will benefit from the *co-ordination and consistency* offered by the network. This should be superior to the level of service they would get by employing a number of individual local firms and co-ordinating the efforts themselves. This, of course, is only true where each of the professional firms is offering the same discipline. Co-ordination of *different* disciplines is often better done by the clients themselves

- Clients can gain access to the firm's resources and expertise and benefit from *economies of scale* in the provision of services such as research

- Clients will be able to get the best professional advice on their problem that exists *anywhere within the network*, not just in their local office. The firm should identify *best practice* in professional skills and administration so that the strengths of the strongest office are available to all

From the firm's point of view a network can help:

- *Marketing* – if the firm develops a well known and well respected brand it can be easier to promote this because the network will receive more attention than a single office

- *Recruiting* – the best people are often attracted to the flexibility and prestige of a network firm

- *Cost saving* – the same point about economies of scale mentioned above means that the firm will be able to carry out certain functions and share the cost

Network co-ordination

A network is different from a group of firms under shared ownership. Within a network the individual firms work together to create mutual benefits. To achieve co-ordination the firm must create mechanisms such as:

- Executive co-ordinators
- Lead office
- International/ central team

Executive co-ordinators

The title of co-ordinator or international manager all too frequently conjures up the picture of expensive overhead bringing no direct benefit to clients. Local offices will frequently complain about the co-ordinators, but without them a major benefit of the network is lost. The co-ordinators will work with the client on developing a multi-office programme but will often face problems getting the offices to play along.

The co-ordinator will have no line management role and therefore no formal power and will also often lack any informal personal network in each office. The co-ordinator is probably best regarded as a client relationship manager whose principal task is to discover if the client is unhappy with any particular local office.

Lead office

The lead office is the one which works closely with the client and then, in essence, subcontracts work to others. An audit of a multi-national firm or a multi-national advertising campaign based on a single creative approach will work this way with one of the firm's offices setting the pace and the others providing assistance.

The principal issue is that of transfer pricing – at what rates do the other offices charge the leader for their services? The best solution is usually for the lead office to agree a basis of charging with them at the start of the relationship. However this basis must be mutually accepted – if a local office is a reluctant contributor because it feels it is being cheated on the fees this will very quickly be communicated to staff and the quality of work will suffer.

Central team

The central team or international office which draws staff from local offices but acts alone runs the risk of becoming an élite which has no real local delivery mechanism. Its members can become isolated and resented by the rest of the firm. However such a team can have a very useful marketing function in identifying and building initial relationships with potential international clients. This sort of structure is probably only valid in a newly created network in the days before the local offices get to know more about each other.

For a specific client project an international 'engagement team' can be created for a short time only and is disbanded at the end of the project. They will have local delivery capability as the members are still seen as being from local offices with local affiliations.

Resolving conflict

A crucial role in operating the network is a mechanism for resolving disputes between offices about transfer pricing, staffing who can go after which clients where and so on. In those firms with a holding company type of structure these decisions are best resolved by the chief executive. In the more democratic partner-ship structure some central committee of office managers will need to be created. It is not possible to appoint an individual as co-ordinator and expect him or her to take such decisions as they will always be ignored with an appeal to higher authority.

Network commitment

Firms must show a commitment to the network idea. Successful multi-national or multi-office projects must be written up and circulated via newsletters and so on. Training sessions must include examples of successful co-ordination. Professionals who are successful in winning and running international business should receive very public praise.

BAKER & McKENZIE

In an article in *Canadian Lawyer* (March 1988) entitled 'The World's Biggest Law Firm', Deborah Watson comments on Baker & McKenzie which now has more than 1,500 lawyers in 50 offices across the globe.

Other firms have tried to build an international network but few have accomplished as much as Baker & McKenzie. At the heart of its success are management techniques that entrench the concept of participatory management.

Partners are compensated using a formula that reflects their overall contribution to the firm and the firm is run by annual meetings of all the worldwide partners who vote on crucial issues.

The annual meetings are run in a parliamentary fashion. When it comes time to vote partners simply press a button and the results are instantly displayed on monitors at the front of the room

THE SHANDWICK NETWORK – FORUM 25

The world's biggest single public relations group Shandwick has a very small central management team but encourages the many companies in the group to communicate and work together by fostering an attitude of strong local autonomy within a family. Chairman Peter Gummer says 'the seamless whole is a lot of codswallop. Most business is local business and we want strong, autonomous local players.' The top managers in the group meet four times a year for up to four days (they call it Forum 25 although there are now more than 25 participants). Gummer says the open meetings are there to 'nip problems in the bud'. He claims that the group creates an informal mechanism for communication between the individual business units.

Figure 5.2   Making the network work

Remove technical barriers to communication. Invest in computer/telecommunications networks. Insist on total compatibility of hardware and software.

Communicate best practice between offices.

Create appropriate co-ordination mechanisms.

Have accepted methods of pricing for shared services.

Establish mechanisms for resolving conflicts.

Show commitment to network idea by top management.

THE ONE-FIRM APPROACH

Some professional firms have a quite remarkable ability to present an identical face to clients and staff in various offices around the world. Frequently quoted examples are the strategy consultants McKinsey, the investment bankers Goldman Sachs and the accounting firm Arthur Andersen but it is also true of other accounting, law and executive search firms. Long before the idea or word 'clone' had entered into the common language these firms were cloning themselves.

The one-firm idea runs deep through every aspect of those businesses which adopt it and can bring with it huge advantages. In many ways the one firm concept could be seen as *the key* management idea for multi-office professional firms. It is dealt with here as it is a very useful mechanism for managing growth although it is also true that the one-firm firms tend to be very profitable and well regarded.

At the most obvious level there are common systems in respect of lay-out of documents, computer systems and methods of working. Below the surface there are often established partnership remuneration systems and firm cultures and mythologies that mean a significant reduction in inter-office politics and a very high degree of global thinking on behalf of the firm.

The one-firm firm will almost always have a global system of partner compensation in that each office will produce surplus revenues which go into a common pool for redistribution to partners. Thus an office which is having a bad year can, in effect, be subsidized by others and all partners will benefit from the success of the overall firm. An outstanding individual in an under-performing office can be suitably rewarded from the common pool. An individual who performs poorly in a strong office does not get a free ride as his or her future promotion prospects will be determined by performance.

The firm is not be broken up into a series of cost and profit centres but will aim to have a common pool of professional resources who generate a common flow of income. The transfer of staff between offices is very easy under this approach as is the sharing of information because of the very low cultural barriers.

The single biggest benefit is probably consistency and quality control of work. Sharing common norms and beliefs, the firm's partners will strive for the same quality in all offices. This gives great confidence to clients who will tend to use the firm as a supplier of first choice everywhere in the world. As clients, themselves, become more international the benefits of the one-firm approach will become even more attractive to professionals as it will enable them to offer clients high quality service in all the areas that the client operates.

Working in a one-firm culture can be both stimulating ('like being in the SAS') and suffocating ('like being part of an army of clones'). What is not in doubt is that these firms do produce excellent work for clients. The difference between the real commitment to clients of the one-firm teams and the relative cynicism and compromise exhibited by some professional firms is very marked.

HEWITT ASSOCIATES

In his article on 'The One Firm Approach' in the *Sloan Management Review* (Autumn 1985) Dr David Maister cites Hewitt Associates, the compensation benefits consultants, as an example of a one-firm firm:

At [Hewitt] de-emphasizing status extends to the physical surroundings; everyone from the newest hire to the oldest partner, has the same size office.

On compensation and having many offices Hewitt's managing partner Peter Friedes is quoted: 'We think having no profit centres is a great advantage to us. Other organizations don't realize how much time they waste fighting over allocation of overhead, transfer charges and other mechanisms created by the profit centre mentality. Whenever there are profit centres, cooperation between groups suffers badly.'

On being team payers Frieds says 'If an individual has ego needs that are too high they can be a very disruptive influence. Our work depends on teamwork and cooperation.'

The *Forbes Magazine* article about McKinsey and Co. (October 1987) makes the point about team players:

TEAM PLAYERS

The absence of stars from the McKinsey roster is by no means purely symbolic. The firm is run in a loose, collegial way. The firm's managing partner has limited clout over fellow partners. His power is that of persuasion.

A successful professional firm which is planning to grow could decide to embark on the one-firm route but in doing so it would have to accept that growth, because of recruitment constraints, will be relatively slow (although potentially very profitable) and that the senior professionals would have to remain wholly committed to the idea. Again *Forbes Magazine* in an article (October 1987) states:

ONE FIRM GROWTH

Building on the foothold of sending an English-educated American partner to open an office in London McKinsey continued to dispatch Americans to open local offices but quickly staffed the offices with local hires. Gradually McKinsey's culture, both in the US and abroad, blended until the entire operation became a single organic world unto itself – the consulting equivalent of IBM.

It is essential that a business adopting a one-firm approach has to be wholly committed to it *all*. It is not possible to go *à la carte* and say 'we want an atmosphere of élitist excellence but we will not invest in training.' Firms with many offices which have been built by acquisition cannot simply declare that as of a certain date they will operate on a one-firm basis. If they are determined to make the transition they must accept that it will take many years.

Figure 5.3 Characteristics of the one-firm firm

LOYALTY

There is a strong sense that the firm itself is in some way special and praiseworthy. A strong sense of élitism and a powerful psychological contract between the professional and the firm. Staff tend genuinely to believe their firm is the best.

CLIENT SERVICE

The firm never stops emphasizing that the client comes first. The commitment to the client by most professional staff is real.

MYTHOLOGY

The firm has a very strong value system. In training and in firm socializing (which is extensive and paid for by the firm) endless anecdotes which illustrate 'the way we do things' get retold.

DEMOCRACY

While there will be a marked difference in compensation levels of firm seniors and junior staff there is, almost always, a lack of status symbols and power games like huge offices and three secretaries demanded by senior people. Junior people are NOT made to feel inferior.

PROFESSIONAL DEVELOPMENT

A real, and expensive commitment by the firm to training and to the internal development of the firm's leaders. There will be little senior recruitment. Nearly all directors will have come in at a junior level and have developed with the firm. Recruitment will be given a very high priority.

FIRM DEVELOPMENT

It is almost impossible to have a one-firm approach if growth has been by acquisition or merger. To keep the culture consistent new offices should be opened by partners from an established one.

COMMUNICATION

A major emphasis on, and again investment in, intra-office communication. Conferences, newsletters, internal training and firm sponsored social events will help people get to know each other.

38

MARKETING

How do you present the firm in the market?
How do you sell the firm's services?

I am not sure we go in for marketing – it sounds a bit like touting for business.

Partner, law firm

The marketing of a professional service firm is no different from the marketing of any other product or service. An analysis of the market place must be made and decisions follow on from that:

- Price of services
- Target customers
- Quality of services
- Promotional spending
- Branding

The issue of pricing is dealt with in part VI, Strategy. The other four elements of marketing are discussed below.

TARGET CUSTOMERS

The people likely to buy a professional service fall broadly into the two groups of regular users and one-off users.

Regular users of professionals

The regular users have an ongoing requirement for professional services and will seek to recruit full-time employees or to have relationships with external firms to provide the necessary help. The regular users are, in effect, faced with a make or buy decision in that they can either directly employ professionals with the necessary skills to carry out a particular service within their own company or they can sub-contract out to a specialist firm.

For small and medium-sized companies simple economics usually dictate that it makes more sense not to have in-house lawyers, advertising executives, public relations people and so on. For very large firms it is more a matter of management philosophy which dictates which route they take to get the best service. Often they will choose a hybrid approach with an in-house department but contracting out certain services.

To reach the regular users a very targeted, highly customer-specific approach is applicable. Most regular users will already have professional firms in place. These existing professionals can be identified. A named individual who is the key decision-maker inside the target company can be located. Winning business from these potential clients is very much a matter of keeping in touch with them and waiting either for the existing relationship to break down or for the workload to expand to a level which justifys another contractor alongside the first.

A special group of regular users are firms who through growth or a change of management philosophy decide to use external professionals *without* any incumbent firm in place. The appointment of a new chief executive who is known to favour contracting out represents a key opportunity. A good example of this has been the UK clearing banks who tended to do everything in-house in line with long-established corporate policy. In many cases a radical re-examination of costs has led to a huge reduction in head office headcount in favour of contractors – catering, public relations, legal services, personnel management and even economics departments have been closed and their functions contracted out.

Being invited to join so-called pitch lists or beauty parades is a key element in reaching potential regular users who will tend to be influenced by the firm's reputation and size when selecting potential candidates.

One-off users of professionals

The one-off users seek professional help for specific projects or in times of crisis – lawyers to help when a writ arrives, architects for a new building, designers for a one-off corporate brochure. These people or organizations will be less sophisticated in their use of professionals, more price-sensitive and more concerned with the professionals' skills in respect of the particular job than their reputation as a firm.

Positioning the firm to this group will require a reasonably high profile, perhaps achieved though advertising. Firms will also do well if they can show a price list approach so that unsophisticated clients will quickly see what they will get for their money.

QUALITY OF SERVICE

A firm must decide just how good it wants its work to be (and therefore how expensive) given the evidence of its clients' requirements.

Professional firms can do work for clients which clients are unable to do because they do not know how – this might be called the *task force* service. Alternatively firms can do work which the client could ask its own staff to undertake but decides not to – this is the *substitution* approach. The creation of a television advertising campaign for a food manufacturer by an agency is a task force service. Providing a simple telephone-answering public relations function would be substitution.

Whatever the firm is offering the *marketing* decision it must make is about quality which is linked to price. In the crudest terms does the client want it cheap and cheerful or expensive and near perfect? The main decision is whether the quality implied in the marketing effort can actually be delivered at the price chosen. Is the quality level chosen clearly understood by clients and staff?

In differentiating themselves from their competitors professional firms must try to explain to clients how the quality/price relationship works, as there is always a risk that clients will select the lowest cost professional firm without fully realizing what extra benefits they would get from a high-cost operator.

PROMOTION

Many professional firms feel uncomfortable with the idea of promoting themselves and their services. Some feel it is an unprofessional thing to do. In England there was much soul-searching when lawyers and accountants were allowed to advertise. However in a market where clients spread their net wide when looking for new professionals some form of profile-raising promotion is critical. Getting the firm known (and respected) is important both for recruitment and winning clients.

If a firm were in the happy position of being quite confident of finding quality staff and winning all clients by word of mouth alone then it could avoid any promotional expenditure and effort.

For most firms, however, some form of promotion is very desirable and there are four main methods available to professional firms:

- Conference appearances
- Signed articles
- Public relations
- Advertising

Conferences

Appearances on conference platforms can provide excellent marketing opportunities for professional service firms. A senior firm member who performs well will be seen to have a high level of expertise in a subject and will often be addressing an audience many of whom are potential customers. It generally contributes to building awareness and positioning the business. The conference circuit is a self-reinforcing system where most speakers are selected following a successful appearance on another conference platform. The best way of breaking in is by direct approaches to conference organizers with an offer of a well-thought out session relevant to their conference subject. For example an accountancy firm might offer to run a session for a transport conference on the economics of truck fleets or it might offer a presentation on the valuation of brands for a conference of marketing directors.

Articles

Signed articles in magazines and newspapers written by members of the firm on relevant professional issues are another excellent way of putting the name in front of potential clients.

By and large the smaller and more specialist a publication the more likely it is to welcome contributions. However the best media are those which are read specifically by clients. For a management consultant, for example, a signed article in *The Grocer* on cost control techniques in supermarkets is of far more value in reaching clients than the same piece in *Management Consulting*.

Public relations

In professional firms PR is mainly aimed at raising the profile of the firm and its professionals as experts in their field. In particular it will involve getting members of the firm used as expert pundits.

Stockbrokers have long used their economists and more recently their sector specialist analysts as expert sources for newspapers, radio and television. A close symbiotic relationship has grown up between the financial journalists and the economists and analysts as the journalists need expert with impartial opinions to support their stories. Just after the 'Big-Bang' in London certain firms paid their economists spot bonuses for being interviewed in the media if the firm received a credit as their employer.

Advertising

This is of particular value to those firms who seek one-off clients and project work where salience of the firm is a key factor in being appointed. However, advertising involves a fixed, minimum cost and is probably only viable where a firm is large enough for that cost to be spread across the fee-earning potential of a large number of professionals so that the cost per professional is low.

A special form of advertising which can have great benefits with clients is recruitment advertising for the firm. The appointments advertisements are quite widely read by executives in many firms partly to see what might be available for them and partly to check their own progress in terms of salaries and benefits. If the firm strongly brands its own job advertisements and stresses its search for quality people this can help in raising its profile in the business community.

BRANDING

A brand tells a consumer what to expect. It conveys messages about a product's quality and value. A professional brand implies that the firm's name conveys important messages to potential clients and staff and helps them understand the firm's values and qualities. And a strong professional brand can help a firm win clients who need the reassurance that the intangible professional services will be carried out by a firm with a good track record. The marketing service group WPP went so far as to investigate having a financial value placed on its main brands, the advertising agencies J. Walter Thompson and Ogilvy & Mather.

In general most of the leading professional brands – Arthur Andersen, Ernst & Young, Price Waterhouse and so on simply convey the idea of large and established without leading to the sort of carefully targeted and differentiated message of consumer brands. Ask most people to describe the difference between the brand personalities of Coca Cola and Pepsi Cola, McDonalds and Burger King or Miller and Budweiser and they will try to give you an answer. The brand messages are universal. The products may be very similar but the personalities are different. Ask the same question about professional service firms and a much more cloudy picture emerges. People are more conditioned by personal experience and word of mouth. When people talk about the qualities of Ernst & Young or Clifford Chance they are, usually, describing the people from those firms they know or have worked with.

For the professional firm the brand is communicated through many relatively passive ways such as through corporate identity, letterheads, office reception area, the way its staff dress, public documents, presentation techniques and so on. Firms can also actively promote a brand by advertising and sponsorship but these usually simply raise brand awareness. It can be hard to communicate a brand personality.

As professional firms get larger and more international having a recognized name or brand will be helpful in being invited to present to potential clients and in recruiting the best staff. But firms must guard their brand and good name very carefully and ensure that the name and any corporate identity is not used in the wrong way which could damage the overall image.

39

NEW BUSINESS

How do you manage the process of winning new business?

There is nothing more exciting than pitching for new business. To be honest I almost don't care what it costs. I just love to win. We all do.

Creative Director, advertising agency

If marketing, as described above, is all about generating new business opportunities then this chapter is about how to convert these opportunities into new client assignments.

The search for new business can be a hugely expensive exercise for most professional firms although often they do not properly identify all the costs involved. Apart from the obvious investment in research and the physical production of new business presentations there is usually a very considerable investment of senior management time.

New business pitches can be very costly, particularly in advertising. *The New York Times* (4 Feb 1991) estimated some new business efforts may cost an agency up to $250,000. The paper cites the specific examples of Chiat/Day which spent $1 million on out of pocket expenses to win the Nissan account worth $150 million in annual billings and of the Levine, Huntley, Schmidt & Beaver agency which spent $300,000 and failed to win the $50 million MCI Communications account.

PITCH FEES

With margins in profesional firms under pressure some are now asking clients to reimburse them for some of the costs of undertaking new business presentations. The *Wall Street Journal* (22 February 1989) reported:

In advertising the speculative creative pitch has been a fact of life for years. Now however as agency margins are squeezed by client pressure some industry leaders are starting to speak out perhaps out of sheer frustration.

The *New York Times* reported (4 Feb 1991) that Volvo had paid three shortlisted agencies $15,000 each to prepare their final presentations.

By far the most important aspect of new business is to focus resources on trying to win only those assignments that are *really* right for the firm. Chasing after everything will not only result in a very low success rate but may also cause the firm to win business it does not really want. The use of the firm's resources to attempt to win new business is an important decision. Figure 5.4 presents a framework for following a disciplined approach to new business.

Increasingly potential clients whether they are seeking advertising, public relations, legal advice, accountancy or architects invite a number of competitors to make a formal presentation. Some firms, particularly in advertising, will spend huge sums on slides, films and props. Some legal firms still just turn up and chat. Even where the end product of a new business process is not a formal presentation, firms should still take the process seriously and go through the steps shown below and detailed in the following pages.

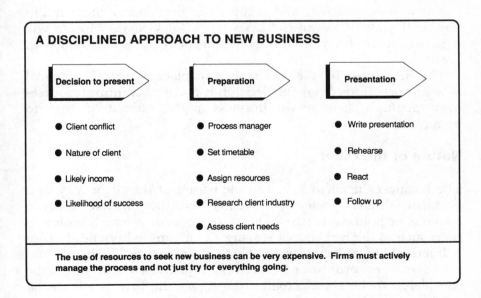

A DISCIPLINED APPROACH TO NEW BUSINESS

Decision to present	Preparation	Presentation
● Client conflict	● Process manager	● Write presentation
● Nature of client	● Set timetable	● Rehearse
● Likely income	● Assign resources	● React
● Likelihood of success	● Research client industry	● Follow up
	● Assess client needs	

The use of resources to seek new business can be very expensive. Firms must actively manage the process and not just try for everything going.

Figure 5.4

DECISION TO PRESENT

A scatter-gun approach of half-heartedly pitching for every potential client around will always fail. Focused firms will come across as far more impressive during presentations and will win more of those highly desirable clients which fit with the firm's strategy and which will be more profitable. The less desirable clients (who may be very small or bad payers) will usually not be targeted by the more focused competing professionals. The scatter-gun approach firm will be more likely to win them resulting in a client register of potentially unprofitable accounts.

It is easy to present a picture of bustling activity with several new business pitches on at any one time which, in fact, conceals a very unsuccessful new business programme.

Client conflicts

Can the client be served even if the business is won? Are there client conflicts? Internal politics can sometimes result in an individual director making a huge effort to win a piece of business without recognizing that it will cause problems with other clients. Most people recognize that Coca-Cola and Pepsi-Cola are in head-to-head competition and it would be very difficult for a professional firm to serve both. It is easy for people to overlook the fact that a certain fast food restaurant is owned by a brewer and that your existing, and competing, beer brand client might object. If your offices in the USA work for General Motors will it be acceptable for your offices in Europe to pitch for, and win, Ford?

The firm must have a mechanism in place to vet *all* potential new business leads *before* the decision is taken to commit resources to attracting a client whose business might, ultimately, have to be refused.

Nature of the client

The business the client is in and the nature of the client may be a problem. Many professional firms will not handle tobacco business or political parties. There are frequently other considerations such as the real cost of serving a company whose head office is hundreds of miles away or which is known to be chaotic and a bad user of professional services. Equally a client might be considered to be a bad credit risk. Again the firm needs to vet opportunities before any decision to commit resources and to communicate clearly to its staff what sort of clients it is seeking.

Likely income

The size of the account and the likely income from it are also critical. Accounts that are too small or too large may not fit the professional firm's own economics. Given the size and nature of the work required by the client – does the firm have the resources to serve the client? If additional recruitment is required, would that be possible in time?

Likelihood of success

Finally how likely is the firm to win in a competitive pitch for new business? Is the firm on the pitch list as a real contender or is it just there to make up the numbers? Is the client just trying to shake up the incumbent or really looking for change? How many other firms are on the short-list? A self-confident professional firm will only pitch to those clients where it really has a very good chance of being appointed.

A structured decision

All this adds up to the fact that the decision to pursue a particular piece of new business is of sufficient importance to be taken by the board or management committee of the firm. Having decided to go for it sufficient resources must be made available and complete commitment ensured. A formal system should be in place through which all potential new business leads are processed.

PREPARATION

The key skill of pitching is to make sure that it really will be all right on the night. This involves a high degree of planning. Again this comes back to the point that having decided to pitch all the necessary resources should be brought to bear to attempt to ensure victory. Despite the high cost of undertaking a major new business project winning four out of five will make the effective cost of new business far lower than winning one out of five with only a small budget for each. Winning a pitch or a beauty parade is more to do with the preparation than the actual performance at the presentation.

Process manager

Pitching for new business is a project in itself. One individual should be given clear responsibility for making everything happen on time and with a minimum cost. This will not necessarily be the person who leads the new business team or actually presents to the prospective client but he or she will be in charge of the process of making the presentation. On balance there are many arguments to say that the process manager should *not* be the team leader as the team leader should concentrate on content (what the client needs to hear) rather than process (the mechanism by which the client hears it). The ideal process manager will understand the firm and its workings and know how to get things done.

All members of the team must be aware of the process manager's role and all should accept that if the slides are late or the taxis do not turn up it will be the process manager who is to blame. Without a process manager it will always be unclear who is responsible for the details.

Being a process manager is a *role* taken on by one of the firm's professionals for the duration of the particular new business project. It is not a *job* within the firm. Even where a firm has a new business director this individual should not be the process manager for all new business projects as this would get in the way of his or her normal client development work and would prevent other firm members from getting new business experience.

Timetable

The first job of the process manager and the new business team leader is to agree, with the client, the date *and circumstances* of the new business presentation. It is important to understand fully the clients expectations in terms of:

- How long the presentation will last
- How many firm members are expected to attend
- Who will be there from the client
- Will the firm have to present credentials (i.e. past work etc.)
- Will the presentation just focus on the client issues or is a more general discussion expected?
- What media are acceptable to both the firm and the client – overheads, 35 mm slides, videos, computer graphics and so on. What does the client advise?

Clients must be consulted about presentations to make them part of the new business process. In most cases there will be an executive on the client side who has been given the job of making the various presentations a success in the sense of ensuring that they address the clients's issues and run to time. The firm's process manager should attempt to contact this person and to work together, *with* them, to ensure that the client's needs are met.

NO SLIDE SHOW

A London advertising agency created a complex new business presentation which it was planning to show to the client in the form of a bound book and hand-held charts. The agency chairman insisted, at the last minute, that the whole thing be redone onto 35 mm slides at a cost of more than £5,000 after numerous changes had been made. On arriving for the presentation they found that not only did the client not own a slide projector but that the client's chairman intensely disliked being shown slides as he objected to sitting in a darkened room.

Having agreed a timetable the process manager should produce a detailed activity plan working back from the agreed date of the presentation, showing what must be achieved by when and laying out clearly the responsibilities of the members of the new business team.

Resources

If the firm takes new business seriously it will assign resources to the team organizing the pitch, such as desk-top publishing time, secretarial support and research time. Equally important is that the professionals working on the project inform the members of any other team they are working on and that they are allowed to schedule a proper amount of time. The process manager and the new business team leader must fight their corner and ensure that all the resources required are made available to them.

A common problem is that a director on an existing client project will resist allowing one of his or her executives to work on new business on the grounds that the current project is real and fee-earning, while new business may or may not be successful.

Research the client industry

Whatever the professional areas of the firm, law, accountancy, advertising and so on it will always help the credibility of the new business effort if the team learns something about the prospective client's industry and reflects this in the presentation. The client will be facing certain issues in its business which may be relevant to the firm's ideas. Food manufacturers face product contamination, detergent manufacturers must deal with green issues, and all organizations which supply supermarkets must deal with the domination of the market by a few large companies. The new business team should read back issues of the client's own trade papers and magazines and should obtain research reports on the client's industry. The client, itself, will often supply all this information.

Assess the client's needs

The firm should not take the client's brief at face value. The firm should question the client as to what is really required by way of professional services, what issues should really be addressed at the new business presentation, and what job does the client really want the firm to do?

If possible the new business team should attempt to interview client executives before any presentation to get a better idea about the client's real needs. Very often the brief written to instruct professional firms will fail to get to the heart of the matter and the firm which wishes to increase the chances of success will invest some time in finding out what the real issues are. Firms should suggest to prospective clients that their new business team should visit client offices and/or production plants and should meet client personnel, even the client's own suppliers and customers, in order to help the firm prepare for the presentation.

Wherever possible the firm should create a team spirit with the client before any formal presentation, so that client executives will already be supporters of the firm before the decision is made.

KNOW THE CLIENT

One international management consultancy specializing in radical corporate restructuring sometimes researches a potential client for months and then presents to the client's board a 'raider's perspective' showing how the company might appear to a corporate predator. A nervous management will often feel it is better to have such formidable skills and insights on its own side and to make changes rather than risk a potential aggressor armed with a similar insight into its weaknesses.

PRESENTATION

The meeting with the client, after which the decision to appoint the firm will be made, can take a wide range of forms from an informal chat to an orchestrated audio-visual show. It will partly depend on the profession, partly on the personality of the firm and partly on the client. Increasingly clients are looking for a formal presentation when appointing professional advisers.

Create presentation

In actually presenting to the client many firms continue to make the mistake of spending too much time talking about themselves and too little on addressing the client's problems and opportunities. The credentials presentation extolling the virtues of the firm and giving confidence in its ability to handle the work should, ideally, be done quite separately from the new business pitch. If it is to be at the same meeting it should be done last and not first.

There is no ideal structure for a new business presentation but firms should probably adopt a structure similar to that shown in figure 5.5 – unless there are powerful reasons to change it because of specific client issues. Above all clients must be left feeling that the firm understands their problem and their business and that the firm's teams have the right set of skills to meet the client's needs. Firms must be specific rather than general. From the client's perspective there is nothing more tedious than spending a day sitting through four presentations all of which talk in general terms about big issues. What brings a meeting alive is when a professional firm starts talking about how it would address a very specific client problem (or opportunity).

Rehearse

Firms should spend far more time on the content of their presentations than on the performance. However, if the format is complex, using a variety of slides, videos and so on then the team should run through at least once to avoid disasters. On a simple logistical point the process manager must ensure that all the necessary things to make the presentation work, such as slide projectors, arrive in the right place at the right time.

Beware of the sort of presentations which are so beautifully scripted and polished that clients feel almost excluded and do not become involved.

Figure 5.5 Structure of presentation

THE CHALLENGE

'The professional problem we are here to help you solve'.

The firm shows it understands what the client wants.

TODAY'S AGENDA

'How we expect this meeting to go.'

Let the client know the structure of the presentation.

YOUR MARKET/ENVIRONMENT

'Issues faced by you and your competitors relevant to the professional services under consideration.'

The firm shows it understands the background.

YOUR COMPANY

'What we understand about you, again, relevant to the professional services under consideration.'

The firm shows it understands the client.

PROFESSIONAL OBJECTIVES

'What will be achieved by the professional relationship.'

The firm shows what it will try to achieve.

PROFESSIONAL ACTIVITIES

'The suggested programme of activity and budget.'

The firm explains the specific work the client will get for the money. Could use case histories of other, similar projects.

PROFESSIONAL RELATIONSHIP

'How we will work together.'

The structure of the firm's team and suggested working relationship with client executives. i.e. who will do what.

THE FIRMS CREDENTIALS

'Who we are and why we can do the job.'

Examples of past work, history of the firm, testimonials etc.

React during the presentation

A good new business presentation will always be a dialogue rather than a monologue. The client executives must be made to feel involved and more than just asking questions should be encouraged to discuss the firm's ideas as to what are the professional issues and how the professional programme should be structured. The firm's team leader must be prepared to think on his or her feet and to offer professional advice on issues which emerge during the meeting. The presentation must almost be a problem solving meeting. The clients should enjoy it and should be made to feel that the professional relationship has already started and that the meeting is a typical example of what will follow.

Follow-up

After the presentation immediate follow-up is essential. The actual decision on which firm to appoint is often not taken for a day or two. If specific questions were asked and not answered during the presentation then answers should be given, in writing, and sent round to the client. If the dialogue in the presentation generated an idea which would be relevant to the professional programme that idea should be followed up. If discussions suggested a change in the suggested timetable or team structure these changes should be made and the client given copies.

In those instances where the firm is successful the follow-up to the presentation will lead directly into the first start-up meetings on the account. In some ways firms should behave throughout the presentation process as if they had already been appointed and the whole exercise was merely part of clarifying the basis of the relationship.

EXISTING CLIENTS

Potentially the best source of new business is to encourage increased spending by existing clients. The reasons this is an attractive source of additional revenue are:

- The marketing costs associated with winning the additional work are likely to be much lower than with new clients with less spent on research, new business presentations and so on

- The firm already knows how the client works and will understand its market-place. This reduces the amount of time required to get up to speed. The firm's team will be able to spend more time on the actual client assignment

- Terms of trade and payment mechanisms will already have been established, significantly reducing the likelihood of arguments over the bill and late payment or even non-payment

- The client is more likely to be happy with a relatively higher proportion of junior people on the team as it will already have confidence in the firm's quality of work and will be easily able to access senior firm members if necessary. This will help create a lower cost structure while still keeping the client happy.

Unfortunately in most professional firms winning additional business from existing clients carries only a fraction of the kudos and rewards of winning new ones.

NEW BUSINESS PASSION

One London advertising agency sends a case of champagne to all those members of staff involved in winning a new account, in addition to cash bonuses for the more senior executives. As a result there is great pressure to become involved in new business work while existing clients are felt to come second.

The major problem for management is that winning new business is simply exciting. People like being part of a race. To get a better balance between chasing new clients and developing existing ones management must take active steps to promote the idea that developing existing clients is important.

Existing client development

One initiative is to budget actively for existing client development as well as for new business. Account managers should be encouraged to get their teams thinking along client development lines. This should not be done indiscriminately for all clients. A short-list of those with real development possibilities must be created by the firm's senior people.

Existing clients likely to develop further will include:

- Those in fast-growing industries or those which are rapidly gaining market share

- Those where management philosophy has recently changed to a more favourable view of contracting out work

- Those known to have several competing professional advisors who might be persuaded to rationalize their relationships

Once certain clients have been targeted a clear programme of client development should be followed. This will include:

- Getting to know senior client executives through both social and professional opportunities

- Mapping out and understanding the client firm. This might even be done formally by asking the client team to make a presentation to the firm's senior management about their client and its industry

- Taking part in conferences and seminars specific to the client's own industry

- Offer to do initial work on relevant business problems and opportunities at no cost to the client. Demonstrate that the firm could add value in these areas if asked

These client development activities should be recorded on time sheets and any expenditure costed to the specific existing client development budget as opposed to new business in general.

It might be argued that clients will find this sort of targeting unappealing and feel hunted. In reality they should welcome it as long as the firm does not become too intrusive. At the heart of a successful professional relationship is the notion that the firm does provide value for money over and above its fees. It could be regarded as a valuable bonus if the firm can find other ways to add value to the client's business by providing more services.

PART VI

STRATEGY

Where to take the firm, and how to operate it in the future?

I have to admit that planning for the future does not come easily to us. We spend so much time on just getting the job done that we barely think about what the firm might look like in five years.

Chairman, market research company

The main strategy questions for the owners and managers of professional service firms are concerned with what sort of services will be most valuable to customers in the future, how to manage the firm to provide those services profitably and how to manage growth. To answer these questions they must develop a very clear idea of where the market is going, where the firm actually is now and what are the constraints on future development. They must then develop an attractive service offering to clients and a business plan which is consistent with delivering this offering.

Strategy is also about change. How to react to expected changes in the firm's environment. How to position the firm to gain maximum advantage from those changes. The implementation of a strategy requires moving the firm from where it is now to where it wants to be. In businesses where people are far more important than plant and machinery to make those moves can be very difficult.

The first issue to consider is that of the probable development of the needs of *customers* in the market place. Is the market growing and if so how fast? Are there attractive and profitable niches? The next issue is the *competitors*. Those already in the firm's own industry sector and those who could become competitors from somewhere else. How are competitors likely to behave? What are the long term prospects for industry–specific resources – for professional service firms this means principally how easy will it be to find suitable people? The third issue is the *company* itself. What are the goals of its owners and managers? What are its skills and resources? Does it have particular strengths or weaknesses? Are there any major constraints on growth?

Having considered these factors it is then necessary to define clearly what the *service offering* of the firm will be. This should be something which customers will want in the future and which the firm will be able to provide more effectively than competitors. This will be in part conditioned by the skills and aspirations of the firm's senior managers as well as by the actual work and positioning of the firm today.

Finally the appropriate *business plan* to deliver this service offering product must be drawn up and put into effect. This will identify the resources required and describe how those resources are to be managed.

In simple terms all the analysis of customers, competitors and the company itself is directed at finding what sort of business the firm should become. The strategy is simply a statement of that desired position. The strategic planning process describes how the firm will get from where it is to where it wants to be. There are many models for formulating corporate strategy; in fact there are probably hundreds of different ways of trying to answer the basic question of where should we take the business. Part VI describes a model which should be useful to managers of professional firms. The model is based on the idea that a successful strategy is aimed at achieving a sustainable differentiation from competitors by

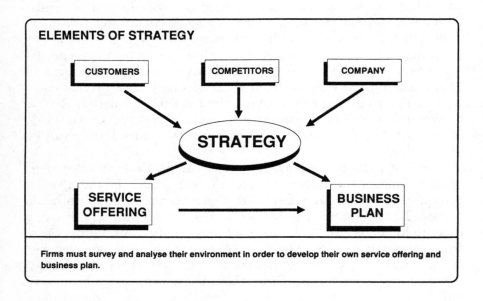

ELEMENTS OF STRATEGY

CUSTOMERS   COMPETITORS   COMPANY

STRATEGY

SERVICE OFFERING   **BUSINESS PLAN**

Firms must survey and analyse their environment in order to develop their own service offering and business plan.

Figure 6.1

finding services and ways of delivering those services that clients are prepared to pay for and pay enough to give the firm a good profit.

The suggested model is shown in figure 6.1. The five elements of the model are:

- Customers – the market place for the firm

- Competitors – the industry the firm is in

- The company – the firm's own goals, skills and resources

- The service offering – the nature of the service(s) the firm offers

- The business plan – the way the firm delivers its services

The strategists of the firm must analyse and understand the first three elements – the customers, the competitors and their own company. They must then take consistent decisions about the service offering and the business plan. For example consider a company whose business is producing annual reports on behalf of clients:

The *customers* could be big, rich, blue-chip international companies or they could be small, price-sensitive new businesses. Both market segments could offer the firm profitable business. The market could be growing as more companies seek external help in producing reports or it could be shrinking as new technology allows them to do the work in-house. More customers could be looking for turnkey services where the report-producing company manages every aspect of the process or they could be looking for a design-only involvement using existing printing, photography and writing contacts.

The main *competitors* will be other specialist annual report companies but there will also be general design firms who have branched out into reports and printing firms who are trying to get more business for their production facilities by offering a report designing service. There will also, potentially, be advertising agencies, public relations consultants and even accountants who could argue that a report would benefit from their specialist skills and that they could manage the whole process. The different types of competitor will present different types of threat. Some will compete on price and others might compete on creativity by offering the services of internationally acclaimed designers.

The *company* might be run by entrepreneurial designers who wish to maximize their own income but enjoy the activity of actually creating reports or it might be owned by shareholders seeking to maximize the value of their investment. It might already have state-of-the-art technology or it might be faced with major investment decisions. Its people may be mainly skilled in design or they could be good at project management.

The *service offering* could be very up-scale: 'we are the best in the world' or very price-conscious 'we know how to bring your report in on budget'. It could be a turnkey service (where the firm takes the risk of subcontracting various jobs like printing but benefits from increased management fees) or it could be a design-only service where the firm simply charges for its own efforts.

The *business plan* would identify the type of people the firm will need. If it is decided that the service offering is to be low-cost computer-generated text and graphics, the firm will need to have suitably skilled computer operators and must invest in the right technology and low-cost premises. If the service offering aims at being top-of-the-market, with no-expense-spared, the firm will have to ensure its operating culture places a high emphasis on absolute quality of work and that it has design people with top reputations.

40

CUSTOMERS – THE MARKET-PLACE

Who are your customers? What do (and will) they want?

Our business is always changing. We have to know what sort of service our clients will need next year so we can make sure we have the right people to do it.

Executive search consultant

An understanding of the needs, behaviour and likely spending of clients and potential clients is fundamental to a firm's strategy. Clients will only pay for what they want and need. What they want and need in two years time may be very different from the position today. Understanding clients will help the firm make its plans.

The first place to start is with existing clients. Why do they use the service, why did they select the firm and not the competition? What do they like and loathe about the firm? All this information should be available as a by-product of the normal process of client relations but should be considered in the context of strategic analysis and not just client service. Feedback from clients about the conduct or quality of the service should lead to immediate changes in the way the firm operates. Information from clients about the way they see *their* business going in the future and the sort of professional services they expect to need should be used by the firm to plan its own future.

The total spending of all the clients with the firm itself and with all its competitors is the total market-place. A firm needs to have some understanding of what this total looks like and what sort of share it currently has and might aspire to.

MARKET DEFINITIONS

To arrive at an exact definition of the market-place of any professional firm is virtually impossible. The degree of overlap of one type of service with another and the potential for services to be wholly or partially carried out in-house by clients means that exact definitions are meaningless. In broad terms, however, it is possible to assess the total size of the potential pool of income available to a firm and to analyse the future direction of this market.

In many cases trade associations and specialist magazines undertake the analysis of the total market and produce league tables of the leading firm ranked by size of income, head-count and so on (the main public league tables for professional firms in the UK and USA appear in the appendix). Assessing market shares for professional firms is particularly difficult because of definition problems. Providing league tables for the top ten law firms or merchant banks involved in hostile takeovers or the ranking of advertising agencies by billings numbers is relatively easy, but to claim a market share is much more difficult and also less meaningful.

A danger of basing any strategic decisions on such standard market definitions and competitor tables is that such market definitions may be useless to the firm. To take an extreme example, a legal firm specializing in copyright law might only appear as number 30 in a league table of law firms with a market share of only one per cent in terms of total fees. In reality, of course, much of the work done by the other firms would be well outside the specialist's chosen market. If the specialist has, in reality, a 25 per cent share of its own chosen market its growth prospects in that market (given client conflict and competitive reaction) might be very limited.

In this example it is obvious that a more focused market definition must be used (often researched by the firm itself) but many professional firms still plan their future without properly answering the question: exactly which market are we in?

To take another example, an advertising agency in a provincial city might have a one per cent share of the national market but a 30 per cent share of its local market. If that agency decides it is going to seek business in the national market it should do its analysis on that basis but clearly recognize in its planning that it must be resourced as a national player with the implications for communications and possible additional offices.

MARKET SEGMENTATION

There are three main axes of definition along which the markets of professional firms can be described (as shown in figure 6.2):

- Geography
- Price
- Service focus

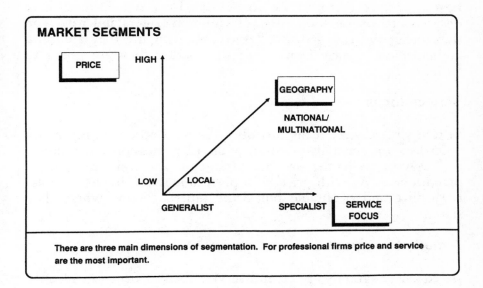

Figure 6.2

Geography

It is often argued that a national market is simply an aggregate of all the local markets. In most professional services it is certainly true that the firm needs to be local to its clients to deliver the service but this localness can be achieved relatively easily by having small satellite offices or simply putting staff up in hotels. Increasingly professional services' markets are becoming national and international as technology makes communications so much easier.

As a general rule *no* professional firms, even very small local ones, should consider the geographical dimension to be too much of a limiting factor. The exact definition of the service they offer, the price and quality are more likely to be the most useful criteria for market definitions. Some firms however might choose to make a virtue out of being local or national and should organize themselves accordingly.

Price

In terms of price there is nearly always a close relationship with cost. Except for those rare occasions when a firm can fool the market by charging high prices for a low cost service, firms will have to accept there are no free rides. They will have to base decisions partly on the desires of senior managers and partly on their belief as to what sort of price/cost structure they are good at managing, which segment of the market they are going to be in.

Service focus

In terms of service, firms broadly have to choose between being specialists or generalists within a broad professional definition, for example whether to be consultant surgeons or general practitioners. As with price both positionings can be very viable, rewarding and profitable but firms must be clear where they stand.

A market segment

Based on geography, price and service focus a firm can identify a market segment which looks accessible and attractive. A law firm could, for example, decide to focus on clients based in London who were price-insensitive and who wanted specialized legal work in family law (divorce etc.). This would have implications for every aspect of the way the firm did business.

In selecting a segment as a target firms should not overlook adjacent segments and should certainly try to form a view as to the prospects for growth and profitability of the various segments which they *could* serve. Firms must be very clear, however, that to move from their current segment into another, potentially more attractive one, is a complex task. They will often find that many other firms have also targeted an attractive market segment for growth and that they will always be a weaker competitor than firms already established in that segment. To continue the above example, a law firm which already specialized in serving up-scale private clients in tax- and estate-planning matters, and which already had prestige offices, would find it much easier to move into the exclusive family law market segment than would a generalist law firm which was, currently, doing mostly criminal work.

A market niche

A market segment is not the same thing as a market niche. A segment is a sub-section of the overall market which can be defined within reasonably clear boundaries – many firms can occupy a segment. A niche is a positioning unique to a firm which has found a defensible and attractive position in a segment.

In many professional firms the niche position is often gained by one or two star practitioners within a firm. A highly creative advertising agency, a technically outstanding tax law firm or a PR agency that really has influence with the Sunday papers is often no more than a statement about one or two individuals. Clients seeking that skill can only access it via the firm.

It follows from this that large firms will find it hard to exploit niche positions although individuals within those firms can do so easily. Indeed the most successful professional firms are those where all the senior players have carved out niches for themselves in the market.

CUSTOMER NEEDS

Segmenting the market, as described above, is about finding a language to describe who your clients are and might be. Having identified a target group the firm must understand what those customers are going to want and what that implies about the size and likely development of the market. For example, a large firm of estate agents needs to take a view about the future volume of house sales. If high interest rates and a slow economy imply that volume will drop, it must assume either that its own firm will contract or that it will stay static (or even grow) by taking market share from competitors. Either course of action requires specific changes to the business plan – in the one case to reduce the cost base by firing people and closing branches, in the other by targeting weaker competitors to attack. If a firm of lawyers specializing in merger and acquisition work believes that a change of government will lead to a marked upswing in M&A activity it must plan for recruitment and expansion if it wishes to grow with or faster than a growing market.

'Megatrends'

Identification of major trends within a professional market such as the abolition of the fixed commission system and the ending of the separation between market-makers and brokers in stockbroking (the so-called Big Bang); the breakdown of the commission system in advertising and the ending of some restrictive practices in the British legal system are important in shaping a firm's strategy. However these big picture factors are visible to all firms and should be reflected in everyone's planning. A strategy based purely on the big-picture issues will look just like everyone else's.

The onset of 1992 in Europe (the date of the harmonization of trade practices in the European Community) has led to wholesale reorganization of many professional firms and to a rush by most of them to develop 1992 products for their customers. Again this is all well and good but unfortunately everyone is doing it.

Specific customer needs

Although firms have to be aware of and take a view on the impact of megatrends it is equally important that they focus on the more subtle developments in customer requirements which might help them to create a service with a clear distinction from the competition.

Formal interviews with current and potential clients must be conducted regularly (at least once a year) to understand how changes in their business are affecting their requirements for professional services. The new business brochures of competitors, particularly new start-up firms and the comments of the trade press, should be studied for evidence of the development of new types of service. Large firms often commission independent market research to gain a better understanding of where their customers are going. Firms should also experiment with new service products to see if they do meet an emerging client need.

EXPERIMENTAL PRODUCTS

A UK public relations consultancy developed a product to provide clients with crisis PR – a pre-planned, quick response in the case of an industrial dispute, an accident, food contamination and so on. The consultancy found that many companies, even those with large internal public relations staffs, felt vulnerable in this area and were very willing to pay fees for an external organization to help them be prepared.

The consultancy launched the crisis management product as a hunch but in trying it with a few customers discovered a genuine client need. As an additional bonus the consultancy was able to make the product using staff resources who were able to claim much higher fee levels than if they had been engaged in other types of PR work.

The example demonstrates a product experiment which un-covered a client need but, arguably, that same need could have been identified from client interviews and a general awareness of the increased sensitivity of companies with the development of intense and rapid media coverage of bad-news events.

The needs of a firm's customers define its market. Most professionals are reasonably good at listening to their client and understanding their immediate requirements – which are reflected in the professional service provided. To be successful in building their firms for the future professionals must also anticipate clients' future needs and seek to build a firm which will be better at meeting those needs than the competition. They must understand how different groups of customers make up the total market and must try to understand the requirements of these different groups.

41

COMPETITORS – THE PROFESSION

What sort of competitors does your firm face?

It would be wrong to say we are always looking over our shoulders at the opposition but we often learn from them in terms of new trends or new things that clients want.

Director, public relations consultancy

This chapter concentrates on how the firm's competitors approach doing business and how they may react in the future.

In developing a strategy to find a defensible competitive advantage, a firm must know how its competitors will react to things it does. It is no use a firm identifying a perfect market niche if competitors are far better able to serve those target clients than it is. One of the biggest dangers in professional firms is a level of complacency and a naive belief that 'we know all about our competitors and anyway there's quite enough business to go round'. The reality is that the fondly-held beliefs about competitors may prove to be badly out of date and with the low and decreasing barriers to entry into most professional areas competition can be intense. In Europe, for example, professional firms may have not even considered the possibility of competitors from different countries seeking to take their clients. In reality that is now very possible. A formal process of competitor analysis will almost always bring benefits to a firm in thinking about its own future. As with other elements of strategy formulation the assessment of competitors starts with a list of questions:

- How inherently profitable is the firm's industry or profession? Is that level of general profitability likely to go up or down?

- If the firm has a well defined niche are competitors going to attack it?

- If the firm's industry is one where competition is, essentially, based on service, what are the chances that someone will start to compete on price alone? Will it lead to a price war?

PROFESSION PROFITABILITY

Within an overall industry profitability can vary considerably by sector and the inherent profitability of a sector will change over time. Those businesses offering a near commodity product often find themselves forced by competition to accept far lower margins than those who enjoy a higher level of perceived specialization. For example an accountancy practice which just does audit work is in close and transparent competition with many other accounting firms for an essentially commodity service – that is all the firms do basically the same thing. Clients will expect those firms to compete on price and thus the potential profits from such a service will be relatively small. An accounting firm which specializes in computerized management information systems however will, if well managed, probably enjoy higher margins as clients will be far more concerned about quality of service and will find it less easy to obtain competitive quotes for identical work.

Long-term profit decline

An overall decline in industry profits can result from a major structural change. In advertising, for example, in the days when most clients accepted a fixed 15 per cent commission on media purchases as the basis of remuneration, profits of agencies tended to be high. As the 15 per cent structure broke down and clients demanded more service for less money profits generally declined. The decline was so marked, in fact, that the less well managed agencies suffered badly and even made losses.

In the domestic estate agency business in Britain in the 1980s firms enjoyed high profits as they charged a fixed percentage commission at a time when house prices were rising by 20 per cent annually and the volume of trade in the market was very high. During the boom period the inherent profitability of the industry was high and many new agents opened up. However when the housing boom ended in the late 1980s the profits of all estate agents crashed and because many of them had been badly managed (poor practices being hidden by the inherently high profitability) many made large losses.

The ending of fixed commissions for stockbrokers in the USA

and the UK resulted in the overall profitability of the industry declining as the income from clients came down far faster than the various firms cut their costs.

Plan for a decline

A firm must take a view about the long-term direction of inherent industry profitability. As a general rule most areas of professional activity will become less profitable over time as competition increases and clients become more aware of what is on offer. Individual firms can still make excellent profits by being good managers and by always moving towards those new services which carry higher margins.

The broad message to managers must be, therefore, to assume absolute profitability will decline and to ensure that the firm's management systems and practices are not wasteful and lax which would mean the firm risked going bust if the overall profit available in the industry declined. Managers in professional firms who hope that they will simply benefit from ever-increasing profitability in their profession are doomed to disappointment.

COMPETITOR INFORMATION

The study of the new business brochures of clients, as well as things like annual reports, corporate videos and advertisements are useful, up to a point, for building a picture of how competitors compete.

Quality standards

All professional firms will emphasize commitment to excellence and the importance of client relationships. Such hyperbole should be, and is, largely discounted by clients and competitors alike.

The key things to look for are those firms where there is a *genuinely* superior attention to client needs. Aside from statements in a brochure this is likely to be manifest by the conduct and attitudes of the firm's professional staff at conferences and in social gatherings. Do they exhibit cynicism about their firm's stance or do they seem to believe and applaud it? Do clients speak well of a firm's commitment to quality work even if they might complain about the arrogance of its professional staff?

The real point of competitive difference will almost certainly not appear in the brochure but there may be hints of it. A firm which goes on, at length, about the *value added* by its services may well have some form of performance-related pay system. Firms which talk about *good value* probably trade on price. Firms stressing *quality* are often expensive but compete by having above-average, highly motivated people.

The quality of the paper and printing of any brochure is, sadly, no indication of the positioning of the firm but bad grammar and spelling mistakes indicate something about the probable lack of attention to detail in the execution of professional services.

New recruits can be from competitors

New recruits are a very useful source of intelligence about a competitor, be they ex-employees or simply have been interviewed by the competitor. It is in the nature of job interviews that the firm must give away a lot about its structure and philosophy in order to have a useful dialogue with a candidate.

General information

At a general level competitors should be watched to pick up major trends such as a move towards a new pricing system, a general relocation to low-cost premises or a rapid growth in size by way of merger and acquisition. For example an early warning of the ending of the 15 per cent commission system in advertising was given in the early 1980s when nothing more than industry gossip had it that certain major clients and agencies had struck deals at well below the accepted norm. The smart managements started to prepare for the breakdown to become generally accepted practice, which took about five years.

How are competitors managing the recruitment function (the supply of good people being one of the firm's major strategic considerations)? Is there any risk that they are building a strong reputation with university graduates which could hinder the firm's own recruitment efforts?

Specific information

At a specific level individual firms should be monitored. Is someone in trouble and if so does that imply that its clients may soon be looking for alternatives? Has a small firm developed a very successful service offering which might be complementary to one's own firm? Should a merger be considered? Is a team of people in another firm known to be unhappy – might they come across as a group? And so on.

ANTICIPATE BEHAVIOUR

In addition to building a picture of how competitors operate the firm should also have a view on *where* competitors are likely to go. Which market segments are they likely to target? What sort of resources does this mean they will be looking for? How are

Figure 6.3   Outline for analysis of competitors

COMPETING FIRM NAME : ....X........

Estimated gross income:
Estimated number of professionals:
Market share:

Professional staff

Young/old? Well regarded? Top heavy?
Recruitment policy
Training policy

Corporate goals

Increase size?
Grow market share?
Increase profitability?
Enter new markets?

Corporate strategy

High/low price
Specialist/generalist
Grow organically or by acquisition
Areas for expansion/entry
Any special service products on offer

Management approach

Structure
Accounting systems
Basis of charging
Philosophy/beliefs

Top management

Age
Succession in place?
Skills

competitors likely to react to strategic moves by the firm? If the firm reduced prices (assuming this would attract clients) would competitors be able to follow or does the firm have a sustainable price advantage?

This sort of information about future direction can be learned from the trade press and from talking to job applicants as described above. It will also be indicated if competitors are known to be looking for specific types of recruit in the future.

Those companies with public shareholders and stock market listings might be tempted to predict their future direction in order to convince the market of the soundness of their future strategy.

COMPETITORS ARE USEFUL

A firm and its competitors define a market-place. The ultimate objective of a professional firm is to serve its clients at a profit. Given this is also the objective of the firm's competitors the firm can learn about new ways of helping clients by knowing what other firms are doing. Unlike some industrial markets where one company's sale is another's missed opportunity, professional firms can *all* benefit from helping their market to grow larger. Professionals should monitor their competitors partly to see if a competitor's weakness may give the firm opportunities but partly to see if the firm can learn from a competitor's strengths.

42

THE COMPANY GOALS AND RESOURCES

What are the strengths and weaknesses of the firm itself?

We used to have very productive strategy sessions working out exactly which way the whole business was going. We came up with great plans for what sort of services we should be offering. The only problem was we had no hope at all of being able to do any of the things we knew clients would want. We just did not have the people.

Director, economic consultancy

It may seem self-evident to say that before outlining a strategy a firm needs to understand itself, but in fact it is often the last question managers ask. Analysis of the customers and the competition will help the firm identify potentially attractive future activities but it must, also, be clear on how well-suited it is for that future and what changes it may need to make internally.

CONSTRAINTS

The firm needs to understand about itself all the things, listed above, which it has tried to understand about its competitors but more than that a firm needs to understand what are its own constraints to following any selected strategic path.

Consensus

The professional and personal wishes of the senior managers or partners are an important factor as indeed are their philosophical and even political beliefs. If there is a consensus among the senior people that they enjoy doing client work personally and really like being part of a small firm it is most unlikely that a strategy based on rapid growth to achieve high leverage of junior staff is going to be successful. If there is no consensus then the firm has a very uncertain future.

Image

The firm must consider its image in the market-place. What do clients feel it stands for? What limitations does this image place on its strategic direction? An architectural firm that is well known for private housing will find it hard to win office development projects even if it is very good at those projects.

Staff resources

A firm can be aware of a future problem with its staff balance if it projects the ages and likely promotion prospects of its people forwards to see what implications this has for future recruitment and required level of income. The skills and experience of existing staff may also be a limit to executing a planned strategy. A London law firm that decides it wishes to build its client base in France will obviously need to find out how many of its people speak French and how well.

Existing clients

A close look at existing client relationships will help planning. Which clients represent growth prospects either because they will spend more themselves or because they represent a valuable introduction to other work? Which clients may be facing cutbacks?

For example, an advertising agency must be very aware of the amount of its business coming from tobacco or drink manufacturers, given the possible legislative threats to their ability to advertise. The flip side of that coin is that sponsorship and public relations companies might regard these types of client as very good prospects.

Operational strengths/weaknesses

In thinking about how and where to compete in the future the firm needs to consider other aspects of its current operation.

- Does it have very low/very high accommodation costs?

- Is its technology up to date?

- Will it be needing to make capital investments in the near future?

- Is the management information system good enough to support a new strategy?

- Does it have special contractual relationships with suppliers which are an advantage or disadvantage?

RESOURCES REQUIRED

A firm needs to understand its own capacity for change and growth.

THE PRIVATIZATION SCRAMBLE

In the 1980s in Britain the government's policy of selling public industries into the private sector by floating them on the stock market was well understood and well signposted. Advertising agencies realized this represented a potential gold mine. As a result many agencies set up privatization teams and spent a great deal of money trying to win some of the business. The strategy of being in this attractive new market was sound but many of the aspirants overlooked the fact that they would have virtually no chance of success.

To win a privatization project an agency would need to show a combination of creative skills and financial literacy and would need to have friends in the City, the government, the civil service and the financial public relations community to convince risk-averse ministers that the agency would perform well. In the event the vast bulk of the Government spending went to a handful of agencies which fitted these criteria – which was more the result of their past development and inherent skills than future strategic planning. Most of the would-be applicants wasted their money.

In formulating strategy firms may see clearly the direction in which their industry is going and may be able to identify very attractive market segments. However if an honest appraisal of themselves and their competitors shows that, because of their current set-up, they will be at a major disadvantage in pursuing the obvious new goal then they should look for some other solution.

43

SERVICE OFFERING/POSITIONING

What sort of services should your firm offer?

We are absolutely clear about what sort of architects we are. We design moderate cost public housing. That's what we like doing, that's what we do best, that's where we can make most money because of the sort of firm we are.

Architect

We are in public relations. We are not a marketing services conglomerate. We stick to what we know.

Chairman, PR group

Having taken regard of its environment (customers and competitors) and its own situation, the firm must decide what to be to its customers.

In a financial holding company it is quite possible to ask questions along the lines of: do we want to be in this industry at all? A holding company can adopt a portfolio approach and put its shareholders' money into any business it feels will be profitable. The top managers could ask themselves: is advertising, public relations, estate agency, executive search (and so on) a *good* business to be in? It may well be that a strategic analysis will convince a holding company that it would be best to exit (or not enter) a particular business. In reality, in professional services, the record of diversified groups is very poor and all the evidence suggests that even for a holding company there should be a high degree of professional focus.

A particular firm, however, has, in reality, no chance of saying this is a business we don't want to be in. For a firm's managers, if they see tough times ahead for their industry, the task is to find some form of service offering (and business plan) that will enable them to prosper while others suffer in difficult conditions.

Defining the product or service is another way of asking the classic consultant's question: what business are we in? For professional firms this question really becomes: what sort of service should we offer?

WHAT SORT OF SERVICE?

A clear definition is important for:

- *Clients*, who need to know what is on offer
- *Staff*, and particularly potential staff, who are making career decisions

The decisions about what services to offer must be made with a view to achieving clear differentiation for the firm; to allow it to be distinct from its competitors and to capture profits by providing customers with valuable service which they cannot find at comparable prices or comparable quality elsewhere.

The firm must decide where the best place to be is along a number of dimensions:

- High price/low price
- Generalist/specialist
- Bespoke/off-the-peg
- Local/national

The two most important dimensions are price point and degree of specialization. These decisions *must* be based on what the customers want, what the competitors will find hard to replicate and what the firm is well placed to achieve. It must be stressed that the decisions about positioning are issues that face a firm at a business unit level. Where to be in respect of any of these trade-offs are not relevant decisions for a holding company, as it might own a number of business units within the same industry each of which would have its own distinct service offering.

A very small firm can have just one service offering. Most firms will have several but to be successful they must be compatible within the overall context of the firm. The problem for management is to ensure that the portfolio of service offerings is consistent in the eyes of clients – that is, they believe the firm can be very good at all of the things on offer. Also the various offerings have to be able to be delivered profitably within the firm's business system and given its resources and the way it is managed. Successful firms are those which find new service offerings which are an extension of, and a logical fit with, their core business.

INTERBRAND

Interbrand is an international consultancy business which specialized in the development of brand identities, selection and legal protection of brand names and so on. It identified the valuations of brands on company balance sheets as a key issue for its clients who might face a potential takeover bid without the real value of their brands being recognized.

Interbrand developed a special methodology for valuing brands and recruited people with the right skills to undertake valuation projects. Accountancy firms lacked the brand knowledge to replicate the product and most marketing consultancies lacked the necessary accounting skills. Clients found this service very valuable and were prepared to pay high fees which made the valuation product very profitable.

Interbrand had identified a customer need and a competitive advantage and they had the mixture of marketing and accountancy skills. They created a service aimed, mainly, at the finance directors of major quoted companies and they assembled the necessary people and resources. They were able to offer a high-price (clients valued it), specialist (very narrow focus), off-the-peg (the same basic product was applied to each situation) service which was required in all main markets across the world.

The above example demonstrates an additional offering which fitted with the firm's existing services in the eyes of clients and was also consistent with the firm's other work. Looking through the corporate brochures of design companies, PR consultancies and some of the mid-sized accounting and legal firms one is faced time and again with claims that the firm is expert at a wide range of specialist services which must raise questions in client's minds as to whether the firm is actually good at any of them.

PRICING

In professional firms pricing usually means the same thing as setting billing rates, project fees or commission rates. These rates can be set either on a cost-plus basis or on a market rate basis. From a strategic point of view firms simply want to charge as much as they can and thus reap maximum profits (assuming they can keep their costs under control). Elasticity of demand – a concern for consumer goods manufacturers – is less of an issue to professional firms. There will be a price at which clients will decide *not* to buy a service but usually the decision is more to do with which professional firm will get the work.

Fees versus commission

The issue of how to be paid – largely a choice between fees based on time or commission based on the value of a transaction completed or goods and services purchased – was discussed in chapter 31 of part IV. From a strategic point of view the key point is that in the client's eyes the *basis* of charging does not matter. What matters is how much it had to pay for the service rendered and how valuable it felt that service to have been.

Cost-plus versus market rate

How much to be paid can be determined by two alternatives – cost-plus and market rates.

Cost-plus means, in simple terms, calculating the cost of servicing a client and then adding a fixed percentage to cover overheads and provide a profit. Cost-plus where the hourly fee represents some multiple of the calculated hourly cost is the traditional way for professionals to price their time. Firms which take a cost-plus approach run the risk of losing touch with the market and in so doing may, on the one hand, miss the opportunity for extra profits by under-charging for the real value of their work or on the other hand find their costs have escalated to such a degree (under the shelter of the cost-plus umbrella) that they can no longer compete effectively with other firms on price.

The problem with the alternative of market pricing is that it involves the firm in a potentially unpleasant negotiation every time it starts a new job. It means the firm and its client must have some idea of the value of highly intangible professional services.

Pricing must, of course, cover costs and yield a profit. The question is how big a profit. The pricing must be flexible enough to allow the firm to capture extra income where its services are particularly valuable. Writing in *Canadian Lawyer* (June 1990) consultant Richard Taylor comments:

> *Currently lawyers set prices according to what the market will bear. The problem though, is that pricing is often based on who the lawyer is, rather than on the value of the work done. You wouldn't hire a heart surgeon to sew up a cut on your hand yet that's what happens when senior, experienced lawyers do work that is below their capability.*

It is unlikely that direct comparisons between the work of professional firms will ever be easy and firms will always be well advised to keep prices as high as they think clients will tolerate.

To decide to compete on the basis of price is almost always going to be damaging in the long run as the firm will tend to make a commodity of the service and cause most competitors and clients to become price–sensitive

SPECIALIZATION

The second dimension in which a firm must position itself is the degree of specialization.

Specialist firms focus their resources and skills and will usually win a specialist project in competition with a generalist but are at risk if there is a downturn in their area and will not be able to grow to the same size as a generalist. Generalists benefit from having a wider portfolio of work and will usually be more profitable as they will be able to achieve a high level of staff utilization over a long period. They may have problems competing for certain types of work as mentioned above and they may not be able to satisfy the needs of senior staff who wish to become expert in a narrowly defined area.

Specialists, by definition, limit themselves to a smaller potential market and need to invest in specific training for their staff. They must ensure that their branding is very clear and well understood by potential staff and clients alike. In most cases they will have to be prepared to serve a large geographical area.

A firm must be clear with itself about where it stands in the specialist/generalist dimension. There is a tendency to tell clients one thing (we specialize in *your* sort of problem) and tell staff another (we expect our people to be able to turn their hands to anything). If it were possible to get away with this it would make a lot of sense from the firm's point of view. In reality, over time, clients will cease to use the firm unless the allegedly specialist services are really as good as those of any genuine specialists.

TAILORED WORK

The standard product costs less to make and will usually (although not always) command lower prices than the one-off solution. The ideal is to find a standard product which other firms find hard to replicate but which appears to be client-specific and commands a high market price. Standard products which are tailored to clients' needs include work such as communications audits done by advertising and PR agencies, cost reduction programmes from management consultancies and brand valuation projects.

Operating with service products is very attractive to the firm but may be less so to junior staff who will lack the variety and learning experiences offered by a series of one-off projects.

IMAGE

The branding of professional firms was covered in chapter 38 on marketing. The issue of overall image in the context of the service offering is a strategic matter because of the impact on the two main market-places in which the firm competes, the market for clients and the market for professional staff.

The firm's image should reflect the reality of where it expects to be in about a year's time. In recruiting staff and winning clients firms should always be looking forward. If top management have taken a decision to specialize in a particular professional area this should be publicized even *before* it is completely achieved as this will help to ensure that the firm is seen in the right way when all the elements finally come into place. Clients who seek that service and professional staff who seek to provide it will be attracted to the firm. A firm must actively manage its communications and not just assume that people will get an accurate idea of what it stands for.

CONTINGENCY APPROACH

In defining their service offering top management must ensure that all elements of it are internally consistent. Where more than one offering exists within one firm they must be complementary.

The point of a *contingency approach* is that firms must organize themselves in such a way that they are best suited to carry out the service offering they have defined. Organization is contingent upon the operational realities of the chosen approach. Having selected its service offering the firm must stick to it and not constantly change in the hope of capturing some new profit opportunity. A change of direction must be carefully considered and its ramifications in *all* aspects of the business be taken into account. In the PR industry, for example, many firms try to be all things to all people and suffer the inevitable decline in profitability.

A typical consumer goods PR firm needs to offer clients a good general service of media relations and event organization. On each account one senior director should provide strategic guidance and maintain the client relationship while a relatively junior (and relatively cheap in terms of salary costs) team carries out the work. The client will pay moderate fees but the firm will still operate profitably. A City PR firm, on the other hand, which might specialize in the publicity attendant on hostile takeovers will have to service each client with a team of very senior, technically skilled (and expensive) people who can provide the 24-hour dedication required. The client will pay large fees and despite its high costs the firm will prosper.

The consumer firm that tries to do City PR will find all its senior people dragged into the fray which, while in the short-term it may be profitable reflecting the high fees, in the medium-term will probably lead to staff resignations and client losses which will destabilize the business. The City firm that tries to do consumer work will meet price resistance from clients and will find its highly paid specialists operating at a loss.

It is quite possible to have clear consumer and City divisions within one firm but culturally this is difficult because of the huge differentials in salaries and logistical back-up required. The 24-hour security, high speed copying and computer facilities required by the City firm represents a cost base which would drag the consumer business down. Equally the low-cost, but quite adequate, consumer businesses facilities would place the City firm at a disadvantage to its rivals.

A CLEAR PROPOSITION

In the early history of service firms it was quite sufficient to hang out a sign saying 'Accountant'; 'Solicitor'; 'Advertising Agent' as the range of professional services provided was sufficiently narrow for any one firm to cover them all. As the professions became more complex firms became differentiated from one another by price, specialization and size. It is now critical that firms define a proposition and service positioning for themselves which allows them to address an attractive part of the market and which reflects their internal strengths so that they can do the work profitably and at least as well as any competitor.

44

THE BUSINESS PLAN

How should your firm put its strategy into action?

Well we do have a business plan somewhere. I am not exactly sure what's in it but we do have one.

Managing Director (successful!), design consultancy

The business plan is the final product of the strategy process – it is the mechanism which puts the strategy into practice. Professional service firms do not have to have a business plan. A small group of professionals can simply concentrate on selling their professional time to clients and can make a good living. However they will find it very difficult to grow the business and almost impossible to grow it profitably unless they clearly plan ahead.

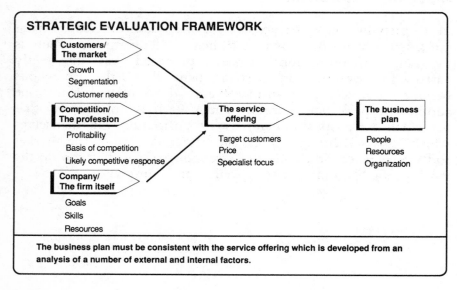

Figure 6.4

Figure 6.4 shows the business plan as the end product of the process of strategic analysis and the development of a service offering.

THE PURPOSE OF A BUSINESS PLAN

In professional firms the corporate or business plan is, in many ways, an amalgam of the individual plans of senior professionals. New business targets and new areas of activity for the firm are nothing more than the aggregate of individuals' targets and interests. The role of top management is to ensure that all the individual plans are going in the same direction. A firm with half the partners seeking to be generalists offering high priced bespoke solutions while the other half aim to become specialists providing standard products will have real problems in the marketplace.

The business plan itself contains more than just the action steps that the firm will follow, it will include a clear statement of the firm's mission, objectives and strategy. These things need to be written down if only to force a degree of consensus among senior people and to remove as much ambiguity as possible about what the firm stands for. It can be easy to get senior people to agree the same action steps while they hold quite contrary views about the firm's real sense of direction.

Many firms shy away from formally writing down things like a mission statement and goals on the grounds that 'we don't need to do that as we all know exactly what we stand for.' Although it is laughed at by some senior professionals as too Californian to go through the mission statement/corporate objectives process, the truth is that most of the outstandingly successful professional firms do have a very clear and well articulated sense of purpose. Without the clear, tangible products of a manufacturer firms need this expression of values and quality to help all members of staff have a sense of what sort of firm they belong to.

Parts of the business plan, such as the financial projections and staff numbers, should remain confidential to the senior management. However those parts dealing with the firm's long-term objectives, target customers and so on should be distributed to all members of staff to give them a clear statement of what the firm is trying to be.

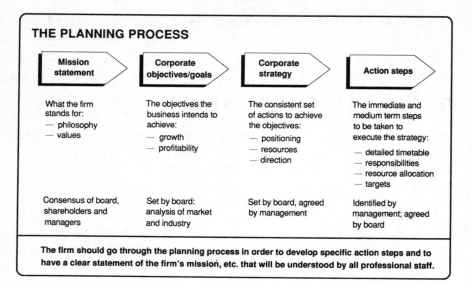

Figure 6.5

THE PLANNING PROCESS

Figure 6.5 shows the four steps of the planning process. A senior partner or member of the board should have the responsibility of drawing up a business plan by going through the four steps. The plan should be updated annually with any changes to the mission statement, objectives or strategy being debated by the board.

A business plan is not a static document but any changes need to go through a process of syndication amongst the professional staff and get formal approval. A business plan cannot be changed in isolation the people in the business must be consulted.

Figure 6.6 shows the chapter headings of a typical business plan. The completed document should be available to all senior managers and newly promoted or recruited senior managers should have it explained to them in detail.

THE BUDGET

The business plan lays out the guiding principles for the firm. It is the source of a budget against which the firm can be managed. The budget should be built up from the smallest level of detail into a simple management summary for consideration by the board. Over the first 12 months covered by the plan the budget should

Figure 6.6 Subject headings of typical business plan

The Firm	Mission statement
	Corporate objectives
	Short/medium/long term strategy
Target market	Predicated growth
	Key influences (interest rates etc.)
Target customers	Needs
	Key influences
	Identities of top prospects
Close competitors	Basis of competition. (Price/Quality etc.)
	Likely response
Firm economics	Revenue targets
	New business targets
	Operating ratios
	Profit forecast
	Cash flow forecast
	Funding requirements
Professional staff	Numbers
	Growth rate
	Salaries
	Skills required
	Recruitment programme
	Training programmes
	Personal development plans
Support staff	Special skills required
	Numbers
Management	Board/committee structure and membership
	Management responsibilities (training etc.)
Premises	Location
	Size to reflect growth
Capital spending	Office equipment
	Computers
	Telecoms
Action steps	Timetable, responsibilities

be done on a monthly basis but for later years can be quarterly or even annual. Preparing a monthly budget is a pointless exercise if managers simply estimate annual figures and divide by 12 – if detail is to be done monthly it must reflect any expected seasonality in the business.

An example of the level of rigour imposed by Mr Martin Sorrell's financial holding company WPP on its subsidiaries in the budgeting process was cited by Alice Rawsthorn in the *Financial Times* (19 June 1990):

> *[After the acquisition of Ogilvy & Mather he] began by introducing WPP's financial systems which involve setting highly detailed, two year rolling budgets. In practice this means that Mr Graham Phillips, Ogilvy's chief executive, once had a general entertainment budget and now has budgets for particular areas like dinner with clients. Mr Sorrell says the degree of detail encourages people to look at every dollar and cent.*

The use of the budget to manage the firm on a day-to-day basis by calculating the variances between budget and actual performance is covered in chapter 28.

IMPLEMENTATION AND MONITORING

All too often a business plan, once written, is left to gather dust and the firm just gets back to doing what it does best which is getting on with professional work. The firm will survive but it will not grow and prosper. The executive committee or board should have the business plan targets as a regular item on their agenda and should constantly test progress against them. Monitoring the financial budget was discussed above but the firm also needs to monitor its performance against recruitment- and staff turnover-targets and needs regularly to test its assumptions about the development of its market-place.

THE BLUEPRINT AND THE YARDSTICK

The business plan should help all the firm's professionals to have a sense of direction and should paint a picture of the future which they all understand and approve of. Firms which avoid having a widely-accepted business plan because they cannot handle the political problems of getting a consensus are storing up problems.

The business plan also helps managers to monitor progress by having quantified goals such as gross fee income, profit margin, number of new recruits and so on which can be followed, over time, to see if the firm is on track.

45

GETTING RICH

How can the senior people in professional firms realize their wealth potential?

I spent 8 years building this business with my partner and then we sold it for US$8 million. Do I feel bad that I'm now just an employee of the company that was my life? No. I just feel rich!

Chief Executive, design consultancy

A crucial issue for the owners and senior managers of professional firms is how to maximize and realize their personal wealth which is tied up in the business. Part of a long-term strategy is often how to get the money out. This final chapter considers how founders and senior managers can obtain the wealth that they have created in successfully running and building a professional firm.

Legally many senior professionals are not employees but are partners. *Emotionally* virtually no senior people in professional firms regard themselves as employees. They will feel a legitimate right to benefit from the wealth creation opportunities of the firm and this must be recognized in providing them with opportunities to benefit from the firm's success.

The issue of *ownership* was considered at the start of chapter 25 in which it was made clear that some firms feel very strongly that selling out is not for them. Those firms must create wealth by keeping all the profits and all the ownership internal. This chapter is about achieving wealth by selling that ownership to someone else.

A professional firm is a machine which will produce revenues and, it is to be hoped, profits out into the future. The owners (often including the management) of that firm can benefit from those future profits by getting a capital sum, up-front, in return for giving up something (the profits) in the future through some form of public sale of stock or a trade sale of the firm. They can, alternatively, seek to participate in that future profit stream with stock options and profit-related bonuses.

The issues of making people wealthy through stock options and profit-related bonuses were dealt with in chapters 19 and 20. The rest of this chapter is devoted to ways of selling the business, which is a strategic decision. The points made about trade sales and earn-outs are, of course, relevant to those managers of people businesses who are contemplating buying firms.

Impact of the style of the firm

There are long-term implications for future staff recruitment and staff motivation of a flotation or trade sale. The effective change of ownership often creates a one-off rich generation of founder managers. Later generations will find that the partnership profits they would normally have expected to share in are being taken away by the new shareholders who made the earlier generation of professionals rich.

This removal of a slice of profits can make the publicly owned company far less attractive to the successful professional than a similar private business. Although a junior member of staff in a private firm will see the partners taking home the profits he or she at least has the chance of becoming one of those partners. In a public company the same junior staff member cannot become a shareholder except by purchasing shares which assumes they have enough money to do so.

In manufacturing it does not create so much of a problem that the original founders cashed in as the new owners (the shareholders) only need professional managers to operate the assets and look after the brand and the manufacturer needed the outside capital for plant and equipment. In professional firms the senior people *are* the assets and, to some extent, the brand in themselves.

Post-acquisition malaise

The worst time to be in a professional firm is immediately after ownership has changed from some form of partnership to public or corporate ownership. The selling partners will often leave the business or certainly lose interest. The layer of management immediately below them, often called the marzipan layer (because they are above the cake but below the icing), will be disenchanted at the loss of their chance to cash in. The junior staff will be worked hard as the new shareholders want to see quick profits on their investment.

It is during this period that the financial health and professional reputation of the firm is at greatest risk. In those cases where the firm has been purchased by a debt-laden corporate parent the pressures are even worse as short-term profit-boosting cost cuts are often made purely to appease the corporate parent's bankers and can have devastating results on the morale and long-term well being of the acquired firm.

PUBLIC FLOATATION

Putting a company onto the stock market will normally result in a loss of majority control by the owners/managers. It also raises issues about the level of financial transparency of the company and its accountability to public shareholders.

The mechanics of public flotation are relatively straightforward, with a choice of going on the Unlisted Securities Market (USM) or the main market of the Stock Exchange (SE). All or part of the company's share capital can be made available. To be quoted on either market a company must file documents to show that its shares meet the necessary qualifications for listing. The rules of the main market and the conditions for listing are far more onerous than for the USM. For the main market a minimum of 25 per cent of the company's share capital must be made available and the company must file accounts for the past three years. For the USM the rules require two years of accounts and ten per cent of the capital to be available.

Having decided to go onto the market it is necessary to create a market in the firm's shares. There are three ways to do this:

- An *introduction* of shares. If a reasonable number of the company's shares are already in public hands (i.e. belong to independent investors and not the management) the shares can simply be listed for trading with no new shares being issued or sold

- A *placing* of a relatively small number of shares with recognized investors will also get shares into public hands

- An *offer for sale* describes the company and its shares in detail and makes them available to any investor who wants them. New shares must be issued

Going to the market is expensive (several hundred thousand pounds at a minimum) and requires a large group of professional advisers, in particular a financial institution (usually a merchant bank) to act as sponsor to manage the whole process and also to underwrite the sale of any new shares (i.e. guarantee to buy them in the event that the investment community does not). Planning a listing, even on the USM, takes at least two years and companies should be making pre-tax profits of getting on for £1 million before it is really worthwhile.

The main advantages of public listing are:

- Existing shareholders can get cash for their shares

- The company can fund future investments and acquisitions using shares

- Senior employees can be given shares which can be easily sold in a liquid market

- Share option schemes are easy to administer as employees can see daily what their options are worth

The main disadvantages are:

- The firm will come under closer scrutiny from investors, competitors, clients and staff. The firm's profits and financial state of health will become public knowledge

- The compliance costs of public ownership can be high. In addition to the annual audit fees there are costs involved in notifying the stock exchange of all material developments at the company, producing annual reports and the management time taken up by investor relations

TRADE SALE

Selling the business to another organization – sometimes a competitor, sometimes a business in an associated area – again can result in the founder managers becoming rich.

Trade sales will be made to corporate parents with three broad groups of reasons:

- Vertical integration
- Horizontal integration
- Conglomerate building

Vertical integration

The new parent already uses the firm as a supplier or as a contractor and comes to the conclusion that it makes more sense to have the resources in-house. This can happen with PR consultancies, design firms and advertising agencies. The main decision for the firm and the new owner is whether the firm will become, in effect, an in-house department with no external clients or will continue to trade in the open market as well as servicing the new parent.

Horizontal integration

The new parent is already in the same business as the firm and is seeking to build a unit with more scale. The main issues here are which culture and set of systems will come to dominate the newly created, larger unit. Will the firm's identity be retained or will it vanish? The issues of post-merger integration were covered in part V.

Conglomerate building

The new parent is seeking to build a portfolio of businesses which may or may not include other service firms. Holding companies like WPP and Saatchi may try to devise mechanisms to generate cross referral of business between various, separate, professional firms. The main issues for the selling managers is whether their firm will benefit and grow from access to other firms' clients.

The future of management

If the principal concern of the selling management is to get the highest immediate price for their business they will probably do that by selling to a competitor who will be able to reduce costs and to whom the business is worth more than anyone else. If top management are intending to stay with the firm (which is usually the case) they will probably enjoy maximum autonomy by selling to a conglomerate which will still leave them in charge, if not in control.

For many people who founded or grew up in a professional service firm the challenge of making the switch from entrepreneur to employee is too great. Despite the best intentions many managers who sell out become very disenchanted and leave the business as soon as their contracts allow.

EARN-OUTS

The most controversial, and one of the most widely used ways of buying professional firms is the earn-out, a mechanism by which the owners of the firm are paid an immediate capital lump sum and then receive future payments over a number of years with the size of the payment depending on the profit performance of the business. The earn-out is *the* mechanism which allowed the growth of the marketing services conglomerates like Saatchi & Saatchi, and WPP, and which has been used widely by many other acquisitive professional firms.

Whilst the earn-out has attractions for the purchasers, in that it offers incentives to the selling managers to continue to generate and increase profits, it can produce very undesirable effects as the managers are tempted to milk the business to produce short-term profits at the expense of long-term success.

Deferred payments

A variant on the earn-out is the use of simple deferred payments. Under this system the purchasing company and the selling firm agree, in advance, the value of the firm and agree the sums to be paid *irrespective* of performance. The top management are usually contracted to stay on and, in many cases, part of the purchase payment is made in shares of the purchasing company which provides an added incentive for the managers to endeavour to make their firm do well even under new ownership. Managers of the purchased firm can be motivated with profit-related bonuses but these can be carefully monitored. Many of the problems of short-term behaviour caused by the performance related earn-out can be overcome.

The problem of paying with shares not cash

The use of shares in an earn-out or deferred payment can be a major problem. The mechanism is that the purchasing company agrees to pay the owners of the firm it has acquired by issuing shares in the parent company rather than making future payments in cash. If the shares of the parent company go up in value this can work very well as the future payments (which have a fixed cash value) can be made by using a relatively small number of shares.

For example, if a corporate parent purchases a design company it might agree to pay the original owners the sum of £10 million *worth* of shares in two years time. At the time of the deal the parent's shares are priced at £2 each meaning five million shares are worth £10m. In two years time those shares might be priced at £4 each meaning that the parent will only need to issue 2.5 million shares to pay off the debt.

If, however, the shares of the parent collapse in value (because of stock market sentiment or poor performance in other of the parent's businesses) then the owners of the acquired company will have to receive a far larger number of shares to meet the payments that are due to them. In the above example if the parent's shares fall to a value of £1 each it will have to issue ten million shares to the previous owners of the purchased company. The shareholders of the parent company will be very unhappy because their holdings will be diluted by a large number of new (low-value) shares that are issued and the previous owners of the acquired firm may be unhappy because they are receiving shares which do not look attractive for the future.

Selling future profits now

The mechanics of an earn-out are relatively straightforward. For example if a firm is making profits of £100,000 per annum then on a *straightforward purchase* by another company it might be decided that the firm is worth a multiple of ten times its current profits, that is £1 million.

Under the earn-out the managers might be paid £200,000 now in cash and be promised that they will be paid a multiple of three times the profits for each of the next three years. Thus the payments might be:

FUTURE EARN-OUT PAYMENTS

Up front payment of £200,000

Future payments assuming a multiple of 3 times profits

£000s	Year 1	Year 2	Year 3	Total
Profits	120	140	160	420
Payment	360	420	480	1,260

This would mean the selling management received a total of £1.46 million but spread over four years – an initial payment of £200,000 with further payments with a total of £1.26 million, as shown above. At the end of the final year the selling managers would have become wealthy and, from then on, the company which purchased their firm would have no more liabilities.

This, of course, is a very simplified model but the basic idea holds true for all earn-outs.

Attraction to the buyer

The great attraction of the earn-out from the point of view of the purchaser is that it locks in the selling management and motivates them to run the business profitably. If profits fall below a certain level then, usually, no earn-out payments are made. If profits go above a certain level there is usually a cap meaning that there is a maximum earn-out payment which will not be exceeded.

In theory, also, the earn-out reduces the buyer's risk. In a conventional purchase the price paid is a reflection of *historic* profit performance with assumptions made about the future. In an earn-out the final price paid reflects the actual future performance.

The earn-out also allows highly acquisitive companies to buy others for very little cash down. The purchasers are gambling on being able to find the money when the future payments become due. If however the purchase is made during a time of great optimism when profit multiples are high and interest rates are low it can prove costly later on if the market conditions deteriorate.

Impact of the purchased firm

Earn-outs are, therefore, potentially attractive to the buying company and to the selling managers but the real question is are they actually good for the business purchased? Performance related earn-outs do produce a number of problems:

- Top managers (of the purchased firm who will benefit from the future payments) become too focused on short-term profits often at the expense of the long-term well-being of the firm

- If profits drop then the selling managers may become very demoralized if they see their capital gain being lost

- Senior employees who do not benefit from the earn-out cash can become very demoralized

- Managers can leave (and often do) as soon as the earn-out period is over

The core problem is that for every £1 generated in profit during the earn-out years the sellers get a multiple of this as their reward. Thus while there is some incentive to grow profits through increasing the overall revenue there is a huge incentive to cut costs and investments. Managers are likely to become increasingly stingy over housekeeping costs and, more worryingly, may persuade employees to keep their wage demands down during the earn-out period by promising them all sorts of 'jam tomorrow'.

It is often the case in earn-out firms that there is a rash of appointments to the board on the grounds that status for the newly promoted people costs nothing and that it will be several years before these new directors start to demand the salaries to match their new positions.

'Earn-out burn-out'

Writing in *The Banker* magazine (May 1990) Victoria Griffith cites an example of earn-out cost slashing:

> *The chief executive of a large public relations company complained of his experience in buying a small marketing firm on the earn-out basis. Eight months after the takeover the manager of the vendor company slashed costs to try to maximise short term gains. A visit to the marketing firm revealed some shocking cost-cutting. There was a queue at the photocopier, since a second copier had broken down and not been repaired. The coffee machine had been allowed to run dry and the offices of two key executives were empty. They had defected in a huff when the vendor sold their company cars. Two secretaries had not been replaced. The offices were in a sorry state.*

The victims of this sort of thing have coined the phrase 'earn-out, burn out' and it is, sadly, common in many firms that have gone through the process. It is particularly exacerbated by very acquisitive holding companies who do not have the time or inclination to become involved in the management of their new firms and often agree to non-interference clauses in the purchase deal which allows incumbent management almost complete freedom during the earn-out period. The leading advertising magazine *Campaign* took a critical look at earn-outs in its editorial column (August 1990):

> *The earn-out deal was the device which fuelled the acquisition boom amongst advertising and marketing groups over recent years, and only observers with rose-coloured spectacles can say that it has been an enduring success. Critics of the earn-out tended to be shouted down when major proponents like Saatchi & Saatchi were building empires based on jam tomorrow. Campaign has counselled its readers on the pitfalls of profit-related purchase formulae recounting the tale of a publisher who discovered the owner of a magazine it was buying was paying off his company's bad debts (from his own*

pocket) by the back door. Every £1 he paid (which then became profit) was worth £7 in the earn-out agreement.

Making earn-outs work

Despite the negative points earn-out can be a good idea if some basic rules are observed:

- The purchasers must *really* understand the business they are buying in terms of its market, clients and operating economics. Only then will they be able to see trouble coming

- The purchasers should not enter into agreements to leave the management to their own devices. Non-interference is a mistake – they should install at least one of their own people (who is a skilled professional in the business in question) in a senior management position – almost certainly on the board. They should agree an operating budget, *based on historical levels,* and must ask questions if cost savings appear unexpectedly great

- *All* senior managers of the firm must be allowed to participate in the earn-out with some form of profit sharing. The jam must not be restricted to just a few original owners

- *All* professional members of staff must be told how the earn-out works (they will find out anyway!) and must be shown why the sale of the business makes sense for them all in the future. For junior people the prospect of being part of a larger group may be very attractive

WEALTH AS THE GOAL

The owners, partners and senior managers of professional firms have the potential to make a very good living by selling their services to clients and by organizing the sale of service by more junior professionals. These senior people can become rich if their firm prospers either by keeping a share of the profits or by selling those future profits to someone else for a lump sum. If people are content to be paid simply as successful professionals they can achieve this by obtaining a position of equity ownership in a major private firm and, as long as they manage the firm well, they will enjoy its profits. If people want large capital sums they will almost certainly have to sell their firm and will have to accept that the character and nature of the publicly or corporately owned firm will almost certainly change.

SUMMARY AND PROPOSITIONS

This book has described the issues that managers of professional service firms must address if they are going to make their firms profitable and if those firms are going to grow and prosper.

While there are considerable differences between the professional services offered by accountants, architects, advertising agents, designers, doctors, executive search firms, lawyers, management consultants, public relations experts and so on, the basic challenges of running their businesses are very similar.

- The key *management* challenge is to track the profitability of individual clients and projects, to avoid subsidizing unprofitable activities and to focus on profitable ones

- The key *control* challenge is to collect money owed rapidly and to manage the cash in the firm

- The key *operational* challenge is to achieve high levels of staff utilization. People are the most valuable (and expensive) asset and must be used well

- The key *resource* challenge is to find skilled staff in the face of a dramatic decline in the numbers of young people. In addition the convergence of various professions means different types of firm are increasingly competing for the same potential recruits

- The key *planning* challenge is to achieve an effective balance within the firm while at the same time increasing the number of people employed in the business, meeting the career needs of the professional staff and finding new clients

TWENTY PROPOSITIONS

What follows are 20 propositions about professional service firms which summarize the main ideas in this book and provide a checklist for managers:

1   Managers of professional firms must understand the *profitability of each client* and/or project. They must have a management information system, based on time–sheets, which allows them to understand how professional staff spend their time.

2   Managers should identify *products* based on consistent standardized services which the firm can offer to clients. These products can be very profitable as the firm can exploit its past experience.

3   Firms should try to increase the *leverage* of their senior staff by increasing the ratio of the number of junior professionals to the greatest degree that is permitted by the requirements of clients and the nature of the market. In general the higher the leverage the higher the profit.

4   Managers should seek to increase the *effective billing rate* which clients pay for professional services in order to increase profits. To do this, however, the firm will have to make its staff more valuable to clients which is usually achieved through training.

5   The main driving force of profitability is achieving high levels of professional *staff utilization*. This does not mean running a sweatshop but it does mean careful planning and marketing to ensure the volume of work closely matches the capacity of the firm.

6   Creating a *profit conscious* attitude in *all* staff is one of the most important ways of achieving profitability in firms where nearly all people have some degree of control over how well the firm is run.

7   *Personnel management* is too critical in professional firms to be done by personnel 'experts'. All executives must regard people management as an important part of their job and all should be assessed on their personnel management skills each year.

8   *Recruitment* is a key process for the firm and should be given a high level of resource and priority. Firms must compete for the best recruits as hard as they compete for clients. Recruitment mistakes are very expensive.

9   *Evaluation* of the skills and contribution of professional staff must be done regularly and on an objective and transparent basis which everyone understands. The evaluation of each person's

level of skill and contribution relative to their peers should be the basis for payment and promotion.

10   The *assignment* of professional staff to certain clients and projects is one of the main management jobs. It directly affects retention of staff, client profitability and staff utilization.

11   *Training* ensures the firm's future growth and profitability. Trained staff are more valuable to clients and can command higher billing rates. Good training helps to differentiate a firm from its competitors, provides a mechanism for communicating the firm's culture and values and will help the retention of key staff. It is also important in building intellectual capital for the firm.

12   To combat the future *people shortage*, professional firms will have to rethink radically their structure and style. The division between professionals and support staff will break down with increasing use of quasi professionals like para-legals. The idea that the only people in the firm with a full-time career are professionals will decline and more tasks will be done by those with part-time involvement such as working mothers.

13   The *leaders* of professional firms have to provide a vision for the future and be professional role models. To be credible they will have to be known as outstanding practitioners with proven professional skills – being a manager is not enough.

14   *Client relations* is crucial to the long-term success of a firm. It must be regarded as an important role for senior professionals and be accepted by them as a professional skill. Firms should create the role of relationship manager to manage the relationship with clients separately from the professional tasks.

15   Investments in *technology* are important for professional firms but they must be coupled with an investment in, and a top management commitment to, building skills to ensure the best use is made of the equipment available.

16   Growing professional firms by *acquisition and merger* is fraught with difficulties because of the problems of a clash of cultures and the politics of who comes out on top. The most successful firms are those which have grown (often quite fast) simply by winning new clients and recruiting new staff. Acquisition of different types of firms to create a professional supermarket does not work. The

highly successful one-firm idea only really works for those businesses which have not grown by acquisition.

17 *Joint ventures* and strategic alliances between professional firms can provide a mechanism for serving clients who require a more comprehensive service than the individual firm can offer.

18 Seeking *new business* is very expensive. Firms must carefully select those clients they really wish to serve and only put resources into those leads. They should not pursue marginal opportunities. Firms must be clear which prospects could become core clients (highly attractive sources of dependable long-term revenues) and which are more likely to result in one-off projects. Existing clients are often a better source of new profitable business than new prospects.

19 The *image* of the firm is important because professional services cannot be easily judged by objective measures. This is why professional firms must be concerned to look the part in terms of having impressive and professional offices and why aspects of the service package such as prompt answering of telephone calls, rapid replies to letters and clear and error-free billing mechanisms are important.

20 A firm must have a distinctive *service offering* which defines its position in the market-place to clients and staff. Managers must ensure that every aspect of the firm – recruitment, training, staff structures, premises and so on – reinforce the firm's positioning and offering.

APPENDIX:
LEADING PROFESSIONAL SERVICE FIRMS

Data on the relative financial performance of professional firms is hard to get. Some professions, like accountancy, are relatively open. Others, like the law in the UK, are notoriously secretive. The following tables are taken from leading trade magazines some of which collect information from firms by surveys and some of which make informed estimates.

Although the data is incomplete it should be useful to managers who can calculate the various ratios for their own firms and make some comparisons.

RELIABILITY OF DATA

The tables are mostly based on the calender year 1990 or a financial year ending in early 1991. The tables are provided here to give an indication of the *relative* performance of firms. Readers wishing to obtain latest statistics should refer to the trade magazines cited.

The data must be taken with a stiff 'health warning' about its accuracy. In some cases the original tables were not accepted by the firms themselves and were the subject of critical correspondence in the various magazines and newspapers. The information must be seen as a rough guide rather than gospel truth. In many cases the definition of terms varies between the various data sources, making direct comparison an unrealistic probability.

In general, data is much more readily available in North American than it is in the UK. For comparative purposes the US data has been converted in UK£ at £1 = US$1.80.

ANALYSIS AND INTERPRETATION OF DATA

The first four columns of each table – gross income, numbers of partners, numbers of other professional staff and numbers of other staff – are mostly those reported by the firms themselves or have been estimated by the trade magazines.

The last four columns – gross income per partner (or director), ratio of other professionals to partners (or directors), ratio of professionals to other staff and annual gross income per professional – have been calculated as described below.

The concentration of the top percentage gives an insight into the degree to which a few big firms dominate each profession.

The calculation of the average performance for the top 20 firms of each profession give broad indications of the underlying economics of the professions but the real message comes from looking at the shape of individual firms. Averages can be very misleading if one or two firms have abnormal numbers because of the way they define things.

Gross income per partner (or director)

The statistic of *gross income per partner (or director)* gives a partial guide to the structure of the firm.

A large figure will usually indicate a firm with high leverage (a large number of other professional staff per partner). It could also be a firm with high overheads to be met from professional fee income. It does not, necessarily, mean that partners in those firms are personally highly paid, simply that there are relatively few senior people.

The very large figures for lawyers (in some cases more than £1 million in fees annually) reflects the fact that legal firms often have high overheads to be covered. The highest income figures tend to be in those firms with a higher ratio of other professionals to partners reflecting the higher leverage: e.g., for Slaughter and May in the UK the 79 partners appear to have an average income per partner of more than £1 million and employ 4.7 other professionals for each partner; the 63 partners of Richards Butler have an average gross income of £746,000 but each partner is supported by only 2.2 other professionals.

This statistic tends to be more revealing for comparing firms within a professional group rather than for comparison between professional groups.

Ratio of other professionals to partners (or directors)

The *ratio of other professionals to partners* is another way of looking at the shape of the staff pyramid or the leverage. Firms with very high ratios will tend to have a high gross income per partner as discussed above.

If a firm within a profession is showing a much higher leverage figure than the others this may indicate it offers clients a different type of service (high leverage would imply large teams of relatively junior people). These high leverage firms will tend to be more profitable but it is difficult for a firm to sustain high leverage for a long period.

Ratio of professionals to other staff

This ratio gives an indication of the structure of a firm's overheads.

A relatively large number of professionals with a small number of support staff will produce a high ratio number implying the firm has relatively low overheads and that the majority of the staff are fee earners. If, on the other hand, there are more support staff than professionals the number will be less than '1'. Large relative numbers of support staff will imply high gross income per professional required to cover the large overhead.

The top UK accountants have relatively small numbers of support staff (secretaries, etc.) and the majority of employees are fee earners. Advertising and PR companies tend to have a larger overhead base but this partly depends on how the term 'professional staff' is defined.

Although the statistics are not available evidence suggests that law firms have reasonably large staff overheads which partly explains the high income per professional as discussed below.

Gross income per professional

This is, in some ways, the most interesting statistic but it can be highly misleading and needs careful interpretation.

Those groups with high numbers (law and, to a lesser extent, executive search and advertising) reflect the relatively high overhead structure to be carried by each professional.

It may well be that the lawyers, search consultants and advertising executives are supported by a larger number of researchers, clerks and secretaries than are the accountants or designers.

The degree of variance of gross income figures *within* each professional group is also of interest. The relatively low variance of the accountants and lawyers implies a homogeneous set of services which tend to be purchased by the customers who are conscious of relative prices. The wider variance of the designers and the management consultants suggests professions with much less homogeneous services where some firms within the same group are doing much higher value work than others.

In the management consultancy group, the relatively lower value-added work done by the accounting firms (often things like implementation of financial systems) shows up in their low gross income per professional figures compared to the strategy consultants such as BCG and McKinsey who do higher 'value-added' work.

Concentration of the profession

The relative concentration of the professional groups can be implied from comparing the combined gross income of the top five to the gross income of the top 20 firms in each group.

It can be seen that the accountants in both the UK and the USA are a heavily concentrated group compared to the much more even distribution, and lower concentration of the lawyers and advertising agencies.

The relatively low concentration of most of the others indicates relatively fragmented professions.

In recent years *all* the professional groups have become more concentrated as the big firms have taken over or merged with smaller ones but the relative ease of starting break-away firms and the lack of true economies of scale mean that most professions will continue to be fragmented.

As a general observation, mid-sized firms in all the professional groups are under threat as they do not enjoy the economies of scale of the major players and cannot achieve the efficiency and motivation of the smaller, more boutique-like firms. As chart 1 shows, there is a marked trend with the gross income per professional being larger in the professions with a lower concentration.

APPENDIX: LEADING PROFESSIONAL SERVICE FIRMS

Appendix: Chart 1

GROSS INCOME PER PROFESSIONAL vs CONCENTRATION OF PROFESSION

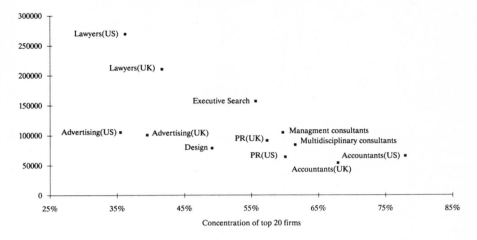

Appendix: Table 1

SUMMARY OF PERFORMANCE OF PROFESSIONS

Profession	Concentration of top 20 firms*	Estimated gross income per professional
Lawyers (US)	36%	£269,624
Lawyers (UK)	42%	£210,278
Executive search	56%	£157,117
Advertising agencies (US)	36%	£105,562
Management consultants	60%	£104,903
Advertising agencies (UK)	39%	£100,806
PR consultants (UK)	57%	£91,671
PR consultants (US)	62%	£84,338
Design consultancies	49%	£78,823
Accountants (US)	78%	£65,674
Multidisciplinary consultants	60%	£64,188
Accountants (UK)	68%	£53,989

* Estimated gross income of top 5 firms expressed as % of the total of the top 20 firms

UK ACCOUNTANTS 1990

FIRM	Gross Fee Income 1990 £m	Partners numbers	Other professionals numbers	Other staff numbers	Income per partner £000's	Ratio Other profs per partner	Ratio All profs/ other staff	Gross income per professional £
Coopers & Lybrand Deloitte	£588	735	7807	2577	£800	10.6	3.3	£68,836
KPMG Peat Marwick McLintock	£467	591	7793	2094	£790	13.2	4.0	£55,713
Price Waterhouse	£377	482	5160	2012	£783	10.7	2.8	£66,891
Ernst & Young	£358	421	5552	1952	£851	13.2	3.1	£59,987
Touche Ross	£295	407	4425	1597	£725	10.9	3.0	£61,031
Arthur Andersen	£269	209	2931	760	£1286	14.0	4.1	£85,605
BDO Binder Hamlyn	£120	231	2042	n/a	£518	8.8	n/a	£52,662
Grant Thornton	£115	247	1952		£467	7.9		£52,433
Pannell Kerr Foster	£85	220	1835		£385	8.3		£41,168
Stoy Hayward	£67	134	1191		£497	8.9		£50,264
Kidsons Impey	£58	178	1227		£323	6.9		£40,925
Clark Whitehall	£57	227	1398		£250	6.2		£34,954
Robson Rhodes	£35	70	523		£500	7.5		£59,022
Neville Russell	£35	87	609		£400	7.0		£50,000
Moore Stephens	£35	123	698		£281	5.7		£42,144
Moores Rowland	£32	95	484		£339	5.1		£55,613
Baker Tilly	£26	59	397		£434	6.7		£56,140
Haines Watts	£20	44	354		£459	8.0		£50,754
Macintyre Hudson	£17	53	338		£315	6.4		£42,711
Saffery Champness	£16	39	269		£418	6.9		£52,922
Concentration of top 20	68%			Averages	£541	8.6	3.4	£53,989

Source: Accountancy July 1991
Other staff estimates for top 5 from Evening Standard 10 July 1990

UK ADVERTISING AGENCIES 1990

FIRM	Gross "Fee" Income 1990 £m Estimated	Directors numbers	Professionals (all) numbers Estimated	Other staff numbers Estimated	Income per director £000's	Ratio Other profs per director	Ratio All profs other staff Derived	Gross income per professional £
Saatchi and Saatchi	£32	n/a	429	286	n/a	n/a	1.5	£74,703
J Walter Thompson	£31		289	193			1.5	£107,308
D'Arcy Masius	£25		216	144			1.5	£115,035
Ogilvy & Mather	£24		221	148			1.5	£107,378
BSB Dorland	£23		237	158			1.5	£98,614
Lowe Howard Spink	£21		163	109			1.5	£127,188
BMP DDB Needham	£19		199	132			1.5	£94,131
McCann-Erickson	£16		148	99			1.5	£110,648
Grey	£16		255	170			1.5	£63,765
Young and Rubicam	£16		189	126			1.5	£85,714
Publicis	£16		175	116			1.5	£90,541
WCRS	£15		124	82			1.5	£119,333
CDP	£14		117	78			1.5	£121,000
Abbott Mead Vickers	£14		124	82			1.5	£111,201
Leo Burnett	£12		148	99			1.5	£83,715
Still Price	£12		119	79			1.5	£100,657
BBH	£12		128	85			1.5	£92,300
GGT	£9		73	49			1.5	£124,898
KHBB	£8		104	69			1.5	£74,350
Yellowhammer	£7		63	42			1.5	£113,643
Concentration of top 20	39%			Averages			1.5	£100,806

Source: Campaign Feb 1991

Assumptions: Gross "fee" or equivalent income is 15% of billings estimated by Media Registar
60% of staff are defined as "professionals" or "fee earners". A different assumption would change figures significantly

UK DESIGN CONSULTANCIES 1990								
FIRM	Gross Design Fee Income 1990	Partners	Professionals	Other staff	Income per partner	Ratio Other profs per partner	Ratio profs/ other staff	Gross income per professional
	£m	numbers	numbers	numbers	£000's			£
WPP Group	£67.5	n/a	865	202	n/a	n/a	4.28	£78,035
YRM Partnership	£27.5		341	113			3.02	£80,645
Building Design Partnership	£27.0		1230					£21,951
Fitch RS	£23.0		420					£54,762
Aukett Associates	£17.7		265	55			4.82	£66,792
Holmes & Marchant	£15.8		116	69			1.68	£136,207
Company of Designers	£14.4		193	194			0.99	£74,767
Addison	£14.3		255					£56,078
McColl Group	£14.1		169	71			2.38	£83,432
Imagination	£12.9		89	111			0.80	£144,944
RSCG Conran Design	£11.5		210					£54,762
Siegel & Gale	£11.5		118	38			3.11	£97,458
RMJM	£11.3		164	98			1.67	£69,146
DY Davies plc	£11.0		110	70			1.57	£100,000
Minanle Tattersfield	£10.0		150					£66,667
Wolf Olins	£9.8		98	57			1.72	£100,000
Sampson Tyrrell	£9.6		94	21			4.48	£102,128
Cambridge Consultants	£8.9		170	60			2.83	£52,353
Landor Associates	£7.0		100	50			2.00	£70,000
DEGW	£6.5		98	28			3.50	£66,327
Concentration of top 20	49%			Averages			2.6	£78,823

source: Design Week   22 March 1991
In some cases no data was given for "other staff"

UK EXECUTIVE SEARCH FIRMS 1989								
FIRM	Gross Fee Income 1989	Partners = consultants	Other professionals	Other staff	Income per partner	Ratio Other profs per partner	Ratio All profs/ other staff	Gross income per professional
	£m	numbers	numbers	numbers	£000's			£
Russell Reynolds	£7.5	22	34	n/a	£341	1.5	n/a	£220,588
Korn Ferry	£5.5	14	24		£393	1.7		£229,167
Norman Broadbent	£5.0	7	10		£714	1.4		£500,000
Spencer Stuart	£4.7	14	22		£339	1.6		£215,455
Heidrick & Struggles	£3.8	14	25		£271	1.8		£152,000
Whitehead Mann	£3.5	10	20		£350	2.0		£175,000
Egon Zehnder	£3.5	11	15		£318	1.4		£233,333
Tyzack & Partners	£2.0	10	18		£200	1.8		£111,111
Saxton Bampfylde	£1.7	5	15		£340	3.0		£113,333
Merton Associates	£1.7	12	20		£138	1.7		£82,500
Carre Orban	£1.3	6	12		£213	2.0		£106,667
Berndtson	£1.2	4	9		£300	2.3		£133,333
Odgers & Co	£1.1	6	9		£183	1.5		£122,222
Boyden	£1.1	6	10		£175	1.7		£105,000
Butterfield Partnership	£1.0	6	9		£167	1.5		£111,111
Welbeck	£0.9	5	7		£182	1.4		£129,857
Baines Gwinner	£0.7	4	7		£175	1.8		£100,000
Christopher Mill	£0.6	3	5		£200	1.7		£120,000
Stephenson Cobbold	£0.6	4	5		£150	1.3		£120,000
Kohnhorst Irvine	£0.4	5	6		£74	1.2		£61,667
Concentration of top 20	56%			Averages	£261	1.7		£157,117

Source: Economist Survey 1990

UK LAWYERS 1989								
FIRM	Gross Fee Income 1989 £m	Partners numbers	Other professionals numbers	Other staff numbers	Income per partner £000's	Ratio Other profs per partner	Ratio All profs/ other staff	Gross income per professional £
Clifford Chance	£164	153	633	992	£1072	4.1	0.8	£208,651
Linklaters & Paines	£113	96	389	712	£1177	4.1	0.7	£232,990
Lovell White Durrent	£98	103	304	638	£947	3.0	0.6	£239,558
Slaughter and May	£86	79	372	569	£1089	4.7	0.8	£190,687
Freshfields	£82	75	308	427	£1093	4.1	0.9	£214,099
Allen & Overy	£74	84	303	513	£881	3.6	0.8	£191,214
Herbert Smith	£70	83	244	478	£843	2.9	0.7	£214,067
Simmons & Simmons	£70	90	231	467	£778	2.6	0.7	£218,069
Denton Hall Burgin	£66	81	193	509	£815	2.4	0.5	£240,876
Norton Rose	£66	82	277	456	£805	3.4	0.8	£183,844
McKenna & Co	£55	58	181	385	£948	3.1	0.6	£230,126
Nabarro Nathanson	£51	70	177	371	£729	2.5	0.7	£206,478
Richards Butler	£47	63	141	244	£746	2.2	0.8	£230,392
Cameron Markby Hewitt	£43	67	160	261	£642	2.4	0.9	£189,427
Evershed Wells & Hind	£43	52	156	292	£827	3.0	0.7	£206,731
Wilde Sapte	£39	44	140	276	£886	3.2	0.7	£211,957
Stephenson Harwood	£35	60	127	238	£583	2.1	0.8	£187,166
Clyde & Co	£35	71	98	291	£493	1.4	0.6	£207,101
Turner Kenneth Brown	£35	59	112	234	£593	1.9	0.7	£204,678
Alsop Wilkinson	£31	66	91	243	£470	1.4	0.6	£197,452
Concentration of top 20	42%			Averages	£821	2.9	0.7	£210,278

Source: Income estimates - Legal Business, Sept 1990 reporting Databank/FT estimates.
N.B. Fee income estimates regarded as unreliable by Legal Business and not confirmed by firms
Source: Number of staff - The Legal 500, January 1991

UK MANAGEMENT CONSULTANTS 1990								
FIRM	Gross Fee Income 1990 £m	Partners/ directors numbers	Professionals (all) numbers	Other staff numbers	Income per partner £000's	Ratio Other profs per partner	Ratio All profs/ other staff	Gross income per professional £
Coopers & Lybrand Deloitte	£150.0	n/a	1465	n/a	n/a	n/a	n/a	£102,389
Andersen Consulting	£130.0		1400					£92,857
Price Waterhouse	£110.2		1323					£83,296
PA Consulting	£86.6		1009					£85,828
KPMG	£73.5		911					£80,681
Ernst & Young	£67.6		620					£109,032
P-E International	£53.5		373					£143,432
Touche Ross	£51.0		500					£102,000
Towers Perrin	£27.5		285					£96,491
Arthur D Little	£26.0		330					£78,788
McKinsey	£25.0		150					£166,667
Capita Group	£20.0		270					£74,074
Hay	£18.3		144					£127,083
Handley Walker	£14.8		210					£70,476
CSL	£13.9		165					£84,242
Doctus	£12.9		126					£102,381
Boston Consulting Group	£12.6		75					£168,000
Booz Allen Hamilton	£11.5		90					£127,778
Stoy Hayward	£9.8		105					£93,333
Butler Cox	£7.1		65					£109,231
Concentration of top 20	60%			Averages				£104,903

Source: Management Consultancy, May 1991
Excludes firms known to be large but for which data is not available

UK MULTIDISCIPINARY CONSULTANCIES	Worldwide data		This is a very diverse group of firms					
FIRM	Gross Fee	Partners	Professionals	Other	Income per	Ratio	Ratio	Gross
	Income		(all)	staff	partner	Other profs	All profs	income per
	World 1989					per partner	other staff	professional
	£m	numbers	numbers	numbers	£000's			£
Ove Arup Partnership	£132.1		2432	1309	n/a	n/a	1.9	£54,317
Mott MacDonald	£91.7		1934	1120			1.7	£47,415
Building Design Partnership	£54.0		1140	420			2.7	£47,368
Sir William Halcrow	£32.0		694	705			1.0	£46,110
Travers Morgan	£32.0		732	250			2.9	£43,716
Sir Alexander Gibb	£32.0		573	556			1.0	£55,846
Scott Wilson Kirkpatrick	£30.0		910	780			1.2	£32,967
The MDA Group	£19.0		215	481			0.4	£88,372
Company of Designers	£17.9		243	230			1.1	£73,663
Oscar Faber	£16.3		310	182			1.7	£52,419
Hunter & Partners	£14.8		187	79			2.4	£79,144
McColl Group	£13.5		221	57			3.9	£61,086
Aukett Associates	£13.0		166	104			1.6	£78,313
Percy Thomas	£12.8		173	172			1.0	£73,988
D.Y. Davies Associates	£12.8		150	94			1.6	£85,333
James R. Knowles	£11.3		145	109			1.3	£77,931
RMJM	£11.3		172	113			1.5	£65,698
White Young	£8.8		127	181			0.7	£69,291
Grove Consultants	£8.4		81	95			0.9	£103,704
DGI Group	£5.5		116	25			4.6	£47,069
Concentration of top 20	60%			Averages			1.8	£64,188
Source: Building. September 1990 , modified by author for simplicity								
Excludes firms known to be large but where data is not available								
This table should not be regarded as an authoritative source because of need for simplifying assumptions								

UK PR CONSULTANTS 1990								
FIRM	Gross Fee	Directors/	Other	Other	Income per	Ratio	Ratio	Gross
	Income	partners	professionals	staff	director /partner	Other profs	All profs	income per
	1990					per director	other staff	professional
	£m	numbers	numbers	numbers	£000's			£
Shandwick	£32.6	96	162	163	£340	1.7	1.6	£126,357
Burson Marsteller	£11.7	28	101	78	£418	3.6	1.7	£90,620
Dewe Rogerson	£10.9	21	116	73	£518	5.5	1.9	£79,343
Corporate Communications	£9.7	37	70	84	£262	1.9	1.3	£90,467
Hill and Knowlton	£7.7	18	87	41	£426	4.8	2.6	£73,048
Grayling Group	£7.6	14	104	48	£544	7.4	2.5	£64,483
Rowland	£6.8	18	88	71	£377	4.9	1.5	£63,962
Countrywide	£6.4	15	71	49	£427	4.7	1.8	£74,419
Daniel J Edelman	£4.4	4	63	20	£1100	15.8	3.4	£65,672
GCI Group Ltd	£3.7	14	39	40	£263	2.8	1.3	£69,434
Biss Lancaster	£3.4	9	29	24	£373	3.2	1.6	£88,342
Counsel	£3.2	14	38	26	£226	2.7	2.0	£60,712
Citigate	£3.1	13	23	19	£238	1.8	1.9	£86,000
Financial Dynamics	£2.9	11	4	9	£267	0.4	1.7	£195,800
Dennis Davidson Associates	£2.3	5	14	14	£464	2.8	1.4	£122,105
Lynne Franks	£2.3	6	33	13	£387	5.5	3.0	£59,462
Hall Harrison Cowley	£2.2	10	36	22	£219	3.6	2.1	£47,587
Cartmell PR	£2.1	4	5	16	£515	1.3	0.6	£229,000
Infopress	£2.0	14	11	18	£144	0.8	1.4	£80,600
Richmond Towers	£1.7	8	17	16	£206	2.1	1.6	£66,000
Concentration of top 20	57%			Averages	£386	3.9	1.8	£91,671
Source: PR Week Survey May 1991								
Other staff data excludes part-time staff. Gross fee income excludes mark-ups on disbursements								

US ACCOUNTING FIRMS 1990

FIRM	Gross Fee Income 1990 $m	Partners numbers	Other professionals numbers	Other staff numbers	Income per partner $000's	Ratio Other profs per partner	Ratio All profs/ other staff	Gross income per professional $
Ernst & Young	$2,195.0	2054	16599	n/a	$1069	8.1	n/a	$117,675
Arthur Andersen	$1,933.0	1268	16472		$1524	13.0		$108,963
KPMG Peat Marwick	$1,929.0	1900	12500		$1015	6.6		$133,958
Deloitte & Touche	$1,900.0	1713	13787		$1109	8.0		$122,581
Coopers & Lybrand	$1,250.0	1253	14747		$998	11.8		$78,125
Price Waterhouse	$1,100.0	920	8510		$1196	9.3		$116,649
Laventhol & Horwath	$345.0	370	2030		$932	5.5		$143,750
Grant Thornton	$200.0	300	1550		$667	5.2		$108,108
BDO Seidman	$178.0	269	1252		$662	4.7		$117,028
McGladrey & Pullen	$168.0	378	1203		$444	3.2		$106,262
Kenneth Leventhal	$165.0	69	781		$2391	11.3		$194,118
Pannell Kerr Forster	$85.5	114	531		$750	4.7		$132,558
Spicer & Oppenheim	$66.0	80	389		$825	4.9		$140,725
Baird Kurtz & Dobson	$53.0	109	343		$486	3.1		$117,257
Plante & Moran	$47.0	80	401		$588	5.0		$97,713
Clifton Gunderson	$45.0	95	464		$474	4.9		$80,501
Crowe, Chizek	$43.0	70	370		$614	5.3		$97,727
Moss Adams	$41.0	66	304		$621	4.6		$110,811
Altschuler Melvoin and Glasser	$38.0	40	300		$950	7.5		$111,765
Cherry Bekaert & Holland	$32.0	64	186		$500	2.9		$128,000
Concentration of top 20	78%			Averages	$891	6.5		$118,214
Source: Accounting Today September 24, 1990					£495			£65,674
Reprinted by permission from Accounting Today. Copyright Lebhar-Friedman, Inc.,						In UK £ at £1 =	1.80	
425 Park Avenue, New York, NY 10022								

US ADVERTISING AGENCIES 1990

FIRM	Gross "Fee" Income 1990 $m	Directors numbers	Professionals (all) numbers Estimate	Other staff numbers Estimate	Income per director $000's	Ratio Other profs per partner	Ratio All profs/ other staff Derived	Gross income per professional $
Leo Burnett	$299	n/a	1378	918	n/a	n/a	1.5	$217,262
Saaatchi & Saatchi	$271		1057	705			1.5	$256,054
Foote, Cone & Belding	$263		1670	1114			1.5	$157,268
Grey Advertising	$256		1441	961			1.5	$177,838
J Walter Thompson	$252		1229	820			1.5	$204,734
Ogilvy & Mather	$230		1298	866			1.5	$176,910
Young & Rubicam	$217		1314	876			1.5	$164,840
McCann-Ericson	$210		1025	684			1.5	$204,896
BBDO	$207		992	661			1.5	$208,812
D'Arcy Masius	$204		1145	763			1.5	$178,546
Lintas	$203		967	645			1.5	$209,988
DDB Needham	$192		1138	759			1.5	$168,600
BSB	$171		802	535			1.5	$212,541
Bozell	$156		962	642			1.5	$161,575
Ketchum	$121		736	490			1.5	$164,899
Campbell-Mithun-Esty	$120		971	648			1.5	$123,842
Ross Roy	$106		572	381			1.5	$185,380
Wells, Rich, Green	$105		419	280			1.5	$250,358
NW Ayer	$99		556	370			1.5	$178,906
Della Femina McNamee	$94		478	319			1.5	$196,989
Concentration of top 20	36%			Averages				$190,012
Source: Advertising Age: March 25th 1991			Assumption: 60% of total staff are professionals			In UK £ at £1 =	1.80	£105,562
Note: In fact the gross income is usually commission based and contains some "mark-up" income								

US LAWYERS 1990

FIRM	Gross Fee Income	Partners	Other professionals	Other staff	Income per partner	Ratio Other profs per partner	Ratio All profs other staff	Gross income per professional
	1990	numbers	numbers	numbers	£000's			$
	$m							
Skadden Arps	$517	197	751	n/a	$2,624	3.8	n/a	$545,359
Baker & McKenzie	$341	432	907		$789	2.1		$254,668
Jones Day	$320	369	683		$867	1.9		$304,183
Shearman & Sterling	$281	123	364		$2,285	3.0		$577,002
Gibson Dunn & Crutcher	$280	194	417		$1,443	2.1		$458,265
David Polk	$240	96	284		$2,500	3.0		$631,579
Sulivan & Cromwell	$230	95	250		$2,421	2.6		$666,667
Latham & Watkins	$223	170	305		$1,312	1.8		$469,474
Cravath, Swaine	$213	64	224		$3,328	3.5		$739,583
Fried, Frank	$213	104	264		$2,048	2.5		$578,804
Sidley & Austin	$213	178	422		$1,197	2.4		$355,000
Simpson, Thatcher	$201	95	289		$2,116	3.0		$523,438
Well, Gotshal	$200	113	344		$1,770	3.0		$437,637
Morgan, Lewis	$198	219	391		$904	1.8		$324,590
O'Melveney & Myers	$198	145	304		$1,366	2.1		$440,980
Paul, Weiss	$195	82	284		$2,378	3.5		$532,787
Kaye, Scholer	$188	94	246		$2,000	2.6		$552,941
Milbank, Tweed	$187	98	300		$1,908	3.1		$469,849
Fulbright & Jaworski	$183	210	372		$871	1.8		$314,433
Cleary, Gottlied	$181	102	240		$1,775	2.4		$529,240
Concentration of top 20	36%			Averages	$1,795	2.6		$485,324
Source: The AmLaw 100 August 1990 copyright The American Lawyer					£997			£269,624
Not to be reproduced elsewhere without permission from The American Lawyer						In UK £ at £1 =	1.80	

US PR CONSULTANCIES 1990

FIRM	Gross Fee Income	Directors	Professionals (all)	Other staff	Income per director	Ratio Other profs per director	Ratio All profs/ other staff	Gross income per professional
	1990							
	$m	numbers	numbers	numbers	£000's			$
			Estimated	Estimated			Derived	
Hill and Knowlton	$120	n/a	676	364	n/a	n/a	1.9	$176,923
Burson-Marsteller	$96		845	455			1.9	$113,609
Shandwick	$95		605	326			1.9	$157,267
Fleishman-Hillard	$43		331	178			1.9	$130,784
Ogilvy PR	$38		244	131			1.9	$154,872
Ketchum	$38		231	124			1.9	$163,380
Edelman	$32		203	110			1.9	$157,483
Manning Selvage & Lee	$29		197	106			1.9	$148,870
Omnicom PR	$27		179	96			1.9	$153,231
Ruder Finn	$24		182	98			1.9	$132,198
Robinson, Lake	$20		95	51			1.9	$215,806
Chon & Wolfe	$13		72	39			1.9	$180,503
GCI Group	$11		75	40			1.9	$150,502
Financial Relations Board	$10		72	39			1.9	$133,427
Corporate Communications	$8		47	26			1.9	$177,450
The Kamber Group	$7		65	35			1.9	$113,846
Gibbs & Soell	$7		53	28			1.9	$136,562
Stoorza, Ziegaus & Metzger	$6		51	27			1.9	$122,880
Earle Palmer Brown	$6		40	22			1.9	$140,447
E. Bruce Harrison	$6		32	17			1.9	$176,138
Concentration of top 20	62%			Averages			1.9	$151,809
Source: J.R. O'Dwyer Company Inc. 1991. Copyright						In UK £ at £1 =	1.80	£84,338
Assumption: 65% of staff are defined as "professional"								

REFERENCES

Sources which may be of interest to those who wish to go deeper into the subject include:

Collard, Edgar, (1980) *125 years at Touche Ross*, Toronto: Touche Ross Canada

Coxe, Weld et al., (1987) *Success Strategies for Design Professionals*, New York: McGraw Hill

Davidow, William and Uttal, Bro. (1990) *Total Customer Service*, New York: Harper & Row

Fallon, Ivan, (1988) *The Brothers. The rise of Saatchi & Saatchi*, London: Hutchinson

Jones Peter, (1989) *Management in Service Industries*, London: Pitman

Katz, Bernard, (1988) *How to Market Professional Services*, London: Gower

Heskett James, (1986) *Managing in the Service Economy*, Boston, Mass: HBS Press

Kleinman, Philip, (1987) *The Saatchi & Saatchi Story*, London: Weidenfeld & Nicolson

Lewis, Michael, (1989) *Liar's Poker, Sevenoaks*, Kent: Hodder & Stoughton

Lovelock Christopher, (1984) *Services Marketing*, Englewood Cliffs, New Jersey: Prentice Hall

McNamara Jay, (1989) *Advertising Agency Management*, Homewood, Illinois: Dow Jones

Maister David, (1989) *Professional Service Firm Management*, Maister Associates, 90 Commonwealth Avenue, Boston, Mass, USA 02116

Normann Richard, (1984) *Service Management: Strategy and Leadership in Service Businesses*, John Wiley & Sons

Parry, Roger, (1979) *The Organization and Environment of Advertising Agencies*, M.Litt Thesis, Oxford University

Sasser et al., (1978) *Management of Service Operations*, Boston, Mass: Allyn and Bacon

Wilson, Aubrey, (1984) *Practice Development for Professional Firms*, New York: McGraw Hill

There are a number of specialist magazines and newspapers devoted to specific professions which often cover management topics. Examples have been quoted from some of these publications. A partial list of the specialist newspapers and magazines which the author has found useful is given on the following page:

Accountancy, Chartered Accountants Hall, Moorgate Place, London EC2P 2BJ [071 628 7060]

Accounting Today (USA), 425 Park Avenue, New York NY [212 371 9400]

Advertising Age, (USA) Crain Publications, 740 Rush Street, Chicago, USA

AdWeek, (USA) 49 E21 Street, New York NY 10010 [212 529 5500]

Building, 1 Millharbour, London E14 9RA [071 537 2222]

Campaign, Haymarket, 22 Lancaster Gate, London W2 [081 943 5000]

Canadian Lawyer, 240 Edward Street, Aurora, Ontario L4G 3S9

Design Week, Centaur Communications, 50 Poland St, London W1V 4AX [071 439 4222]

Legal Business, Legalease, 3 Clifton Road, London W9 1SZ [071 286 1890]

Marketing Week, Centaur Communications, 50 Poland St, London W1V 4AX [071 439 4222]

Management Consultancy, VNU Publications, 32/34 Broadwick St., London W1A 2HG [071 439 4242]

PR Week, Haymarket, 22 Lancaster Gate, London W2 [081 943 5000]

The American Lawyer (USA), 600 Third Ave New York, NY 10017 [212 973 2800]

INDEX

needs, determining 15–17, 295–7; satisfying 49–50, 127, 160
profitability 53–4, 57, 64–71, 181–3
relationship audits 54–5, 198–202
relationships 21, 39, 89–90, 196–204
resources 17
service package 37, 40–2
service teams 162–7
service techniques 39–40
Clifford Chance 273
commission systems 11, 29 *see also* payment *and* pricing
comparative performance 62
competitive pitches 17, 69, 274–85
competitors 298–303
complaints *see* client feedback
computers 217–19
consistency of service 3, 36
consultants 69
contracting out 97
cost allocation 3, 51–2, 182–3, 259
costs
   client-related 65–6, 179–84
   communications 11
   external 65, 66
   marketing 11
   premises 95, 212–15
   product 75, 183–4
   salary 2, 7
   staff 4, 7, 26
cost sharing 259
counselling *see* staff
creditors 188–9
cultural indoctrination 133–5

day-to-day management 147–8
debt
   collection 20, 148
   monitoring 187–8
decision-making 167–70
delegation 78–9
designers 9, 69
desk-top publishing 218–19
disputed expenses 92
distribution businesses 12

earn-outs 324–9
economics 24–32
electronic mail 36
Ernst & Young 202, 272, 273
executive recruiters *see* headhunters